GUESTS

IN THEIR OWN

HOUSE

THE WOMEN OF
VATICAN II

Carmel Elizabeth McEnroy

Foreword by Bernard Häring

A Crossroad Book
The Crossroad Publishing Company
New York

1996

The Crossroad Publishing Company
370 Lexington Avenue, New York, NY 10017

Printed in the United States of America

Library of Congress Cataloging-in-Publication Data

McEnroy, Carmel.
 Guests in their own house : the women of Vatican II / Carmel
McEnroy.
   p.   cm.
 Includes bibliographical references and index.
 ISBN 0-8245-1547-1 (pb)
  1. Women in the Catholic Church.   2. Vatican Council (2nd :
1962-1965)   3. Sexism in religion.   4. Catholic women–Religious
life.   I. Title.
 BX2347.8.W6M44   1996
 262'.52–dc20   95-44250
                                                        CIP

DATE DUE

FE 20 '97			
JE 18			

DEMCO 38-296

GUESTS

IN THEIR OWN

HOUSE

With *gratitude,*
to the twenty-three women auditors
officially invited to Vatican Council II,

With *love,*
to my immediate family and in-laws —
Bernadette and Frank McGovern, Sr. Gabriel McEnroy,
Ann and Brian McEnroy, Noreen and Brian Smith,
Margaret and Ignatius McEnroy; Rita and Padraig Fitzgerald —
who have glimpsed the vision of Vatican II and are determined that
it cannot and will not die but must come to fruition
in the next generation of sinners, saints, and scholars,

With *hope,*
to my religious family, the Congregation of
the Sisters of Mercy of Ireland and South Africa,
as they promote the dignity of women and challenge
all unjust structures in church and society

CONTENTS

FOREWORD

═══ ❖ ═══

I read Carmel McEnroy's book with special attention to what biblical scholars explain to us about the historicity of the Gospels. Mark, Luke, and Matthew had contact with eyewitnesses who thousands of times would tell the stories about Jesus, what happened, and what he said. Of course, they told the real stories, but always with an eye to the situation of those who listened to them. When we, after two thousand years, read the Gospels, we have three dimensions of reference: (1) What did Jesus really say at *that time?* How did he respond directly to people? (2) How did the evangelists tell the same stories in view of the joys, sorrows, and problems of their readers *in their time,* thirty, or perhaps even sixty years later? (3) How can we transmit the same message to people *today,* sharing their joys, hopes, sorrows, in full faithfulness to the original message, but also to our task of making ourselves, our hearers, and our readers contemporaries of Jesus, without taking from their present situation?

Carmel McEnroy's whole book is to be read from this perspective. Her method is above all to let the council mothers speak about how they experienced the council and how they tried to spread the message and experience dynamically in the period after the council. McEnroy shares with the women who experienced the council as auditors and in conciliar commissions the same concern: to bring the council with its dynamics to the readers of today. It is a matter of good *translation,* as are all our efforts to live as contemporaries of people today and at the same time as closely as possible to Jesus in his time. Reading the book refreshed many of my own memories in a way that I can easily and fully identify with what is said. I also share substantially the concern of the author and those she interviewed to keep the spirit of the council alive.

I consider McEnroy's book both important and necessary. As far as I can see, up to now very little is said by historians of the council about the absence and presence of women in Vatican Council II. Not much is to be found on the even more vital question: What did the council mean and what does it still mean about the role of women in church and society, for women and men of today and of the time to come? I dare to foretell that the present book will find great interest for a long time.

The few women who were present in the council have spread the message and done much to keep the conciliar spirit alive. What would have happened if hundreds of women of the same caliber had been actively engaged in the council! Even so, women in the church, sisters and laywomen, are guarantors that the spirit of Vatican II will be kept alive with all its dynamics. Our holy women are in the service of life. They are sharply opposed to its abortion. Then let the spirit of the council not be aborted by men more concerned for law and order than for growing life.

At the synod on consecrated life in the fall of 1994, the presence of women was a prophetic event. There was no inferiority or superiority complex. Thanks be to God that we have so many mature and dedicated women who never allow life, fullness of life and freedom, to be stifled. At the end of the second synod, Angelo Cardinal Sodano, secretary of state (what a title for a churchman!), admonished the sisters that those who love the church will never criticize the pope. In the past, holy women did criticize popes and rendered a great service to the church. I just mention St. Catherine of Siena. If women are *never* supposed to criticize the pope, implicitly they are thus supposed not to be mature, not to have a share of responsibility within the church.

In Carmel McEnroy's book, highly competent churchwomen do express criticism. That means they show discernment and sincerity. Only a blind man will not see that they do so with astonishing maturity and peacefulness. The question, What kind of priests and what kind of women does the church want? is intimately related to the question, *What kind of church does the Lord want for the world?* The present book gives convincing witness to this spirit. Thank you, Sister Carmel! Thank you, great ladies!

BERNARD HÄRING, C.SS.R.

ACKNOWLEDGMENTS

Some of my married women friends and former students, Mary Ann Mertz, Rosemary Cavanaugh, Pat Sexton, and Patty Blair, told me that writing a book is like giving birth. You must breathe and relax, breathe and relax, and when the time is right, push.

The idea for my book on the women of Vatican II was conceived in 1988. I started serious work on it during a half-year sabbatical in 1989. There was time to breathe and relax after a fashion between then and my next half-year sabbatical in 1993. I found that devoting myself to my primary interest, full-time teaching, left very little time for my own research. By the time I had reacquainted myself with it during vacations, it was time to return to school, so it's been a long pregnancy. As other members of my family say, "If there are nine straightforward ways to do anything and one complicated way, we will pick that one. It's in our genes." And so I followed the family tradition of an uncharted route.

An African proverb claims that "it takes a whole village to rear a child." I claim that it took a whole church — at least in miniature — to write this book. The specific contributions of several people will become obvious in the following pages. Here I acknowledge especially the cooperation of Léon-Josef Cardinal Suenens, Archbishop Andrea di Montezemolo, Archbishop Augustinus Frotz, and Bishop Charles Buswell for their auxiliary role in a work that spotlights female protagonists.

Research projects that involve international travel are costly. Even more so if one does not read or speak all the languages involved. I was not daunted by the fact that auditors came from fourteen different countries, and I did not know Italian or Spanish. French, German, Latin, and English were a start, and my Gaelic was a bonus. I am grateful to the Abigail Quigley McCarthy Center for Women's Research, Resources, and Scholarship for a research grant in 1993 and to St. Meinrad School of Theology for grants from the Adrian

xi

Fuerst Faculty Development Fund during both of my sabbaticals. These grants partially financed my travel expenses and translations. My Congregation of the Sisters of Mercy of Ireland and South Africa just got less money when there was less to give. Many, especially from my original Ballymahon community, sustained me by their interest and presupposition that I could complete anything I started.

Just as my teaching career in St. Meinrad was aborted in May 1995, my book came to full term. I greatly appreciated the midwifery of Michael Leach and the Crossroad Publishing Company, especially Gwendolin Herder's European perspective and John Eagleson's relentless pursuit of clarity and accurate details. The original tight deadline I received appeared more like a Caesarean section. My breathing became more rapid. Relaxations were fewer. I knew the time had come to push. Blessings on Ellen Twibell for making sure that I had special things to eat during the final week's crunch. Pam Ford Smith and Doris Rapp came to the rescue as usual with their welcoming "home away from home" for my dog. My newly discovered family, Sister L on the Internet became an important standby solidarity group, thanks to Peggy Thompson and friends. Sisterhood (and true brotherhood) are powerful.

My sincere thanks to the Vatican II women and all those mentioned in my book who led me to them in any way, as well as to anyone I may have inadvertently overlooked. Without their wholehearted cooperation and encouragement, the whole project could have miscarried at an early stage. Rosemary Goldie was outstanding in all of this and deserves special mention, as do Sig. Gabriele Turella, librarian at the Pontifical Council for the Laity, and his staff for their gracious reception of me during two intense weeks of working in their archives.

Bernard Häring gave significant input for my research, and I am honored that he has written the Foreword for my book. Above and beyond that he has proven himself to be a courageous, compassionate, and encouraging theologian who continues to speak the truth in love for the church. I respect and admire him.

Many friends and some colleagues at St. Meinrad School of Theology stood by me to the bitter end. A few deserve to be singled out. Damian Dietlein, O.S.B. (Assumption Abbey), was my computer expert, who even talked me through difficult maneuvers by long distance phone calls during his sabbatical in Claremont. Mark Ciganovich, O.Carm., a trusted colleague and partner in theological dialogue over the years, gave me a critical reading of the text, as did historian Isaac McDaniel, O.S.B. I also appreciate Isaac's advance publicity for my book through his course on Vatican Council II. Bridget Clare McKeever, S.S.L., having resigned her own teaching position in the cause of justice, was pastoral care giver and counselor *pro bono* at any and every hour. Cajetan White, O.S.B., came through with Spanish translations with incredible promptness and generosity with his time. Students may not realize just how much their reception of the human interest stories about council mothers energized me to complete the project. This was especially true of those in the Continuing Education courses.

My family in Ireland and in Canada have always been there for me, keeping my theology earthed in human experience and often reflecting me encouragingly at least at twice my natural potential. The younger generation of nieces and nephews frequently asked when I would be "launching my book," and that kept the dream going. Finally, where would I be without the unconditional love of my dog Maeve? No matter what the level of achievement or frustration, I could always count on the sound of one tail clapping.

Somewhat like Mother God in her creation of order from chaos, I brought forth my book, christened it in the name of the women, and Crossroad saw that it was good. Moladh le Dia!

Abbreviations

$$= \diamond =$$

CCCC	*Centrum Coordinationis Communicationum de Concilio*
CDF	Congregation for the Doctrine of the Faith
CFM	Christian Family Movement
COPECIAL	Permanent Committee for International Congresses of the Lay Apostolate
CTSA	Catholic Theological Society of America
DH	*Dignitatis Humanae,* Declaration on Religious Freedom
GS	*Gaudium et Spes,* Pastoral Constitution on the Church in the Modern World
ICO/CIO	International Catholic Organizations
LCWR	Leadership Conference of Women Religious
LG	*Lumen Gentium,* Dogmatic Constitution on the Church
MIAMSI	International Movement for the Apostolate in the "Independent Milieux"
MIJARC	International Movement of Catholic Agricultural and Rural Youth
NCCM	National Council of Catholic Men
NCCW	National Council of Catholic Women
SCRIS	Sacred Congregation for Religious and Secular Institutes
UISG	International Union of Superiors General

UR	*Unitatis Redintegratio*, Decree on Ecumenism
WCC	World Council of Churches
WELG	Women's Ecumenical Linkage Group
WFCYWG	World Federation of Catholic Young Women and Girls
WOC	Women's Ordination Conference
WUCWO	World Union of Catholic Women's Organizations

GUESTS
IN THEIR OWN
HOUSE

Introduction

===❖===

This detective project started with one name and a healthy dose of anger. The name was Mary Luke Tobin. The anger was triggered by Alberic Stacpole's wonderful book *Vatican II Revisited by Those Who Were There*.[1] The twenty-three essays by men who were at the council evoke the memory and excitement of that event, but they give no inkling that there were any women present, other than an occasional Protestant observer's wife. Stacpole relates "light-heartedly" Margaret Pawley's method of measuring ecumenical progress by how the observers' wives were treated. She is the widow of Canon Bernard Pawley, an Anglican observer and first representative of the archbishop of Canterbury at Vatican II. No wives were invited to the opening of the first conciliar session, October 11, 1962. They were invited to the closing of that session but were located way in the back with neither books nor kneelers. They were invited to the opening of the second session and were seated a little farther from the back. By the closing of that session, they were closer to the front and had kneelers. Pawley concluded, "Thereafter...we moved further forward — as in grandmother's footsteps — and were progressively given kneelers and then books."[2] Why does the only reference to women have to be "light-hearted"? Isn't there a substantial problem here, not only from an ecumenical point of view, but anthropologically? Neither Stacpole nor Pawley (as quoted) mention the significant factor of Roman Catholic women being invited to the third and fourth conciliar sessions and how that could have impacted the treatment of observers' wives. Furthermore, some ecumenical women were present in their own right, not as anyone's *wife*, toward the end of the fourth session.

Stacpole's book has no essay by any layperson, much less a woman, although there were twenty-nine laymen and twenty-three women present as officially invited auditors. The men arrived a year ahead of the women and were there from the second session onward.

Jean Guitton, French philosopher and friend of John XXIII, was the
only layperson invited to the first session. John had told him to come
and see what he thought. My critique of Stacpole is that he makes no
reference to such historical events as the restoration of a lay presence
at a council, a regular phenomenon in the earlier church councils,
when dignitaries were permitted, which happened also at the Council
of Trent (1545–63), but which was omitted at Vatican I (1869–70).
Women, however, were never permitted at a council before the third
session of Vatican II in 1964.[3] That is at least as newsworthy as the
presence of ecumenical observers for the first time invited as friends
with something to offer, not as renegades being asked to return to the
Roman fold. But the observers were men, and they were given more
prominence than any of the women. Without wishing in any way to
undermine the significance of the positive progress of ecumenism, I
have to say that the more basic *world problems* of injustice, poverty,
violence, and war are at the present time most directly related to
unequal perceptions and behavioral patterns in sex relations. There
is a direct carryover from this mistreatment of women (inferiors) to
the treatment of men who are perceived to be inferior because of
their race, culture, class, sexual orientation, etc. They are treated as
women, that is, they are not understood or listened to, they are dis-
criminated against, they do not count in important matters, and they
are expendable.

Vatican II occurred at a crucial moment in history both in terms of
a socio-historical juncture for humanity as a global community and
also for the interrelated emergence of a *world-church.* According to
German theologian Karl Rahner, the shift taking place was comparable to what happened only once before when the young movement
of Judaeo-Christianity confronted the Greek world and was forced
to adapt to Greek philosophy and culture if it was to survive.[4] Since
then, Catholicism became wedded to Roman culture and law and
later on to Neo-Scholastic philosophy. It was thus that Christianity
was exported to missionary countries all over the world, destroy-
ing rather than assimilating native cultures. In a new age of national
pride, identity, and liberation in previously colonialized countries,
foreign religion also came under fire or fell by the wayside in the
new awakening and development. In an attempt to defend the faith
against error, church authorities equated unity with uniformity. Vatican I was convened to "stem the tide of modernity" and try to keep
the church apart from threatening secular influence. The spiritual

bulwark of papal primacy and infallibility was erected to compensate for the loss of temporal power in the papal states, and the pope became the prisoner of the Vatican. One can hold a finger in the leaky dike just so long. Eventually the torrent broke through at Vatican II.

That council was called to read "the signs of the times" in the light of the gospel, to look critically at the church's own record, life, and mission, to see what spring-cleaning needed to be done, what unnecessary baggage needed to be discarded so that the pilgrim people of God could move about more easily, efficiently, and unencumbered. Yes, the church had a message for the world, but it could also learn from the world. In the process, the church, previously equated with the hierarchy, came to recognize the other 99.9 percent of its membership — *the laity*. In fact, the church assembled in council realized how foolish it looked without them. Laity too were church, and the whole body could only be enriched by listening to them and enlisting them in missionary activity. Next came the realization that *women* make up more than half of humanity, and they were totally left out of church leadership, discussion, and policy-making, although they were the silent majority of churchgoers, fundraisers, childrearers, churchcleaners, educators, health care workers, and missionaries. The church was a predominantly female space dominated by males. So that the whole church might be represented in council, the women too needed to be brought in visibly. Hence, Paul VI's emphasis on the *symbolic presence* of a few women.

True, the conciliar women were small in number, constituting less than 1 percent of the total gathering, but that is all the more reason why they must be included in the historical records. My experience has been that *most women* even in Catholic church and theological circles are completely unaware that there were *any* women at the council. That is even more true of men. As with most history, women are seldom mentioned, and the impression is given that they were not there or they did nothing worth recording. The more serious problem is that women, *all of us,* were so conditioned that we did not expect to find ourselves there, and we did not miss ourselves when we were left out.

Apart from the *Council Daybook,* newspaper and periodical articles, and interviews from the conciliar years, when the women auditors made headlines for a while, very little is known about the historical breakthrough that was in fact made in 1964. If this progress is not known, how can we build on it? We search and research as if we are always starting from scratch in a process that post-Christian feminist philosopher Mary Daly calls, the "kitty litter box syndrome of patriarchal scholarship."[5] Daly further explains this re-search as "a function of patriarchal scholarship (including pseudofeminist scholarship): circular academented game of hide-and-seek: pseudosearch for information which, in fact, has been systematically hidden by previous re-searchers, and which, when found, is then ritually re-covered by succeeding investigators, only to be re-discovered and re-covered endlessly." I would not go as far as Daly in saying that the cover-up is "systematic." I think it is more in the nature of neglect, omission, and trivialization because it is not perceived to be important. It stems from a mentality conditioned to think, what would a bunch of women, unschooled in philosophy and theology, know about the council discussions that took place in Latin? Folks, I have news for you.

I would have been in the same state of ignorance regarding the conciliar women had it not been for circumstances in the 1960s. Newly arrived in the United States, I was studying at Marillac College in St. Louis, 1963–66. I was more concerned with adjusting to American culture, climate, and my new surroundings than getting excited about the council that was in session. I was boarding with the Sisters of Loretto, and I recall their excitement in 1964 when their mother general, Mary Luke Tobin, was invited as an auditor. I remember the sisters going to Webster College to hear Tobin's report from the council. I knew that some other women were also at the council, but I had no idea how many or who they were. I also recall how Marillac's president, Sister Bertrand Myers, cancelled classes one afternoon, called a general meeting, and announced that Ma Mère, Suzanne Guillemin, would soon visit the Daughters of Charity community. Little did I think that thirty years later I would be writing to Marillac's archivist for information on council auditor Suzanne Guillemin and trying to find out what transpired during her visit.

So Tobin was my starting point. I met her at the Loretto motherhouse in Nerinx, Kentucky, in April 1988. Four names figured prominently in our first conversation: Rosemary Goldie, Suzanne Guillemin, Bernard Häring, and Gregory Baum. Baum was "stellar" in the media interviews. Häring was responsible for getting women involved on the working commissions. Guillemin was a farsighted woman religious, but unfortunately she died shortly after the council, before she was able to carry out some important work assigned to her by the Vatican. Tobin was emphatic, "You must meet Rosemary Goldie. She is an Australian and a fund of information." Prospects of a trip to Australia were exciting, though financially daunting. Later, I learned that Goldie was still in Rome. I wrote to her at the Lateran University and received an immediate reply, as I have always done on the many occasions since then when I wrote for information or clarification. I also wrote to Häring at the Collegio Sant' Alfonso in Rome. He was about to leave his position in Rome and return to his native Germany, so he was in the throes of packing, sorting files and belongings, and presenting five candidates for doctoral defenses within two weeks. Nevertheless, he promptly replied to my letter with valuable information from behind the scenes in regard to the women's conciliar involvement, which I cite in chapter 4. In the meantime, I had begun to piece together a list of the auditors with the assistance of the *Council Daybook*.[6] With Goldie's aid and *Lay Apostolate* bulletins,[7] I completed the list. There were no addresses or phone numbers. In the case of the women religious, their community initials and the position they held were given. The laywomen were listed with the organizations they headed. In some instances, I had nothing to go on but a name and a country: e.g., "Hedwig Skoda, Czechoslovakia."

Naively, I presumed the Vatican archives contained a great body of material with the women's addresses, the precise reason particular women were invited, at whose instigation, day and date of their coming to Rome, the contribution they made to various committees, copies of their invitations, and a host of other relevant data, which I in my limited knowledge of the topic had not thought of asking about. My main dilemma was how to access this gold mine of information. The smile on Goldie's face at our first meeting spoke volumes in response to my enthusiasm. "Archives?" she said. "There are no archives on this topic, other than the few folders of material I saved and collated according to major topics on the laity. I gave my best copy to the Vatican library and another to the library of the Pontifical Council for the Laity. We [the auditors] compiled the updated lists for the press and published them in the *Lay Apostolate* bulletin."[8] Without Goldie's assiduous work, the Vatican archives would have revealed nothing to me other than perhaps the text of the invitations and some fragmentary correspondence of acceptance. So much for my demythologization of the Vatican archives! Thanks to

Goldie's influence and the gracious librarian at the Pontifical Council for the Laity, I was able to spend two weeks there going through Goldie's complete files on the lay auditors. "She's gone with half our archives," laughed Goldie, as I left with a hefty pile of photocopied material in Latin, French, German, Italian, Spanish, and English.

Goldie introduced me to Alda Miceli and acted as my interpreter during the interview. Goldie also made arrangements for me to meet Ida Grillo in Tortona, Constantina Baldinucci in Milan, and Pilar Bellosillo in Spain. I thought I had figured out a system for negotiating my correct bus stop on the way home from the first day of interviewing Bellosillo in Madrid. Realizing that I would be returning home after dark, on the way over I counted the brilliant water fountains — there must have been at least five along my route, the last being within a block or two of my destination. What I did not count on was the fountains being turned off at 9:00 p.m. All my landmarks were gone, and I got off my bus about ten blocks too soon, my first night out on the town in a strange city! After that, I was cautioned to take a taxi. My next stop was Rue du Bac, Paris, in search of information on Suzanne Guillemin. Marie-Thérèse Van Lunen Chenu, also in Paris, gave me useful secondary references. Denise Peeters in Brussels talked about Sabine de Valon and her whereabouts in Lyons. On another trip, Helga Sourek, Gertrud Ehrle's former translator, rendezvoused with me at the Cologne railway station as we both converged from different directions. During several hours of Sourek's home hospitality, Ehrle took on flesh and blood in my mind. More hospitality and limousine service awaited me in Dernbach, where the sisters of Juliana Thomas's community, Poor Handmaids of Jesus Christ, filled in some blanks about her. On my third visit to Rome, Goldie arranged a meeting with Lucienne Salle in the Pontifical Council for the Laity, and through her I became acquainted with the memory of Marie-Louise Monnet, the very first woman auditor.

Back in the United States, the National Council of Catholic Women (NCCW) and specifically Margaret Mealey, its former executive secretary, put me in touch with Catherine McCarthy in San Francisco, and a meeting was arranged.

Never before did I realize how many variations there are on religious communities associated with the hearts of Jesus and Mary, and the designation of Sisters, Servants, and Handmaids was crucial in helping me eventually establish the whereabouts of all the sister auditors. Once I located the right community for Claudia Feddish, they gave me Jerome Maria Chimy's address, and when I eventually met Chimy, she was able to fill me in further on Feddish. Ida Grillo gave me the address of Amalia di Montezemolo's son, Andrea, and so I had him, the papal nuncio in Montevideo, furnishing useful information on his deceased mother, setting up an interview for me with his two sisters in Rome, and becoming further engaged in the detective project by locating Gladys Parentelli, formerly of Uruguay and currently in Venezuela. Through a member of the extended Icaza family in San Antonio, I obtained an address for the only married couple at the council, Luz-Marie and José Alvarez-Icaza. It took a second trip to Mexico City before I could connect with them, and Betsie Hollants in Cuernavaca salvaged my first trip with her helpful information surrounding the council. After several of my futile attempts at contacting their communities, Pamela Dowdell of the International Union of Superiors General (UISG) in Rome gave me the correct addresses for Marie-Henriette Ghanem in Beyrouth and Marie de la Croix Khouzam in Cairo. I was delighted to discover both still living, able and willing to correspond with me and to issue gracious invitations, which I could not accept because of political unrest in the Middle East.

Through all of my challenges, accomplishments, and frustrations, I experienced great excitement every time I received foreign mail that heralded the discovery of an auditor hitherto missing from my contact. The puzzle fell into place, and there is only one piece missing — Hedwig Skoda, whose whereabouts I have not yet been able to determine, despite Gertrud Heinzelmann's and Rosemary Goldie's efforts in resurrecting fragments of information. By now, I feel a personal bond with all the women, even those I have met only through letters, and I would go a step further and say even with those who are deceased.

I asked each of the auditors the following basic questions:

1. Why were you invited?

2. How did you experience the council?

3. How were you received by council fathers?

4. What did you contribute?

5. How did the conciliar experience affect you?

6. Have you any anecdotes that capture the conciliar scene?

7. What is most important for me to include in my book?

8. How do you perceive the church's direction today in relation to Vatican II?

My intention was to use those questions as a springboard for gleaning the maximum information from the women. Where some other points of interest arose, I followed that lead. The general outline of my book follows the questions more or less as they are listed. After some preliminary information on women's general situation prior to Vatican II and specific factors that contributed to the new "emergence" of women (chapter 1), I lead off by introducing the women and the reasons they were chosen (chapter 2). This is followed by their reception and experience (chapter 3). The logical sequel is the contribution they made both formally in the working commissions and informally by their very presence (chapters 4 and 5). There is a carry-over of new experiences and contributions in my discussion of ecumenism (chapter 6). The conciliar impact and sense of responsibility and mission follows as the women leave the council and go out to tell what they have heard and seen (chapter 7). Who can predict the future? I conclude with some implications from the general direction charted by the council with the presence of women and their own conviction that the future *can, must, and will* see better days, more visibility, and necessarily more inclusion of women as full church members. The "signs of the times" are written in capital letters and inclusive language. The pilgrim people of God are discovering a new Pentecost, immersed in their daily struggle for meaning in life, and they are reading and spelling the text out loud, while Roman authorities remain trapped in the tower of Babel, attempting to hold hostage the bishops of the world and silencing anyone speaking in a non-Roman tongue.

I am aware that in the course of writing my findings on the women, some are given more space than others, and there is an uneven distribution of citations from each in the various chapters. That is inevitable, as I used the material on hand. Women whom I met in person had a decided advantage of getting fuller coverage because of the dynamic of conversation that often takes unexpected turns as one remark leads to another, and specific points can be unearthed and elaborated in a way that is not possible in written correspondence, where the questions posed may not always press the right buttons to draw out the most interesting stories. When I spoke to the women themselves, they were more likely to talk about their conciliar experiences. When I spoke to others about the conciliar women, they were likely to know more about the women themselves and less about the specific details of their actual experience and concrete participation in commissions. Women who wrote articles or books or were interviewed by journalists at the time of the council are more likely to get a more accurate portrayal. In fairness to all the women, I have attempted to utilize all the material I collected, regardless of the unevenness created within the different chapters. I am aware that women from special interest groups, such as Dorothy Day and Eileen Egan from the U.S., though not auditors, were prominent around the council. Unfortunately, space limits prevent me from dealing with them at length.

Part of my approach to determining how the women were received and perceived at the council involved writing to a few bishops and *periti*. I informed them that in this study, they would be *in the background,* while the women would be center stage. Léon-Josef Cardinal Suenens, Archbishop Augustinus Frotz, Archbishop Rembert Weakland (though not a council father), Bishop Charles Buswell, Gregory Baum, and Thomas Stransky replied promptly. I was able to meet in person with Bishop Donal Lamont in Dublin. I also wanted the perspective of live journalists to fill out the many reports and interviews I had read. I met with Eva Jung-Inglessis in Rome and Seán Mac Réamoinn in Dublin, talked to Eva Fleischner by phone in Grailville, Ohio, and corresponded with Bonnie Brennan in Ottawa.

The result is not just a book for women. It is intended to be a historical contribution to the mainline ecclesiology of Vatican II. The whole church belongs to everyone and should be of interest to everyone, women as well as men. Women need to know that they were represented by women at the council because knowledge is power, and women need to claim their own power, especially in an age that is attempting to diminish it further through hierarchical clout. Men need to know that women were at the council because the men in power invited them there. Men need role models of church leaders who courageously dared to do something new because the Spirit working through the signs of the times demanded it.

This book is not just for Catholics. Some of my Protestant friends have told me how significant Vatican II was for them and their churches. Besides, the Protestant observers at the council had a strong impact on the women, and I presume they experienced an equally enriching reciprocation. The Brothers of Taizé figured prominently in the experience of several women. Furthermore, there was the unique breakthrough when the first women's international ecumenical meeting took place during the final conciliar session between some of the auditors and various invitees of the World Council of Churches.

I got an enthusiastic response from the women I met. "The story needs to be told," they said. "It must be the Holy Spirit that inspired you to do this." I am convinced that the story needs to be told fully. The women need to be listed together — for the first time in English, as far as I can determine. The conciliar lists were fragmentary, as the new auditors were named, a few at a time. In many respects we are presently experiencing a chilling winter blowing in from Rome and gradually killing off the spring shoots of Vatican II, including the daring, prophetic action of Paul VI in inviting women to a council for the first time in history. We need to evoke what is fast becoming a *dangerous memory* because women moved several steps closer to the altar and to being taken seriously as full church members.

Women today need to be encouraged by that action in the past. A pope can turn things around in the church, no matter what his predecessors have done. Unfortunately, that can also work against progress. But the seed that is planted and dies for a time will spring forth to new life in another season. Young women of the present and future need to know that those of us who lived through the council, the dinosaur generation, have more than gripes to pass on about the church. Let those who have ears to hear, hear. Those who have eyes to see, read my text. Those with a tongue, create a forum and spread the word. There once were *council mothers* as well as fathers, and the hour is coming when all women will claim their full equality in the church as elsewhere in society, when the Spirit is let loose again, and a new day dawns.

CHAPTER ONE

WOMEN MUST COME CLOSER
TO THE ALTAR

═══ ❖ ═══

Not *That* Close, Please

"The church is not racist, but it does *not* admit *women* to its council." These words made headlines in a Belgian Catholic newspaper during the first month of Vatican II (October 1962).[1] There were outsiders taking stock of the council and its omissions. Within, a Protestant observer, United Church of Christ representative Douglas Horton, missed women from the beginning, especially since his wife, Mildred, was not permitted to join him at the first conciliar session. In the earliest reflections in his *Vatican Diary,* he recounted a meeting of non-Roman observers held at the Waldensian theology college (October 18, 1962).[2] It was mostly for men, "but when it came to the light refreshments at the close, gracious ladies suddenly appeared (as they seem to in every part of the world) with laden trays — this time with pastries for which Rome is famous."[3] He later mentions invitations to the Foyer *Unitas,* an ecumenical organization within the Roman church. With it are associated certain "Women of Bethany," an order of nuns begun in the Netherlands, who take vows like other nuns but dress like ordinary women, work for the promotion of ecumenism, and run a hostel in which many of the observers resided while in Rome.

Within his first month in the council hall, Horton had a flash of recognition that something was even stranger than his insertion as a Protestant among a sea of Catholic bishops.

> It suddenly came over me, as I sat looking at this vast assembly of almost three thousand people today that it has about it an

air of artificiality and that the main reason for this is that there is not a single woman in the whole company. Up and down the nave you look and into the transepts, nothing but men. It is an abstracted body, incomplete, a torso of true catholicity, speaking more of an outmoded past than of the living present. Let us hope that the world will see something of Rome's strong women at Vatican III.[4]

The winds of change descended on the council a little sooner than he expected.

Journalist Eva Jung-Inglessis recounted a true story.

The German bishops were holding a national meeting before the council, and other people were present also. The floor was opened up. "Any questions?" A young woman at the back said, "I wonder if the women will be invited to the council." People thought, what a silly question! It was self-evident that no woman could ever be invited to a council. We were all indignant about such a question and thought, what a shame that a woman gets up and asks such a stupid question. The bishop who directed the meeting was perplexed for a moment and did not know what to say. He finally responded, "Now, to this council, no, but to the third Vatican Council, yes." So all were happy. Theresa Münsch put the question to provoke thinking about it.[5]

The seed was publicly planted.

"Women must come closer to the altar, to souls, and to the church in order to gather together the people" (cited by Archbishop Paul Hallinan in written text, October 1965). Thus spoke Giovanni Battista Montini, archbishop of Milan, on February 11, 1961, suggesting that at least one Roman Catholic church leader was finally acknowledging its discriminatory practices in regard to women and the need to reverse them. Later, as Pope Paul VI, he broke with tradition and invited twenty-three women as a symbolic presence of officially invited auditors at an ecumenical council *for the first time in history*. This action was then perceived as just a beginning. Others would follow until women would no longer be treated as minors but as full and equal members of the church. In his encyclical *Pacem in Terris,* John XXIII had already recognized the changing social and cultural roles of women as a "sign of the times" that could not be overlooked by the church. But how close is too close?

Given the postconciliar actions of Paul VI, it is difficult to imagine what he had in mind in bringing women "closer to the altar and to souls."

This chapter title brought a smile to Bernard Häring's face, since he knew Rome's attitude toward women.

> In 1949, the Vatican issued a "very important Instruction," approved by the pope, on three issues: private chapels and above all altar "boys." It said there — no joke — "only when there is no man, women, including consecrated women, can give the responses but only *ex longuinquo,* that is, from a distance." It was explained that a woman who during Mass would come close to the altar would commit *grave sin* (which meant of course mortal sin). The Instruction also said, "All moralists *agree* that a woman coming closer to the altar beyond the communion rail, would commit a grave sin."[6]

With the aid of his smart students in Gars, Häring went through all the manuals of moral theology since the Instruction. "We found only two culprits who really 'taught' this. Bad enough, but worse when the Vatican then said '*all.*' "

During the second conciliar session, both Douglas Horton and his wife set out for Rome together. Mildred, like other guests, was fortunate to be given tickets for the opening ceremonies each morning and for some special celebratory occasions, but not the working sessions, so she had to be in her place by 7:30 a.m. She was not permitted to sit with her husband in the observers' special seats in the rotunda. Observers and their wives were taken on special outings to Assisi and Monte Cassino. In each case, history was made as sex barriers were broken, the cloister was lifted, and for the first time in history (with perhaps a few exceptions for some queen or another) women ate in "what is usually the desolately male refectory of the monastery."[7] One advance led to another as the Reformation women prepared the way for their Catholic sisters to take back some of their own church space. Horton talked about a "rumor" that at the next session there would be "five women — repeat, *women* — among the auditors."[8] It was common knowledge that when the first list of auditors was brought to Paul VI, he expressed surprise that no women were included. Apparently, they were intended to be on the papal guest list, but someone else controlled the list. Horton continued, "so next time it is likely that another giant step in *aggiornamento* will be taken."[9]

Prior to Vatican II, women could clean church sanctuaries, and after church hours they could come close enough to strip altars and spend long hours mending, washing, starching, ironing, and replacing linen altar cloths, priests' amices, albs, and purificators (the last only after the priest had given them the initial rinse, lest women's hands should come in contact with any residue of consecrated wine).[10] Women sacristans could remove, clean, and polish the sacred vessels — chalice and ciborium — but only while wearing white gloves. They could arrange flowers, remove candle grease, and replace candles, especially in the long white metallic interior-sprung variety, which were lit mainly for High Mass, Benediction, and Forty Hours Exposition, and were likely to jump from their moorings if not properly secured, much to the terror and dismay of unsuspecting altar boys. So what else had the revolutionary Paul VI in mind for women's role in church?

In 1972, the tenth year of his pontificate, the pope issued his apostolic letter instituting readers and acolytes to replace clerical tonsure, minor orders, and subdiaconate, and to maintain clear distinctions between the *institution* of lay ministries and the *ordination* of clerics. The idea was to flesh out the greater involvement of the faithful in liturgical celebrations in keeping with their baptismal priesthood, as specified in the conciliar documents and in keeping with liturgical renewal. In reality, the minor order mentality, seeing reader and acolyte as stepping stones to priesthood, prevailed in the papal document, despite its protestation to the contrary. Otherwise, how can one account for the inclusion of norm no. 7: "In accordance with the venerable tradition of the church, institution in the ministries of reader and acolyte is reserved to men"? Here "men" was not used in the so-called "generic" sense. It clearly meant *male* persons, and no reason was given beyond that of the age-old tradition. It would seem that literacy to the extent of being a good reader is the main requirement for public proclamation of the word in church, while adequate mobility and a reverential disposition suffice for acolyte. One would be hard pressed in this latter half of the twentieth century to claim that *men* are better qualified as a group for these services than *women* as a group. What appears to be operative in this legislated discrimination is the residue of the Levitical priesthood and its taboos about ritual purity, mainly the fear of menstruating women, although this does not account for banning little girls from being altar servers.

In the years following the council, most parish churches included women with laymen as readers and distributors of communion with or without formal installation ceremonies, as common sense prevailed over the letter of the Roman law, and baptism was recognized as the primary requirement. In 1976, Paul VI approved the publication of *Inter Insigniores,* the declaration against the ordination of women, a text that ignored even the modest conclusions of his own Pontifical Biblical Committee, which claimed that Scripture alone could not decide the issue one way or another.

In 1994, John Paul II finally agreed that girl altar servers were permissible, at the discretion of the local bishop. On May 30, 1994, the pope issued a "definitive" apostolic letter, *Ordinatio Sacerdotalis,* restating the past, present, and future exclusion of women from ordination, while extolling woman's dignity and vocation as "holy martyrs, virgins, and the mothers of families." The papal letter added nothing new and simply repeated the old prohibitions and reasons without any reference to contemporary scholarship. The text is generally seen as a reaction to progress in the Anglican Church of England, which voted to accept women for ordination and actually followed through by initially ordaining thirty-eight women. The ordination of three women to the diaconate at Christ Church in Dublin, Ireland (June 1994), made headlines because it was the first time in over nine hundred years that *no men* were ordained. Rome perceives women's ordination in the Anglican Church as an obstacle to ecumenical progress between the two churches.

Ordained Anglican married men defecting to Rome in protest against their own church's ordination of women are received with open arms. By way of contrast, ordained *women* from another Christian tradition who join the Roman Church forfeit their ordination under all circumstances. Furthermore, the Barnabas Society provides monetary and emotional support for the newcomers, their wives, and families until they become financially stable.[11] Meanwhile, celibacy continues to be mandated for Roman Catholic men seeking ordination, and priests who have left and married are barred from ministry. The only altar to which women are drawing closer appears to be that of ongoing self-immolation and sacrifice as they endure new onslaughts of blatant and disguised sexism.

Women before Vatican II

For many women in the past, entrance into religious life meant up-ward mobility, as priesthood did for men, who would otherwise never have the opportunity of higher education. At the same time, the sisters were often the indentured servants of the hierarchical church, since their life structures were patterned after the patriar-chal society and were regulated by Canon Law and a Rule that had to be approved by Roman male authorities, with regular checkups of canonical visitation by the local ordinary, the diocesan bishop. In addition to staffing schools and hospitals, sisters were also in de-mand as the domestic staff in boys boarding schools and seminaries. Women were not permitted to earn degrees in theology. When they were finally accepted into the doctoral program at Catholic Univer-sity of America, women were permitted to hear the lectures only while sitting in the hallway outside the classroom. When Protestant women were first permitted to attend the Master of Divinity classes in Toronto, their grades were not posted outside the classroom door with the men's because they were higher.

In the United States, sisters often worked for less than one thou-sand dollars per year in the Catholic school system, with no pension plans and few, if any, health care benefits. Most were poorly pre-pared for the teaching they were expected to do as soon as they joined the community. The religious habit, rather than a university degree, was their passport to the classroom, while they began to work on their degree on the twenty-year plan through the summer school phenomenon. One's major area of study was frequently deter-mined by the courses available rather than one's interest or aptitude. This continued until the revolutionary Sister Formation movement of the 1950s.

As late as 1960, despite more than forty years of suffrage, no woman had ever served in a significant position either on the fed-eral or state level. Women had little to say in the political system and the voting record for women was significantly lower than that for men. In state politics man was king, and woman was little more than a silent consort. In the sphere of domestic policies, man was also master of his own castle. Divorce and child custody laws were rigid for women, and they had few or no rights concerning do-mestic violence or sexual abuse. There was little hope of escaping from an abusive spouse. The overall response to the situation was denial. Battered wives recalled how the Roman Catholic Church's response was to send them back to their abusive husbands with the exhortation to try harder to please their spouse. For numerous unrecorded wives, this eventually led to further abuse, rape, and even death.

Women served on school committees and fundraising groups and participated in endless parish school carpools. Few, if any, had a say in the financial or administrative tasks of the parish. Theologically, they were still viewed mostly in terms of their reproductive processes. The practice of "churching" women after childbirth persisted, re-inforcing the stereotype that sexuality and childbirth made women ritually "unclean," while no such ceremony marked the participation of the male in the procreative act. A girl who became pregnant in high school had to drop out, while the boy who impregnated her did not. In many churches women and men were segregated to opposite sides of the church, and the odd couple who deviated from this norm was seen as an anomaly.

Prior to the council, journalists sounded out notable theologians and some laity on their expectations from the forthcoming ecclesiastical gathering. Rosemary Goldie was among those tapped for her opinion. She responded briefly:

> When we speak of "the layman," we may hope that the term will be taken to include a mid-twentieth-century version of "woman's place," not only in the home and in society but also in the church; that it will be wide enough and flexible enough to extend from the "ordinary" Catholic to that somewhat hybrid class — to which I belong — of lay full-timers at the service of the church: that it will be studied also in the context of modern life at all levels: local, national, international.[12]

In the days preceding and following women's presence at the council, there was much talk about women "emerging" in church and society. One could only ask, emerging from where? The truth is that women were there all the time, but no one took notice of them. When the church hierarchy began to look in women's direction, they saw a throng *emerging from the fog of clerical mental blindness*. They numbered more than the series of 144,000 numbered in the Book of Revelation. In the in-between time — between Cardinal Suenens's conciliar call for women's inclusion and the actual nomination of women — women also emerged as subjects of journalistic articles and interviews. *Ave Maria* magazine contacted a panel of ten women from different parts of the U.S. and various walks of life and published a series of ten articles from the findings about the emerging "New Catholic Woman," the new opportunities afforded her, her vocation, her work, her marriage, her children, her concerns, her relationships to men, parish, council, and society. The information was gathered before it was publicly known that Rome intended to invite women as auditors, although the publications took place during the third session, when women were arriving in dribs and drabs. Some of the women said it was the first time anyone had ever asked for their opinions on church and parish.[13]

The panel's responses indicated that the tide was turning for women, although the old mentality lingered. It was being critiqued, and new visions were emerging. Some women resented the "bill of goods being sold by the Betty Friedans, Simone de Beauvoirs," and other books on the "woman problem," claiming that "with every door now open, woman is nevertheless supposedly trapped by her biological function...still enslaved by that monster, 'male-man.'"[14] The "ideal woman," which is usually a male construct, is obviously internalized by the woman who hopes that "maybe we're at the tag end of the feminist movement and we'll swing into a wildly feminine era," in which all will realize that "woman has power only when she remains a woman."[15] In truth, the new feminist wave had barely begun. Generally, the women recognized a radical change in their circumstances, compared to their mothers or grandmothers, although they claimed that the Catholic woman herself remained basically the same, with her primary vocation as marriage, her primary responsibility childbearing and childrearing, her primary duty to her husband and family, her primary fulfillment within that realm, and with the husband as primary authority. There were shades of agreement that for a woman a career and marriage did not blend, and there was some suspicion of a woman's motives for working outside the home, although some women might need the challenge, while for others it was an economic necessity.[16] Some women's basic distrust of other women was manifested in the reaction to women's ordination. One admitted that the very thought of it "leaves me cold.... The thought of going to confession to a female priest strikes terror into my soul."[17]

Women with a new vision claimed the *vocation to marriage* on equal footing with what was previously called "vocation" in the exclusive sense of meaning religious life. They saw the new Catholic woman becoming even more Catholic by carrying her mission beyond the parish ghetto into the social and cultural world, where she could find kindred spirits among non-Catholic women. The ideal modern Catholic woman was *one* (integrated), *holy* (trying to perfect herself), *catholic* (universal in interests outside herself), and *apostolic* (trying to bring Christ both home and abroad).[18] She advocated educating women for freedom and responsibility. She was critical of the parish that did not answer the needs of educated women, either in the liturgy, sermons, or parish organizations. Women needed to hear about social justice issues and responsible parenthood, instead of seeing medals pinned on the parents with the most children.[19] Emphasis should be placed on developing women as complete human beings before and after marriage, instead of blaming women's "immaturity" for family breakdown and at the same time training them to remain infants intellectually and spiritually.[20] Women were looking for mutual partnerships and shared parenthood in marriage rather than male "heads" for their female "hearts," as pre-Cana conferences taught. The home needed "two hearts for children" and division of authority along lines of expediency.[21] The complex and multidimensional art of parenting, in which many women chose to specialize instead of working outside the home, was grossly undervalued. Some early feminists were also guilty in this regard, so that instead of bonding with the grassroots majority of women, they made the mistake of pitting themselves against them.

One of the most notable changes perceived in the new breed of woman was that *she read* widely and avidly. While the married woman continued to be totally committed to her family, she also recognized the need for private outside interests, which, rather than detracting from the family well-being, actually contributed to it by taking some of the heat off husband and children for meeting the woman's needs in a parasitic way.[22]

Far from fleeing from responsibility, new Catholic women wanted to give more service to the church. They finally realized that the official church was ignoring their existence, and they saw that as "a modern scandal." The women concluded that the whole church will be the loser if the Vatican Council misses the opportunity for hearing women's voices.

Sexism in Seminary Formation

The ambiguity toward women in the 1950s, which still persists, though less obviously blatant, is hardly surprising when one considers the attitudes toward women engendered in seminary formation manuals and practice. Woman was the temptress and had to be excluded as a potential threat to the celibate vocation of the candidates for priesthood. Since women were not permitted to take theology courses, there was no question of their being seminary professors, no more than laymen in that exclusively clerical role. Many American seminaries were established in remote, rural locations, thereby facilitating the exclusion of seminarians from contact with the "outside world," especially where women were concerned. The only safe women from a formational standpoint were vowed women religious, properly habited and veiled and generally constituting the kitchen staff. "Glorified maids we were," said sisters in my own community.

I heard a true story about sisters who worked in a seminary in England. Apparently, the boys and young men were locked in their rooms at 8:00 p.m. and could not leave until morning, lest they become involved in unspecified naughty conduct in the toilets during the night. They arose early each morning and went to meditation. The sisters put on their aprons, went to the male students' rooms, and emptied all the chamber pots. Then they removed their aprons, washed their hands, and they too went to meditation. When a newly elected superior refused to let the sisters continue to act as chamber maids, the seminary rector was not pleased, but the superior was adamant and finally won the day. Small wonder that clerics who went through this system have difficulty relating to women as equals and accepting them as peers in theological faculties of colleges, seminaries, and universities. Popes who went through this system as young men could not possibly see how women could "signify eminence of degree [ordination], for a woman is in the state of subjection...by her nature."[23] Ironically, clergy today often lay claim to the servant model of priesthood, while women — models of servanthood par excellence — who have been and still continue to be at the service of family, church, and society at large, are automatically excluded from ordination, on the grounds that they are *by nature* incapable of imaging Jesus, the servant of humankind.

Social manuals for seminary students published in the 1900s exemplified clerical attitudes toward women in seminary formation.

Manuals warned that seminarians are to be guarded in their "social intercourse" with women, observing scrupulously the guidelines for contact with "the fairer sex." Women who chance to visit the seminary must be met only in the parlor or in another suitable public place. The young men were warned that "custody of the eyes" is of paramount importance in dealing with women.

Several noteworthy male saints in the Christian tradition equated misogyny with virtue. For example, Bonaventure in the thirteenth century wrote in his rule for novices, "Shun the society of women as you would a snake and never speak with a woman unless necessity compels you. Do not look at any woman's face, and if any woman speaks to you cut her off as quickly as possible."[24] That explains a lot. "Three hundred years later, St. Robert Bellarmine wrote that there were three classes of people who could grasp no more of theology than the sound of the words. These classes were country folk, idiots, and, you guessed it, women."[25] Unfortunately, such attitudes are not all past tense.

Critics of feminism in the 1960s voiced the concern that it would lead to the church becoming more effeminate and woman-oriented and would thus alienate more males. The complaints ran that "there are already too many feminine influences — the effeminate statues of Christ and the saints, the sugar-coated hymns, the lace-curtain approach to liturgical vestments and altar cloths. Why make matters worse?"[26] At least one medical authority privately opined that the so-called "feminine exaggeration" in the male-dominated church is due to compensation and sublimated sexual repression. "Priests and seminarians grow up feeling that sex is either dirty or devilish nice, in either case forbidden. When the day comes that they realize that their own mothers must have had sexual relations, they turn to the Virgin Mary as the only pure symbol. In these circumstances the emphasis on purity and Mary by celibate priests is the logical consequence."[27] Presuming the correlation between the downgrading of women, undue effeminateness, and devotion to Mary, Schalk hazarded a guess that "perhaps by giving women their rightful place in the church, Momism and its opposite number, clericalism, would be considerably reduced because there would no longer be the need on the part of a celibate clergy for continuous compensation for this lack."[28] He concluded that feminism is going to increase, so "whatever the outcome, the mere fact that there are grave problems, serious theological difficulties, and enormous emotional hurdles is not sufficient reason to make this subject of women in the church taboo."[29] In retrospect, one can see how accurately Schalk was reading the signs of the times in this regard. Rome's failure to do so has not stemmed the tide of feminism, and the attempt to gag the church at large in this regard is merely the sexist, clerical death rattle. The 1995 statement of forty U.S. bishops indicated that they have heard this menacing sound, and they called for ongoing discussion on ministerial topics necessary to save the church, such as the possibility of ordaining women and married men, as well as the need to respond more practically to the real-life issues of the faithful.

Given the fearful, sexist indoctrination to which clerical students have been subjected for centuries, the wonder is not that the clerical church has been and sadly continues to be in many ways so misogynistic but that so many priests and bishops managed to develop a moderately humane pastoral approach toward women at all.

Ecumenical Forerunners to Women as Laity

The idea of laity as an ecumenical subject and the awareness of ecumenism as a responsibility of laymen and women as well as hierarchy came from the World Council of Churches (WCC), not Roman Catholicism. "The pioneers of this 'ecumenical movement' came indeed to a great extent from the lay movements dating back to the last century, in particular the YMCA and the World Student Christian Federation," stated Rosemary Goldie, and "in the great confrontation of the churches with the modern world 'the layman [sic] was more important than the theologian.' "[30]

That did not mean that full representation of women and laymen came easily either in the WCC or its respective members. The first assembly of the WCC in Amsterdam in 1948 expressed concern for participation of the whole church in its committees on "The Life and Work of Women in the Church," "The Significance of the Laity in the Church," and its youth delegation. The "delegates affirmed that 'the church as the body of Christ consists of men and women created as responsible persons to glorify God and to do His [sic] will.' However, as they acknowledge, 'This truth, accepted in theory, is too often ignored in practice.' "[31]

The concerns expressed in Lausanne and Amsterdam led the WCC to establish the Commission on the Life and Work of Women in the

Church in 1949 and more widely through the member churches following the WCC's second meeting in Evanston in 1954, which led to the establishment of the Department on the Cooperation of Men and Women in Church, Family, and Society.

Some Catholic lay groups were stirring in the early 1920s, but while they involved women, there was no explicit platform to address issues of women's equality. Ecumenism was not a major issue either for the first two World Congresses for the Lay Apostolate, although they raised the issue of Christian unity. Laypeople were encouraged to pray for that unity, while being bound by the papal instruction of December 20, 1949: "the only legitimate union is that of the return of the dissidents to the Roman Church."[32] Nevertheless, ecumenical contacts and friendly exchanges increased between some Catholic and Protestant lay groups and also between COPECIAL and the WCC. Eventually, this led to a changed ecumenical climate in Rome.

The Incoming Tide Lifts All the Boats

French Dominican theologian Yves Congar, one of the last giants of Vatican II, who died in 1995, produced a landmark book in the early 1950s. It was translated as *Lay People in the Church*,[33] a title that does not do justice to the author's intention in the original French, *Jalons pour une théologie du laïcat*. Experts claimed that Congar had in mind something more dynamic and tentative, "signposts" for a theology of the laity at a time when sound theology was needed for the shift from church as hierarchical institution to the more inclusive communal model (Introduction, xvi). Congar noted his omission of anything explicitly about women. He presumed that "a complete theology of the laity will be a total ecclesiology: it will also be an anthropology, and even a theology of the creation in its relation to Christology" (xvii). In other words, no one could afford to be left out any longer. This was the basis for the inclusive theology of Vatican II, its emphasis on the priesthood of all believers through baptism, the universal call to holiness, involvement of the whole church in both the spiritual and temporal realms without dualistic compartmentalism, the pervasiveness of the Spirit in the entire Body of Christ, and the consequent infallibility of *all* the faithful, including women.

Congar was well schooled in the practical theology of the laity because he was a *peritus,* or expert theologian, at the First World Congress for the Lay Apostolate in 1951 with participating delegates from seventy-four countries and thirty-eight Catholic international organizations. Vittorino Veronese, a layman, had taken the initiative to organize that with the able assistance of Rosemary Goldie, who then organized a second congress in 1957 and a third congress to coincide with the first Bishops synod in Rome in 1967. The significance of the two congresses in the 1950s cannot be exaggerated in terms of preparing the way for lay involvement in Vatican II and especially the gradual inclusion of women, some of whom were in the front line of action at the congresses and in the various Catholic international organizations, while the vast majority of their married sisters were immersed in trying to make a go of homemaking, and women in religious communities distinguished themselves as "religious" over against "seculars" living "in the world" outside the convent walls. Conciliar women, such as Rosemary Goldie, never lost the sense of women being primarily *laity* in the Roman Catholic Church, so that whatever pertained to laity pertained equally to women and men. This was the way into women's recognition as active members of the church.

Through his words and actions Pope Pius XII recognized that "the hour of the laity has struck." The biblical term *laos* meant all the people, but in the course of history, the church became clericalized to the extent that church became synonymous with hierarchy or clergy. In 1922 Pius XI in his encyclical *Ubi Arcano* gave a major impetus to what came to be known as Catholic Action as an extension of the apostolate of the hierarchy. Thus began the official rehabilitation of the laity. They were intended to be elastic organizations, such as the Jocists, the Jeunesse Ouvrière Chrétienne, an organization of factory workers begun by Abbé Joseph Cardijn in Belgium after World War I (1914–18), the Legion of Mary begun in Ireland in 1921 under Frank Duff (later an auditor at Vatican II), and the Grail Movement begun in Holland in 1929 (Rosemary Goldie was a member of the Grail).[34]

In the 1950s and early 1960s, the controversy raged over what constituted Catholic Action, and heated discussions took place at the Second World Congress in 1957.[35] In his address to the First World Congress for the Lay Apostolate, on October 14, 1951, Pius XII "traced the development of the modern lay apostolate back to the

Council of Trent, to the first Marian Congregations and to Mary Ward."[36]

This background material is important because it locates old battles that resurfaced at the council and were handled more expeditiously because of the preliminary discussions at the congresses. Keenly aware of this, Goldie named this era as the first of three stages in the remote preparation "of the work of the Conciliar Commission on Lay Apostolate, which not only drafted the decree *Apostolicam Actuositatem,* but also collaborated with the Theological Commission in drafting chapter 4 of the constitution *Lumen Gentium* and, especially, in preparing the Pastoral Constitution on the Church in the Modern World."[37] Goldie stated unambiguously: "If, for the first time, an Ecumenical Council had dealt explicitly with the laity and the lay apostolate, the fact was largely due to active sharing in this mission by lay men and women over the preceding decades; but it was a sharing in close communion and collaboration with the Pastors of the Church."[38] Continuing in this vein, she further explained:

> In the remote preparation for Vatican II, the part played by the growth of a mature sense of Christian responsibility among lay people is mainly discernible in the work of the lay movements. These emerged into fuller visibility after the second world war with the foundation or development of nearly forty Catholic International Organizations (C.I.O.) active in almost all fields of Christian endeavor and with the two World Congresses for the Lay Apostolate held in Rome, in 1951 and 1957, and preceded or followed by regional meetings in the different continents.[39]

This gold mine was used as a primary source by the conciliar Preparatory Commission on the Lay Apostolate, according to its secretary, Msgr. Achille Glorieux.

During the third conciliar session, when Englishman Patrick Keegan addressed the council on behalf of the auditors, he could truly say: "This schema [*Apostolicam Actuositatem*] marks for us a point of fulfillment in the historical development of the Lay Apostolate. We sincerely hope that it marks also the beginning of a whole new stage of development. The schema...is also the result of the progressive discovery by men and women of their responsibility and role within the whole apostolate of the church." The schema epitomized the practical questions laity had been asking for years, and it gave signposts and opened doors to the future for both women and men.

Goldie gave an eyewitness account both from within the World Congresses and from her vantage point in Rome at COPECIAL, which was set up by Pius XII in 1952 and served as a general clearing house for preparatory conciliar material on the laity in the absence of a specific department or office for that. The basic texts prepared for the Second World Congress in 1957 dealt with mission and lay vocation. Texts prepared by theologians at the request of the laity later provided a *status quaestionis* as the starting point for much of the council's work concerning the laity. Other texts laid the groundwork for *Gaudium et Spes*.

Most importantly, the studies undertaken by lay women and men conscious of sharing responsibility for the church's mission created a climate in which the council became possible. Speaking from experience, Goldie concluded that "long before the council, lay movements had provided in their international gatherings... the only forum — where awareness of the pastoral problems of the universal church could grow in shared reflection of hierarchy, clergy, and laity. Some of the bishops, many of the *periti*, and most of the lay people attending the council had shared this experience."[40] As a result, when such bishops found themselves at the council discussing topics concerning the laity with no laity present, they became profoundly embarrassed by this absurdity and took steps to have it rectified. To borrow a phrase from John Henry Newman, "the church [assembled in council] looked foolish without them."

The Second Congress for the Lay Apostolate took a giant step toward consulting the laity in matters that pertained to their lives when Pius XII took the unprecedented initiative of referring to the laity for consideration "a 'suggestion' concerning the terminology and structures of 'Catholic Action,' which had been submitted to him"[41] by Suenens, a rising star who was to shine brilliantly at Vatican II, where with Montini he became the architect of an overall conciliar plan with John XXIII's blessing. The papal "suggestion" thrown out to the laity in 1957 would have come to nothing if it had been allowed to die with the pope in 1958. COPECIAL sent out a worldwide questionnaire about Catholic Action, and it passed on the replies to the Preparatory Commission in addition to its own studies.

The International Catholic Organizations set up study groups to deal with such specific topics as international Catholic action, woman's place in church and society, laity's difficulties in social action, the Christian in a world of technology, pastoral problems of the intellectual milieux, and chaplains and organizations for the apostolate.

Other national and international organizations sent in documentation on ecumenical work among the laity, general Catholic Action, the St. Vincent de Paul Society, and cooperatives in the lay apostolate. The most ambitious project was the "Panorama of the Organized Lay Apostolate in the World," a text distributed to the council fathers on October 22, 1963, with the express intention of illustrating for them the concrete reality of the schema that they were discussing. That was during the second conciliar session, when the first laymen were present but no women as yet, although the tide was rising.

Goldie, writing in 1963, expressed disappointment at the further delay in inviting women because they too had been active in organizing and participating in the world congresses and national and international committees.

> When the male auditors were appointed, Catholic women rejoiced.... It was, however, inevitable that the women should wonder...why this small group did not include any female auditor...(the fathers need not be afraid that there would be a "March upon the council" of enraged suffragettes!). But it still remains rather a pity that a very good opportunity was missed for an action that would clearly mean *aggiornamento*.[42]

The discrimination was blatant to Goldie, whose co-worker, Mieczyslaw de Habicht, within the same office, was invited a full year ahead of her. Goldie was the last person to look for personal privilege. Her focus was laity first and women second as a vital part of the laity.

With the eyes of the world on Rome and the publicity given during the second session to discrimination against journalist Eva Fleischner, such extreme methods of exclusion became untenable. Bishops were asked embarrassing questions before the press and could offer no satisfactory answers. The time was ripe for a breakthrough.

Once the women were there the symbol began to function. Speaking about the impact of this small group of women — less than 1 percent of the council — Catherine McCarthy stated quite matter-of-factly, "Well, it showed that women were part of the human race. Half of it was being forgotten. Even though recognition was slow in coming, this was a real step to show that women were a part of the church. It showed the big mistake they were making in not considering us."[43]

The Preparatory Commission's drafts of texts contained nothing on "the Women's Problem." Rosemary Goldie recognized that "Nuns — teaching, nursing, and missionary nuns especially — exert considerable influence (a formidable influence, you may think) over much of the Mystical Body.... And yet, not one mother general was called in by the Preparatory Commissions for the Ecumenical Council."[44] This kind of untapped lay resource has contributed to the impoverishment of a clericalized church. Not a single mention was made of women in the first conciliar session, not even when *De Ecclesia* was discussed for the first time. Two interventions were made during the second session. At least fifteen interventions were made during the third session and ten during the fourth. Not all were positive or contributed to women's advancement, but the most important point was that *women were present in the flesh and could no longer be ignored.* African bishops, mindful of the absence of African women, brought forward some of their specific problems and issued prophetic calls for an end to slavery by promoting the full liberation of woman in the church as elsewhere. The "listening women" in St. Andrew's tribune[45] let forth murmurs of approval or disapproval as the bishops took to the microphone.

Women who had been functioning as Christian leaven in all the key sectors of the world were now perceived to be "emerging." They were there all along, but the hierarchical church, lost in the land of Oz, had to remove its blinkers to see who was really in the vanguard of progress in the service of the human family and the world's poor, sick, and ignorant. Women who were capable of organizing, pioneering, and leading religious communities with their missions and secular projects on a world scale had no recognition or visibility in their own church — a church whose founder had died for the cause of inclusivity and had commissioned his woman friend, Mary Magdalene, to "go and tell Peter and the others" the astounding news of his resurrection. Picking up on this foundational tradition, Paul VI recommissioned women as "experts in life" to give their input for church renewal in a way that no bishops could.

When John XXIII was opening Vatican II, he commented that he felt he was launching a big ship that someone else would have to take out to sea. Whether one views the incoming or outgoing tides in Galway Bay, Botany Bay, the Gulf of Mexico, or elsewhere, the pattern is the same. Oceanbound liners, fishing trawlers, tugboats, sailboats, currachs, and dingies of all shapes, sizes, and cargo all rise or fall together in the same water. And so it is with humankind, male and female. Vatican II demonstrated this by growth in degrees of inclusivity. There was a cumulative effect. With the formation of the WCC, the lay tide began to rise, and women too were sighted in the current. Catholic laity took note and started to swim on their own and with hierarchical assistance. Giovanni Roncalli's ecumenical experiences during his Vatican assignments in Bulgaria, Constantinople, France, and elsewhere prior to becoming pope convinced him of the need for human bonding and friendship on all levels. By the time he convened Vatican II as John XXIII, he resisted curial opposition and opened the doors of St. Peter's to Protestant and Orthodox observers. Next came the internationally known active church laymen. The obvious question followed: *Where are the women?* A beginning was made that can never again be ignored for long. All the boats have begun to rise, stir, and tug at their moorings. Even when Peter's barque withdraws into dry dock, as is currently happening, it cannot remain there forever.

Bringing the Whole Church into a "State of Council"

The report of the "Fribourg Meeting" was an important document prepared mainly by laity for the conciliar Preparatory Commission. On the initiative of the president of Pax Romana–International Catholic Movement for Intellectual and Cultural Affairs (the graduate Movement of Pax Romana), Prof. Ramon Sugranyes de Franch, a meeting was held in Fribourg, Switzerland, on July 17, 1960, with the express purpose of bringing together for the first time an international lay group to contribute to the work of Vatican II. There were twenty-two participants, including four priests involved in international activity, and three women. All the laity were active in many areas — political life, UNESCO, education and the university, youth, workers movements, etc. There was one representative each from Africa, Asia, North and South America, and Australia, and the remainder were from Europe. François Charrière, bishop of Lausanne, Geneva, and Fribourg, accepted the invitation to preside over the secret meeting. Goldie, the Australian participant, recounted how "the confidential synthesis of the discussions is introduced with these words: 'The whole church is from now on *in a state of Council.*' "[46] It was an overstatement to think that the *whole* church was as interested and informed as the group that made this declaration, but the fact that such a meeting took place as a lay initiative demonstrated their intention to claim their place in the forthcoming council. The majority of the faithful had some awareness of the "seismic shock for Christendom" that was on the way.

The meeting was *secret* in the sense of not wanting to attract publicity that could hinder its purpose. It was not a case of laity plotting behind bishops' backs. The organizers wanted an open meeting where they could discuss their real problems in the presence of a bishop. What emerged dealt with the status of laity in the church, Christian unity, church-state relations, peace and the international community, church government, pastoral problems in the workplace and intellectual milieux, training of priests for working with the laity, and the church in newly emerging nations.

Many people were responsible for bringing the whole church into "a state of council." Foremost among those deserving mention were lay journalists who interpreted the aims and later the workings of the council for the thinking public, creating a climate of interest and understanding without which deliberations in Rome could never have caught on. The ICO provided regular information for its members and organized a campaign of prayer during the year immediately before the council. COPECIAL launched a worldwide study on unity. Bishops in Belgium and Holland engaged the laity enthusiastically in conciliar preparation. In Canada, in 1964, Philip Pocock, archbishop of Toronto, welcomed the opinions published by twenty-five laymen and women — including housewives, university professors, lawyers, business executives, and trade unionists — when they spoke their minds in constructive dialogue on a variety of topics, including political freedom, labor problems, sexual ethics, ecumenism, theology for lay people, and three approaches to "woman's role" in church and society. In French-speaking Canada, lay consultation began as early as 1961 with special meetings in about ten dioceses, starting with Montreal. One hundred laypeople responded to Bishop Gerard-Marie Coderre's invitation to meet after several months of preparation in the diocese of Saint-Jean. Given this lay input, it was not surprising that the Canadian bishops were in the forefront of calling for declericalization of the church and promoting the cause of women. Bishop Alexander Carter of Sault Sainte Marie complained that laity were consulted "too little and too late" on the schema about lay apostolate.[47]

"So great was the chasm between hierarchy and people when Vatican II began that the thought of lay involvement was hardly mentioned. This was a reflection on the church's withdrawal from the world, of the defensive, rigid, and patronizing attitude the hierarchy had developed following the Protestant Reformation."[48] Once the council started, ghosts from the past, such as John Henry Newman, began to emerge in terms of consulting the laity. Once the "people of God" model of church surfaced, the pyramidal, hierarchical model began to topple.

> A great ferment marked the first session of Vatican II, in 1962, as the progressives discovered how numerous they were. Midway through the session, Pope John suddenly sent for Jean Guitton, a philosopher from the Sorbonne in Paris and a member of the French Academy, whose learning in history, Scripture, theology, and philosophy is astounding. "Tell him to come immediately, immediately!" said Pope John. "He will cast a ray of sunshine across the council."[49]

Guitton came, and the council planners did not know what to do with him, so they located him among the Protestant observers. He was writing a commentary at the time on Newman's doctrine on consulting the faithful. "The layman will no longer appear as a mere adjacent member of the church."[50] A breakthrough had been made in the four-hundred-year-old clerical image of the Roman church, and a return to the tradition of antiquity meant that laity would be present and heard at the council. Clearly this meant *male laity.* Roche cautioned:

> No one is holding up as a model the Second Council of Nicaea in 787, convoked and partially presided over by the Empress Irene. [And why not?] Yet neither is Vatican I (1869–70), which ignored the laity, commendable. Since a council represents the whole church, says Father Bernard Häring, the great moral theologian who preached the pope's retreat this year, "the representation is imperfect, if not invalid, if the laity is totally absent."[51]

In the second session, more male auditors joined Guitton, but they were not truly representative of the majority of church members.

> They are rather removed from the interests of the man-in-the-street [sic]; the first group of auditors, top heavy with intellectuality and international Catholic organization presidents, conceded they were not representative. Since the council was already sprinting for the finish line when the list was augmented, the functions of the new auditors will be mainly to act as window dressing, thus placating the feelings of nationalities, women, and religious.[52]

The most noteworthy factor was that *some laity* were present. A beginning had been made. Laity can no longer be "regarded as foot-soldiers for the clergy," as Bishop John J. Wright of Pittsburgh remarked. It was part of Vatican II's retrieval of a forgotten tradition. "The witness and commitment of many laymen throughout the world, including two Americans named Norris and Work, have helped the church to turn a softer face to the world."[53]

Early in 1963, the board of directors for COPECIAL (Goldie was executive secretary) meeting in Rome, received an official request for collaboration and sent in proposals to Fernando Cardinal Cento's commission for improving the general tone of the schema on the laity, plus specific points pertaining to relations among hierarchy, priests, and laity; coordination of lay apostolate; formation; Catholic Action; international apostolate and social concerns, etc. Collaboration was rather hurriedly sought also from the ICO. Goldie prepared an unofficial English translation of the schema for COPECIAL. Once the laymen came to the council in 1963, they had more direct input into documents. This was also true of the women when they arrived in 1964, but it must not be forgotten that, as Pilar Bellosillo informed me, "We were already living the council for two years *from the outside.*"[54]

Friends in Court

While the tide was turning in Rome in regard to ecumenism and the laity as an essential part of a total ecclesiology, laity themselves, especially women, could not have scaled the Aurelian Wall without assistance from the inside. They were dependent on bishops to take up their cause and speak on their behalf. This remained true for the most part even after the laity were present as auditors. The breakthrough came on October 23, 1963, during the discussion on the church as people of God (*Lumen Gentium*). Léon-Josef Cardinal Suenens, archbishop of Malines and a council moderator, said that systematically excluding women from active church participation made no sense in an age when they go almost to the moon. He called for increasing the number and range of lay auditors. He continued: "Women too should be invited as auditors: unless I am mistaken, they make up half of the human race."

Next day, October 24, the Melkite Archbishop George Hakim of Galilee picked up the same theme, criticizing the schema on the church for its silence regarding women, giving the impression that they did not even exist. He reminded the council of the tremendous advantages accruing to the church from the dedicated service of women. The timing of both interventions was no accident, following as they did right on the heels of the document distributed the day before on the organized lay apostolate in the world. The two speeches brought the question into the open and made way for Paul VI's decisive action. Lobbying took place both within and outside the council. The women arrived a year later. Suenens led the way in acknowledging the missing half of humanity; Hakim picked up the theme; a chorus of other voices followed once the women were present.

Years later, Suenens recounted the story from his perspective, giving the specific context.

> The mention of charisms during the debate on the draft of *Lumen Gentium* triggered a reaction from Cardinal Ruffini, author of at least one hundred statements. He now asked that this word be suppressed; he felt that charisms were all very well in the primitive church, but their mention as something that might still be relevant today could easily lead to abuses. I felt, to the contrary, that this mention was necessary, and that the charisms of the Holy Spirit are an integral part of Christian life. The council adopted this point of view, and mention was made of charisms in the council text, with a wording that was wise and discriminating, but definitely positive.... In calling for the recognition of charisms for all the baptized, I had deliberately emphasized that the term "baptized" referred to both men and women. I concluded my call to openness by saying that "unless I am mistaken,

women make up half of the human race." To this, on the mor-
row, a journalist added, on his own initiative, that "women are
also responsible...for the other half."[55]

Suenens continued:

> It is hard to believe to what extent such truisms, and their prac-
> tical applications, were still not obvious in those days. I had to
> speak personally to Pope Paul to request that the few women
> who were present as observers at the council be allowed to re-
> ceive Communion from his hand. And I was unsuccessful in my
> attempts to ensure that Barbara Ward — the well-known and
> remarkable economist from Columbia University — should be al-
> lowed to speak at a Council meeting. She wrote a paper which
> was read by the American observer, Nolan [the wrong name is
> used here for Norris]. In later years, she spoke at a post-conciliar
> synod; many doors have opened since.[56]

Suenens was rightly hailed as the champion of women's cause, to
the delight of some and the fear and opposition of others. Looking
back to the council from 1988, he stated, "at the council time attention was concentrated as such on our Christian duties as baptized
people, and the specific role of the women was not on the order
of the day. In fact, I insisted on their presence in the council, but
my own attention was concentrated in the apostolic renewal in our
active religious congregations, as you know."[57]

As already indicated, Theresa Münsch broached the subject of
women's presence at the council even before the opening of the
first session, but it was not until council fathers took up the cause
publicly that people began to think seriously about why not. This
was true also of many women and their organizations. In 1961,
Margaret Mealey, executive director of the National Council of
Catholic Women in the U.S., expressed some expectations from the
council.

> The Catholic women of America need explicit directives delin-
> eating women's work in the lay apostolate and establishing areas
> for their work in Catholic Action....It is evident that women's
> contribution...is commensurate with the encouragement and di-
> rection given to them....The question of women's role in the
> apostolate can never be answered, of course, without a descrip-
> tion of the role of any lay person in the apostolate. Therefore,

Catholic women want to know: What is this role? Is there one apostolate or are there many? How can the lay apostolate be most effectively organized? Specifically how does the lay apostolate differ from the apostolate of the hierarchy? How can a climate of trust be created between those who fulfill religious vocations and those who follow lay vocations?[58]

The general thrust of Mealey's input was looking toward the hierarchy for role definitions in regard to women and their apostolate, family life, childrearing, education, and liturgical participation. The prevalent understanding was that the church and its apostolate belong to the hierarchy, who decided the terms for lay participation. Their inclusion was seen as a *privilege,* rather than a natural baptismal *birthright.* That was also the mentality with which the women auditors received their invitations to listen in on the council in session, while keeping their mouths shut.

At least an editor for *America* was bolder than the women dared to be. We read: "The biennial congress of the National Council of Catholic Women, Nov. 3–7, in Detroit, invites reflection on the all-male gathering of church leaders in Rome for the Second Vatican Council. What about the status and role of the Catholic woman? Was there a subtle irony in the fact that the first heroic-size statue of a saint to meet the eyes of most bishops, as they filed into St. Peter's to begin their labors, was that of St. Teresa of Avila?"[59] The writer commented that while the sixteenth-century Spanish mystic and later proclaimed doctor of the church was not clamoring for "women's rights" in her day, times have changed. She referred to "the staggering achievements of lay and religious women, at almost every level of operation," in education, welfare, and social action.[60] She then fell back on the usual consolation offered to women in Mary, the one woman who, *alone of all her sex* (a title later used by Marina Warner in her excellent book about Mary), was so different from everybody else that she made the grade in getting some church recognition and pedestal treatment. Douglas Horton commented on all the references made to Mary as the "beloved patron of the Church of Silence," referring to Christians in persecuted lands.[61] She could also be seen as the patron of the silent female auditors in St. Peter's.

While theologians were not council fathers in the sense of speakers or voters, they were often the "holy ghost" writers of bishops' speeches and conciliar texts, so they too played a part in creating the climate that hastened or retarded women's becoming visible in the church. One bishop was heard referring to the gallery where the *periti* sat as "the rebels' roost."[62] Noteworthy among such *periti* was German theologian Karl Rahner, whose own position on women's role in the church evolved over the years.

> Everything the church is proclaiming today about the lay apostolate and its worldwide mission should be applied also to women, says Karl Rahner, S.J.... "Theoretically, this position of equality is no longer being disputed, but in practice much still remains to be desired...." "Because of the lack of priests, the church today is compelled to call on women to occupy posts in the hierarchical apostolate... Care should be taken by the clergy not to look upon these women's tasks as subordinate auxiliary jobs, but rather consider the women as independent, respecting their dignity and communal responsibility for such work."[63]

Such progressive theological stances were not appreciated by Alfredo Cardinal Ottaviani, the faithful watchdog of the "Holy Office" (now called the Congregation for Doctrine of the Faith). Someone with a touch of wit and rhyme captured the climate of hostility toward the hasteners of *aggiornamento* and wrote:

> Congar and Rahner and Küng
> Are names that are frequently süng.
> But Ottaviani
> On some fine *domani* [tomorrow]
> Will see all the three of them hüng.[64]

While the prophecy was not literally fulfilled, conservatives who opposed the conciliar vision lashed out vehemently against the powerful German theologians, including Häring. The time was right for a change. The challenge was issued, and Paul VI responded courageously but cautiously by bringing in a small, symbolic presence of women. At the close of the second session, Horton was glad to get home. He wrote: "Mildred's presence with me has redeemed the experience of being the exile it would otherwise have been.... It is stimulating to feel that one is witnessing a majestic turn of the tide in history."[65]

Guess Who Is Going to Rome?

"I think the really big excitement will come when, some day, the curia finds out there are women in the church. And I have a feeling that moment is now nearing." Thus wrote Katherine Burton in April 1963, six months before the question of conciliar women was openly faced in the aula. Burton was referring to "a clerical — and masculine — concept which, consciously or unconsciously, rules out any possibility of a serious contribution on the part of women."[66] Burton's observation was that "the ecclesiastical circles concerned are just not thinking about women at all."[67] Goldie added her "Amen" to the wake-up call when the church begins to take women seriously.

The beginning of a new day dawned seven months later. It was not a concession that had to be wrung from the pope. He wanted to be more inclusive of women in the church. As pope, he was disappointed that no women's names appeared on the first list of proposed auditors. Goldie, with her finger on the Roman pulse, cited a reliable source, Msgr. Vincenzo Carbone. Apparently, the campaign for women following Suenens's speech actually delayed the pope's invitations. Bernard Häring, C.SS.R. testified that "Suenens stirred up great displeasure among conservative bishops, especially Italians, so that it took a lot of courage on Paul VI's part to invite auditrices."[68] A low-key approach would have been less threatening to conservatives and less likely to give the appearance of a weak pope acceding to popular demand.

Adolph Schalk captured the climate that greeted women's coming as auditors:

> One of the jokes floating around the council last fall dealt with women's place in the church. A group of powerful Catholic women's organizations, the apocryphal story went, got together and fired off a formal protest to the Holy Father over the inferior role that women play in the church. In no uncertain terms they demanded a greater say in church matters. The Holy Father (a nonexistent one, let it be said at once, and no irreverence is intended), greatly disturbed by the letter, called a special meeting of the College of Cardinals. He had the letter read aloud to them and they all agreed that it was a grave and delicate matter. "Obviously," said this fictitious pope, "we can't give in to these demands. Tradition is against it. Christ and the apostles were all

men. The church was from the beginning guided by men. It is a man's church. We must not let women gain a foothold! But before we reply to these women, charitably but firmly, let us pray for guidance: Hail, *Mary*, full of grace.... "[69]

The "joke" is only partially apocryphal. In point of fact, the conciliar preparatory commission did receive a formal protest-petition, "Wir schweigen nicht länger" (We Won't Keep Silence Any Longer), from Swiss lawyer Dr. Gertrud Heinzelmann, on May 23, 1962 — five months before the council opened. This was no joke. It started as follows:

> Certain recently published articles which have presented a somewhat anti-feminist view (primarily Herder's *Wort und Wahrheit*, a report...which contains the charge that the church has been undergoing a harmful "feminization" — despite the fact that women have had nothing whatsoever to say about church policies) have inspired me to address myself to the Preparatory Commission of the Vatican Council. I speak as a woman of our own times who, through her studies, her profession, and her many years spent in the work of obtaining for women their rightful place in society, knows the needs and the problems of her sisters. I turn to you with the hope that this petition will be given the consideration warranted by its seriousness and its importance. In what I have to say I am a sister to all other women. I should like my words, therefore, to be understood as a protest and as an indictment brought by one-half of all humanity — the feminine members of the human race, who have been suppressed.'[70]

Critiquing Roman Catholic theology's sexism, stemming from Thomistic underpinnings and defective Aristotelian biology whereby woman was perceived to be a defective human being contributing nothing to the genetic generation of other humans, Heinzelmann called for opening the ordained ministries to women on an equal footing with men. She was a member of St. Joan's International Alliance, founded in England, the first organization to speak of women's ordination and equality in the church. Its visionary members maintained a presence around the council and set the parameters for more cautious progressives. Having women present at the council was no joking matter for Heinzelmann. "I suffered horribly as a child," she says, "because I found it incomprehensible that I could not become a priest merely because I was a member of the female sex."[71] As a lawyer, Heinzelmann devoted her life to promoting the cause of women and other disadvantaged persons in society and church. Her presence around the council was part of this ongoing work. Recounting the jocular version of the serious petition, Schalk commented,

> If the reader does not laugh, it is just as well. For, alas, there is indeed more truth than humor in this joke, which illustrates, if in a bizarre way, a rather puzzling anomaly that characterizes the church. For does it not seem strange that the church which gives such unparalleled homage to the Virgin Mary is the same church which, if the truth be told, more often than not relegates women to an inferior status? As a prominent Catholic (male) physician said to me during the third session of the council, "the church has made women second-class citizens. Why, they can't even be altar-boys!"[72]

Schalk continued his analysis of women's exclusion from church positions that count:

> Unlike the other reforms, however, the feminist changes are proving to be slow going. A great many prejudices and hardened thought processes will have to be overcome, and enormous adjustments made before women are genuinely accepted as equals in the church. Even the council, which leaves one dizzy from the whirlwind speed of its reforms, has been proceeding most cautiously, even ponderously, before giving a voice to women.[73]

After the female auditors came, Schalk noted that changes began to take place,

> and one can even say that the feminist movement has really begun to come out into the open. Where it will all lead even the women themselves don't know, but one thing is certain, we are going to hear a lot more about the subject. The voices are getting louder, more numerous, and more articulate. So we might as well start making adjustments now. For the women are rising as an army in battle array, determined to be put into their place even if nobody, themselves included, quite knows what that place should be.[74]

It was clear that things had to change. Schalk quoted a woman who had devoted most of twenty years to Catholic lay activities:

> Part of the reason why women are not given a real share in the council may be because the council is run by celibate bishops, who are accustomed to putting women "way out there." Women are an unknown quantity, forbidden territory, and just trouble-makers and gossips in general, as far as parish work is concerned. They are good enough to scrub the church and prepare spaghetti dinners but are seldom if ever consulted on policy matters. I number many priests as good friends, but as far as the work of the council and the church are concerned, I think the general idea is that they believe women don't have much to contribute.[75]

Schalk recognized that "now the church has the beginnings of a full-fledged feminist movement on its hands.... Once the council prodded open the doors and windows of the church, even feminism could not be held back."[76] I commend Schalk for his accurate perception of the movement that was quickening at the time of the council. Unfortunately, it was almost a stillbirth in terms of actual movement for women *within the church,* after the conciliar euphoria died down, although women's spirits continued to rise, and they began to hear one another to speech in theological and pastoral circles. Paul VI's invitation to female auditors was the symbolic start.

Betsie Hollants, former editor of a major Belgian newspaper, had a journalist's nose for smelling out a good story. She resided in Rome during some of the sessions. She was aware of the Latin American bishops' difficulty in getting together to exchange ideas, and they had to practically get permission from Rome to meet. In Rome, "each was in his own cubby hole," said Hollants. She tried to get a room near the Vatican with a coffee pot where the bishops could meet, but that fell through because of too much red tape involved. But Hollants was not about to give up. She knew many of the bishops from her work with Ivan Illich in Cuernavaca, where they ran a program for preparing prospective missionary sisters, priests, and brothers from Canada and the U.S. for their work in Latin America. She had also traveled extensively in Latin America. Since her plan for the bishops club fell through in conciliar Rome, Hollants started to invite bishops to her apartment. She explained what a venture that was.

I had no maid, and I am no cook, so this was rather risky, but you know in Italy you can always go and buy salad, rolls, coffee, and soup broth. I know better how to make soup, but during the war we never learned to prepare meat, so meat was out of my personal life. From the second session on, every day of the council meetings, I invited twelve, fourteen, or sixteen bishops and an odd mother superior or father general to my apartment for lunch. They got wholesome, simple meals and of course wine. A friend of mine once said, "Betsie, aren't you going to be ashamed when you leave this apartment, and the owner of the place is going to see how many empty wine bottles are in the place?" You know, the wine was less expensive than mineral water. You know the water in Rome, so I wasn't going to poison bishops. They all came and loved it, not just Latin Americans but others. There was always room for everyone who came, and they served each other. One day there was not enough room because an extra bishop came. We put the ironing board between two chairs, and that solved our problem of table space. You see my style. I never withdrew. I was always there, and I heard all the conversations, so I knew everything that was going on inside the council![77]

Hollants had occasion to meet with Paulo Cardinal Philippe on business pertaining to Illich. He would not look at her, and when she mentioned that women should be at the council, he assured her that would never be possible. "What about baptism?" she said, and he had no answer. Hollants explained to me further: "My original idea was that sisters should be sent to Rome to get to know all they could about the council. I told the mother superiors to send those with doctorates — the more degrees the better. Let them be willing and humble enough to run errands for bishops, be their secretaries, etc., and in that way hear what's going on." That is what many of the smart priests in Rome at the time did. According to Archbishop Lamont, "Manning, Law, and Baum from the United States were the small boys carrying the briefcases for the cardinals, so they were on the periphery of the council."

On September 8, 1964, the pope told a group of women religious and members of secular institutes at Castel Gandolfo about his intention to invite women auditors. He announced:

We believe that the time has come for the religious life of women to be given more honor and to be made more efficacious. We

have given instructions that a few qualified women should assist as auditors at several solemn rites and at some of the general
congregations ... during which questions will be discussed that
might particularly interest the life of women. In this way we will
have for the first time, perhaps, a feminine representation, not
numerous of course but significant and quasi-symbolical of you
religious women first of all and then of the great Catholic organizations of women, so that they may know how much the church
honors woman in the dignity of her being and in her human and
Christian mission.

In this way, the pope leaked the news to the public a week before the council reopened for the third session. It gave the opposed,
the reticent, and the fearful a few weeks to brace themselves psychologically for the actual appearance of the women in council. The
women, preoccupied as they were with overcoming their own timid-
ity before this awesome gathering of dressed-up men whom they
equated with church, thought only of the privilege that was theirs
in being admitted to see and hear. Little did they realize the trauma-
tizing effect their presence had on many bishops. Not knowing and
not identifying with the seminary textbook definitions of themselves
as temptress, the devil's gateway, etc., little did the women realize
the iconoclastic alarms set off even by their silent, self-conscious
presence.

One might think that when the pope spoke his word was law
(*Roma locuta, causa finita!*). Not so. As Xavier Rynne reported:

The cardinal's [Suenens] reference to the attendance of women at
the council, of course, immediately evoked a number of ironical
comments in the press. The cynical right-wing *Il Borghese,* in
an article entitled "Il Feminismo di Sua Eminenza" conjured up
all sorts of supposed horrors that would result from taking the
proposal seriously, from the resurrection of the scabrous days of
"Popess Joan" and "furtive Boccaccio-esque encounters" to the
dire prospect of an "Aristophanian Parliament of Women." It
cited the editor of *The Tablet* (London) to the effect that "I had
hoped in the near future to be included among the lay auditors
at the council, but it appears now that my wife will beat me to
it," as a result of the intervention of "the paladin of ecclesiastical
neo-feminism."[78]

There is nothing very exciting or daring about inviting twenty-three women as silent spectators to a gathering of some three thousand men, until one specifies that the event is an ecumenical council of the Roman Catholic Church and that never before in its history have women been present at one of its councils. Even the empress Theodora was not permitted to exercise her lawful right and call the council of Nicea (325). Instead, she had to defer to her husband, who became emperor only through his marriage with her. Horton recalled how "no woman had been present at any ecumenical council since the Empress Irene summoned and ratified the acts of the Second Council of Nicaea in 787 (and I am not sure that she looked in on the business sessions even then)."[79] Meanwhile, women have always constituted at least half of humanity and more than half of church membership. With Vatican II, at least women were set on the road to Rome. There is no turning back, no matter how long the journey, how many the roadblocks, how frequent the guerilla warfare, how painful the insults, or how devious the religious legitimations that try to deflect them from achieving full church membership in keeping with their baptismal calling.

CHAPTER TWO

THE MISSING HALF
OF HUMANITY SURFACES

=❖=

Alone of All Their Sex

The twenty-three women who finally made it to Vatican Council II were there, not because they scaled the Aurelian Wall, but because they were, like the Protestant observers, Paul VI's invited guests — except that the women were guests in their own house. Their presence was different from that of the other Catholics present, the bishops and even their lay counterparts, the twenty-nine male auditors. The women were a "symbolic" presence of the other half of humanity, hitherto absent from the male-dominated councils for most of two thousand years, although some women were present at the local Synod of Whitby (664 C.E.)

Their presence created a stir at first. It is difficult to say who was more shocked by the record-making papal decision to invite them — the Roman curia or the women themselves. "We are delighted to welcome among the auditors our beloved daughters in Christ, the first women in history to participate in a conciliar assembly." The papal welcome resounded through St. Peter's as part of Paul VI's plenary address at the opening of the third conciliar session on September 14, 1964. Ironically it highlighted his momentous decision to invite female auditors because none were present to receive his welcome. Bishops and reporters looked in vain for women in the still all-male tribune of St. Andrew. Douglas Horton, who had been keeping score for every female appearance, noted on September 15 how eight auditors had taken communion at the 9:00 a.m. Mass, "but among whom, alas, there are as yet no women to be seen." Recalling that the schema on the Blessed Virgin Mary was to be discussed next day, he continued, "I cannot think of a more appropriate moment for the women to take their seats here."[1] Next day, he watched again. "Some women — five of them — took communion this morning, but this is nothing new. It happened last year. They left the basilica before the debate began. Still no women auditors."[2]

First of all, no women had as yet been officially named. Second, because of the formalities involved in conveying unconventional invitations to women in various parts of the world, the women themselves often got the message secondhand. A reliable source recounts how "a Council official less than enthused about their [women's] presence had held up publication of the names because restroom facilities were not adequate."[3] This was not an uncommon problem experienced by women pioneering in the hitherto all-male space of medical schools, seminaries, and the Lateran University, as Goldie testifies.

A week after the papal welcome to women, Horton wrote:

> No woman has as yet been admitted to a working session of the council, but today's papers say that one has been appointed — Mlle. Maria Luisa Monnet of France, president of the International Federation of the Independent Social Welfare Organization. Pope Paul VI announced her selection yesterday at a Mass in St. Peter's. Announcement had previously been made that a few women, both religious and lay, would be invited to the council as auditors, but only to certain meetings, when the subject under discussion would be of special interest to women. This is surely a break from yesterday, when women's concerns were supposed to be limited to drawing room music and the things of kitchen and nursery, before it was generally known that intelligent women are likely to be appealed to by the same causes as intelligent men. Here a strong dose of *aggiornamento* would seem to be in order.[4]

The First Woman to Cross the Male Divide

"On September 25, 1964, my sixty-second birthday, I entered the council for the first time," said **Marie-Louise Monnet.**[5] Horton did not miss the grand entry. "It was just before the Mass that I glanced over at the auditors' tribune, when what to my wondering eyes should appear but — a woman! Though I could not be sure of recognition at that distance, I judged from pictures I had seen

of Mlle. Monnet that it might be she."[6] Monnet's friends recount
an amusing story of how she came to be the *first* woman auditor
to enter St. Peter's. She was well known to French bishops from her
founding of Catholic Action groups for youth and adults. In October 1961, Archbishop Angelo Dell Acqua, then substitute secretary
of state, had said to Monnet during conciliar preparations, "Come to
the council so as to get to know the bishops and become known to
them. Come also and meet the observers from other Christian com-
munions. I will help you." The fact that meetings with bishops were
facilitated for Monnet, even before auditors were appointed, illustrated the climate that was developing, especially after John XXIII
set up a preparatory commission for the lay apostolate on Pentecost
1960. The French bishops nominated Monnet as an obvious choice
for auditor.

Paul VI knew Monnet, "La petite madame de Paris,"[7] from her
setting up of MIAMSI while he was secretary of state. On September 20, 1964, members of the constituent assembly of her movement
(MIAMSI) attended the pope's Mass in St. Peter's and were received
in audience. When the pope recognized and greeted Monnet, she cut
through the red tape and thanked him for his willingness to admit her as an auditor. What could the pope do but make a public
announcement to the group?[8] Underlining the importance of lay participation in the council, he added: "I can tell you already today in
confidence that your president is on the list of persons whom we
have the intention of inviting to the council as an auditor." Gladys
Parentelli was present. She said the pope

> raised his eyes from his prepared text and looking at us, made
> the announcement in his deep, hoarse voice. Then he continued
> to read his printed text, but we were so overcome with emo-
> tion that we heard nothing, as we whispered to one another how
> we were witnessing a historic moment — the appointment of the
> first woman ever to enter an ecumenical council.... On purpose,
> we bought *L'Osservatore Romano* next day, to see Marie-Louise
> Monnet's appointment in print, but it was not there, despite
> the fact that they had transcribed the pope's discourse of the
> previous day, but not the phrase that he had added.[9]

On September 25, Monnet entered the council, even ahead of the
president of the World Union of Catholic Women's Organizations!

"It was a big, happy surprise for her to be invited as an auditor," recalled Lucienne Salle, who was a young woman associated with Monnet at the time of the council through her own work for the youth movement and who now works in the Pontifical Council for the Laity.

> She never made much of it that she was the very *first* woman to enter the council. For her, it was something very natural that women were there inside the church at the council, and they didn't need any more recognition. If they were doing something more, that was fine, but Marie-Louise was not someone to be pushing more for women's rights. She always wanted to be "an ordinary woman." She was really an ordinary woman the way she dressed and lived. Nothing of that changed when she went to the council. She was not good in languages and only spoke French. She was not an intellectual woman, but she could understand and correspond with many different people. In her generation, women were not supposed to do prolonged study.[10]

Monnet's family experience shaped her for life. She tells how her father dealt in the international business of brandy, *eau-de-vie*. He owned the Cognac Monnet firm, and the whole family was shipping this famous Cognac all over the world. (It is now owned by another company, although there are still some bottles that say, "Cognac Monnet.") The whole family was open to the world because of that. The connection between selling Cognac and being a conciliar auditor is not immediately obvious, but it will unfold. "At that time [in the early 1900s] it was not customary to receive clients at a hotel or restaurant. It all took place at the family residence."[11] From a very young age, Monnet experienced her father's hospitality as a mode of negotiating with customers from many different countries, including Germany, Scandinavia, Japan, Canada, and the United States.

Her brother, Jean, was a political figure already involved in the early organization of the United Nations. He is sometimes referred to as "Father of Europe," since he was actively involved in recovery efforts in Europe after the war. He was the English-speaking secretary general of the UN in Geneva and asked Marie-Louise to help him manage the house and entertain guests from the different countries attending the UN meeting. This gave her an open mind. She wondered why Catholics were not involved in this international work of fashioning the world of tomorrow and why they were not interested in the meetings among countries and furthering the mission of the church. From her own experience, she became convinced of two things: (1) that the church needs to be open to the whole world, and (2) that the church is and has to be universal.

In 1931, as Monnet was approaching her thirtieth year, which she saw as a turning point in her life, she went to Lourdes to invoke Mary's assistance in deciding her future. She met the Young Christian Workers (JOC) from Belgium, who had come to celebrate the twenty-fifth anniversary of the priestly ordination of its founder, Fr. Joseph Cardijn. From that encounter, she discovered the concept of peer ministry, the apostolate of similar people ministering to each other. It was not just an apostolate *to* or *for* youth, but also *by, with,* and *among* youth. They could reach each other by their example of a Christian life in factories, schools, and other places where the clergy were not present. The primary apostles to workers were workers.[12] In this way they would be spreading the reign of God everywhere in the world. Monnet decided that what Cardijn was doing for youth needed also to be done for the middle class, the bourgeoisie, and the aristocracy.

She saw this as an obvious response to Pius XI's call for Catholic Action to transform the social milieu by a real conversion of heart followed by authentic Christian living. In this way, the whole social ambience would be changed slowly and profoundly to such an extent that the people in it would recover the connection between the faith of Christ and their own everyday lives. No one knows that milieu better than those living in it. Monnet started with the youth group in France and was president of the Young Christian Female Independent group. She remembered that her father had taught her to "see, observe, hear, and speak to those you meet; thus you will learn more from paying attention to others than you will read in any book."[13] As youth members grew into adulthood, she saw the need to continue an adult group for them, so she became involved with the Independent Catholic Action (ACI). This later expanded and developed into an international group that was finally approved in the church and officially named the International Movement for the Apostolate in the "Independent Milieux" (MIAMSI) in 1963. Her experience was that life itself had become a place for encountering God, so that living was a religious adventure in a very profound sense, and a workplace could truly be experienced as a "state of grace."

From her experience as a "nomad" in the independent milieu,

traveling especially to various parts of Africa in the 1950s in response to Pius XII's 1957 encyclical *Fidei Donum,* calling for the evangelization of that continent, Monnet recalled how "in the early days of the church, it was the traders, the magistrates, the soldiers, the functionaries, and particular individuals whose names remain unknown...who spread the gift of faith they had received."[14] Monnet saw that same process being renewed before her eyes with the new communication and exchanges among nations. And here the connection with the Cognac international business becomes relevant, as no doubt more than brandy was exchanged in the hospitality of the Cognac Monnet household, where people got together, listened, and talked. More than brandy was brought back to the ends of the earth through this basic model of evangelization in the independent milieux of the open world. It was a social, collective event that went beyond the personal vocation Monnet discovered for herself back at Lourdes in 1931. Artificial barriers between the sacred and profane created the real de-Christianization of society and had to be pulled down as a complete ecclesiology was realized through the collaboration of clergy and laity. Monnet explained how

> the point of departure for the organized apostolate in the independent milieux was situated in my own life at the confluence of two joint encounters: the encounter with the call of the church, launched by Pius XI, and the encounter with the young Christians being responsive to that call in their milieu by way of their peer apostolate. It is at that juncture of those two routes — that of the church and that of the world — that the birth of the apostolate in the independent milieux took place.[15]

A key principle of Monnet's involvement in various forms of Catholic Action was "nothing without the bishop."[16] Another was in keeping with the newly emerging spirituality of the laity: "Nothing has to be added to our life; it is not a question of introducing supplementary actions; it is a question of recognizing Christ at work, living in us, in everyone we meet,...allowing him to transform our minds,...our outlook,...our actions."[17] Salle explained,

> That's why she wanted the international movement, MIAMSI, and that's why when the Vatican Council opened, she [Monnet] was in Rome all the time. She stayed there at the Columbus Hotel near the Vatican because she wanted to have contact with as

many people as possible. She was very good friends with Alan and Guite Galichon, and they invited many people to their home. They had bishops from everywhere, especially Africa. They were very close to the church in Africa. So Marie-Louise's invitation to the council was a big surprise, and yet it was very normal.

Archbishop Joseph-Marie Martin of Rouen was the first to salute auditors as "brothers and sisters,"[18] or as Horton says elsewhere, "laity in both kinds."[19]

The fact that Monnet was the *first* woman to enter Vatican Council II was not planned that way. Several invitations were issued at the same time, and it so happened that she was there on the spot and ready to respond immediately. In retrospect, it was fitting that this "ordinary woman" who worked on the largest canvas of the world — "ordinary daily life" — should be the first symbolic presence of what should be the church's all-inclusive arena. Within that, all other specialized apostolates are located.

Global View of Thirty-Six Million Women

At the appointed hour on January 27, 1989, I arrived at the Bellosillo residence on Felipe IV in Madrid to find my host already in place with her solid brass hexagonal timepiece prominently displayed, and Julio, the translator, equipped with tape recorder, poised and ready for action. Within the first ten minutes, I received our schedule for two solid working days, punctuated by lunch and tea breaks, a Sunday evening working-social meeting with local scholars and friends, plus an outline of the major topics to be covered in her prepared text. It became immediately obvious to me how this great eagle-eyed, highly organized woman, **Pilar Bellosillo**, was chosen as the president for the WUCWO, a position she held for thirteen years. The clock was a gift from her predecessor, the outgoing president. Bellosillo was wearing a gold watch, a recently acquired gift from a local television station, on the occasion of her presentation on John Paul II's meditation, *Dignitatis Mulieris*. Over the next three days of reliving the conciliar experience, analyzing the main themes, and critiquing their implementation from the early post-conciliar era up to the present, I discovered that this woman had a sense, not just of time, but also of the "signs of the times."

With a feeling for contextual theology, she began with a note on the unique situation in her native Spain, with its marriage of church and state in the 1960s. It was the age of 100 percent Christianity, national Catholicism, "proselytizing by force," and bad law. Vatican II's openness to the modern world, to non-Catholic Christians, and even non-Christians, was both a surprise and a disappointment to the bishops of Spain, including Archbishop Vicente Enrique y Tarancón. It caught them off guard and left them disconcerted. Against this backdrop, the full impact of the council with its ecumenical thrust and Declaration on Religious Freedom (*Dignitatis Humanae*) can be grasped only by someone who lived in Catholic Spain during the reign of Franco's dictatorship.

During the Spanish Civil War (1936–39), graphically immortalized in Pablo Picasso's *Guérnica* — not one of Bellosillo's favorite art pieces — on display in an annex to the Prado Museum across the park from her residence, her parents took their nine children to Lisbon for safety. Her father and eldest brother returned to Madrid, where they suffered much, including imprisonment. By the grace of God they were not killed. Bellosillo points to a picture of the Sacred Heart on the dining room wall, where it has hung for more than sixty years. She believes the Sacred Heart protected them, despite how the rest of the house and their beautiful belongings were ravaged. Now she and her sister, Carmen, live on the third floor of the large house that once belonged entirely to their family.

Bellosillo was part of the lay delegation chosen to attend the solemn opening of the council in 1962, and she was expected to be an auditor. After all, WUCWO represented about 36 million women worldwide, and she was its president. Communication lines between Rome and Madrid were not the fastest, and others got the word before she did. Her hairdresser was the first to break the news to her. He had scanned headlines in the morning paper and gleefully informed his celebrity customer, "I think you are one of the women who are going to the council." She probably got an extra good hairdo that day.

La Bambina Vaticana

Australian **Rosemary Goldie,** in her usual self-effacing manner says, "I was there; it would have been hard not to invite me." True, given Goldie's Roman and worldwide involvement prior to the council. Sometimes referred to as *la bambina vaticana* (the child of the Vatican), she is "tiny, wise, spirited and elfin."[20] I hoped I would recognize this conciliar celebrity among the throngs of people risking their lives as they battled Roman traffic crossing the Via del Plebescito at Piazza Venezia on a hot July day in 1988. I expected to meet an Amazon. I did, under the guise of *la piccinina* (tiny little thing). This was John XXIII's description of her as she was pushed to the front line for a picture and almost fell at the papal feet during an audience of COPECIAL in 1961. Later, in January 1989, I learned that heavy theological discussions could take place even as we dodged traffic crossing the Tiber, with me defending the cause of women's ordination from two paces behind my fearless leader.

Goldie referred to herself as belonging to "a category that is closed forever... 'woman auditor at Vatican II.'"[21] She was the only woman invited among a group of special guests (not auditors) at the Extraordinary Synod of 1985 commemorating the council. The group was constituted solely as a memory of the council and consisted of nine cardinals, a bishop from Eastern Europe, three theologians (Hans Urs Von Balthasar, G. Martelet, S.J., and Max Thurian of Taizé), and Stefan Swiezawski, a lay professor from the Catholic University of Lublin, who had been an auditor.

In her office in Piazza San Calisto, overlooking the church of Santa Maria in Trastevere, Goldie displays a picture of John Paul II visiting her there in 1979. She tunes in daily to Vatican radio at 2:30 p.m. "to hear if the pope has done anything spectacular." While technically retired from teaching at the Lateran University, she still directs students' theses at Regina Mundi, and she is in constant demand as guest lecturer on subjects ranging from John Paul's *Dignitatis Mulieris* to cults and sects. She continues to be a consultant of the Pontifical Council for the Laity and the Secretariat for Promoting Christian Unity. She was part of the Vatican's delegation to the WCC in Canberra in 1993.

Goldie played several pioneering roles during her lifetime, or, as she said, her "three lives," referring to her experiences in Australia, France, and Italy. She was born in Sydney, the only daughter and youngest of six children of world-traveling journalistic and theatrical parents, who returned annually to Australia or New Zealand for the birth of a child, then left the children to be raised by their maternal grandmother. Goldie first went to Europe in 1936 on a French government traveling scholarship, studied at the Sorbonne, and returned home as the Second World War clouds were gathering. In 1945, she returned to Paris on a traveling scholarship to work on a doctorate in French literature. She was among the first civilian passengers to pass through the Suez Canal after the war began. She signed a document relieving the crew of the *Moreton Bay* of any obligation to deliver her safely to her destination. Before she could complete her doctorate, her membership with the Grail led her to accept a four-months' job at Pax Romana in Fribourg, and this extended into six years. When Pius XII set up a permanent committee of the laity in Rome to give "lasting fruit to the 1951 World Congress," Vittorino Veronese from Pax Romana headed the committee, and knowing Goldie's expertise, efficiency, and multilingual skills, invited her to Rome. She traveled to organize meetings on the lay apostolate in Africa, Asia, and Europe. She also organized the second world congress on the laity in 1957.

After Veronese left the committee to become director of UNESCO in Paris in 1958, Goldie inherited his work — without his title. After several months of deliberations, she was made executive secretary of the COPECIAL, working with a board, rather than general secretary as Veronese had been. Goldie explained, "I'm not the right type to be a feminist — I'm not a fighter." It is partly true that she is not a fighter — at least, she could not understand my aggressive approach to bargaining with the open-air vendors, something she could never do. However, she protested that while she may not be a feminist, she is not outmoded either. Her own experiences of sexist and clerical discrimination have sharpened her sensitivities. She is convinced that the job discrimination in COPECIAL was for no other reason than that she was a woman, and that hurt her deeply. A woman of her caliber and prominence in the lay apostolate was well known to Cardinal Montini (the future Paul VI). Her committee served as a clearing house for many conciliar matters, including nominations and arrangements for a lay delegation to the solemn conciliar opening ceremony, the arrival of male auditors in 1962, and a communications center outside St. Peter's. Some council fathers had already solicited her personal input on documents, especially pertaining to the laity. Even with living in Rome and working within Vatican City, Goldie's invitation, dated September 21, 1964, and signed by the council's secretary general, Pericle Cardinal Felici, took two days in transit and reached her an hour before it was announced to the press.

Goldie's primary identification is as a layperson. Her inclusive orientation comes from a long history of working for the cause of laity, rather than specifically women's groups, as she tried to bring all sides along. She is also aware that all women in the Roman Catholic Church are laity, not clerics, so that everything pertaining to laity also includes women, a point she often repeated at the council.

Goldie has worked in Rome for over forty years, as executive secretary of COPECIAL for nine years, then undersecretary of Concilium de Laicis, a position she shared jointly with Mieczyslaw de Habicht from 1967 to 1975, so she holds the dubious honor of having been the only "curial woman" for nine years. She was also lecturer at the Lateran for nineteen years, where she said, "I taught a subject I never studied formally (pastoral theology), in a language I never studied formally (Italian), to priests." Citing G. K. Chesterton, "anything worth doing at all is worth doing badly," she claims to have done so many things she was not prepared for, "but one does what one can." She is a living embodiment of encyclopedic knowledge, especially of the laity and their Roman connections for more than four decades.

The New Phenomenon of Secular Institutes

Italian **Alda Miceli** was president of the Centro Italiano Feminile (the Italian Women's Center), a coordinating group of Catholic women in Italy, and international president of Secular Institutes, the Missionaries of Christ the King. Her own main activity was in the international Italian women's center, which was involved not only in formation work but also in the social and political field, but not party politics. Miceli, on a trip to the Holy Land in September 1964, came down from Mount Tabor for lunch and was greeted by a Franciscan priest who was reading the newspaper. "Look what's happening in Rome," he said. Paul VI has appointed women to the council. One is an Italian named Alda Miceli. Do you know her?"

In her elegant apartment with its abundance of huge indoor plants, large poinsettias, and many pictures of the animals she loves, Miceli has her own way of creating the outdoors inside, in the heart of Rome and close to a busy, traffic-packed roadway. Prominently displayed in her study are her favorite pictures, an antique painting of the Madonna and Child and a picture from Vatican II with cardinals and auditors. It was really as president of a lay secular institute that Miceli was invited to the council.

When pressed to tell me something personal about herself, Miceli responded:

> I'm from Calabria, but my family was a family of patriots who worked for the unity of Italy. From two or three years of age, I was in Rome. I was educated by the Sisters of Saint Dorothea, who helped me a lot in growing up and in my religious education. I studied arts at the university. While I have been living in Rome, I kept up my contacts with Calabria. As a student at the university I was involved in the FUCHI, that is, the Italian Catholic University Federation, where my brothers were already involved. It was part of the movement of university students, which is a part of Catholic Action. When my brothers and I were students, the national ecclesiastical assistant was Msgr. Montini, who later became Paul VI. He was a great friend of my family. I also met the Gioventù Feminile, that is, the girls branch of Italian Catholic Action. Personally, I preferred the university movement, which had a more open spirit. I was able to collaborate with other young women in Catholic Action, and it was there I came to know Amida Parrelli, a great figure in starting the Gioventù Feminile and its work. Through Parrelli I came to know Fr. Jamelli, the Franciscan, and her co-founder of the Catholic University in Italy. This was influential probably in deciding my own vocation. Through these contacts I was drawn to consecration in a secular form. In the girls Catholic Action, first I was a member, then a leader, and finally I was president. As president I had much contact with Pope Pius XII, who became almost my spiritual director during that period.

For eighteen years Miceli worked with the Centro Italiano Feminile, during which she appreciated Msgr. Montini's interest in the movement. For eighteen years she was president of the Secular Institute of Christ the King, to which she belongs. "I am a member of Catholic Action in my parish, a member of the Centro Italiano Feminile, and a member of the secular institute, so I am back to grassroots, 'on the ground floor,'" she added, "and I am happy there after all the years in leadership positions."[22]

The U.S. Contingent

A total of three women from the United States attended the council, **Mary Luke Tobin, Catherine McCarthy**, and **Claudia Feddish**. Feddish was invited because of her rite rather than her nationality, so I will speak of her later in that context. Unsuspectingly, Tobin was halfway across the Atlantic aboard the *Constitution* on her way to Rome, "just to see what was happening around the council," when she received three shipboard telephone calls from reporters, asking how she felt about being invited by the pope as an auditor. That was the first she had heard of it. Tobin was the superior general of the Sisters of Loretto at the Foot of the Cross, an all-American community founded in Kentucky in 1812. Tobin was invited because she was the newly elected president of the Conference of Major Religious Superiors of Women in the United States.[23] She explained,

> I was elected just in time to be an auditrice, and had it been a few months earlier I would not have been because they took whoever was president that year. I remember when we gathered after the election, and the group suggested that I go to Rome, listen, find out all I could about what was happening about religious life, and bring it back. I never expected to go and stay, although there was talk about women being invited.[24]

Tobin was walking in the fields when I met her at Nerinx. She had just finished a series of talks to young women candidates considering becoming Sisters of Loretto. She told them about the council and her meeting with Dutch theologian Edward Schillebeeckx. Topics of conversation included problems facing religious, formation programs for young people, the novitiate, etc. One thing in particular stood out for her: "A novitiate should be a smiling and sunny place." In subsequent years, Tobin did her best to make it such, as she led her community as a pioneering group in the direction of renewal. Her own talks frequently reflect her fascination with Karl Rahner's deep theological ideas based in human experience. "Everything stems from this," she says, "that 'every human being is the event of God's absolutely free, radical, self-communication,' and when people get that, they have a sense of who they are."

Coupled with this Rahnerian foundation is Tobin's immersion in the writings and spirituality of Thomas Merton, and she has been co-ordinator of the Merton Center for Creative Exchange in Denver for many years. Her concern for peace and justice issues is well known nationally, and she has actively participated in nonviolent demonstrations at Rocky Flats, Lowry Air Base, and the U.S. Air Force Academy, besides participating in international missions for peace, justice, and solidarity in Ireland, England, France, Netherlands, El Salvador, and South Vietnam. When asked if her political awareness was an outgrowth of the conciliar experience, Tobin said no. "I went into the council with that agenda."

Tobin combines a deep seriousness and concern for all human, environmental, and global concerns with a lightheartedness that makes it all bearable because of the ultimate source to which she is so consciously linked. While she can be on the picket line, or receiving the U.S. Catholic award "for furthering the cause of women in the church" or the Prophetic Voices award from the Women's Ordination Conference, or giving a seminary convocation address or a challenging presentation at the Future of the American Church Conference, she can just as easily slip into her old ballet shoes and engage in a liturgical dance, as she did during the celebration for her eightieth birthday a few years ago.

The other U.S. woman not belonging to a religious community who was a conciliar auditor was Bostonian **Catherine McCarthy**, now living in San Francisco, who was president of the National Council of Catholic Women — a branch of the National Catholic Welfare Conference, the coordinating agency of the U.S. bishops. Her husband died in 1949. McCarthy was recognized for her outstanding contributions to the church when she received a Pro Ecclesia et Pontifice medal from Paul VI in 1964 and a special Dominican Tertiary award because of her outstanding service in Catholic Action. "Mrs. McCarthy's life is a record of service to God and neighbor."[25] Margaret Mealey was executive secretary for NCCW when McCarthy was president. Their teamwork during the interview[26] gave me some insight into how these two strong, accomplished women cooperated in the leadership of their national organization and were able to steer it through a significant era of its history, especially during Vatican II and its aftermath. They explained to me how the NCCW, as a federation of fourteen thousand Catholic women's organizations, represented ten million American women, and it had representation in WUCWO with its headquarters in Paris. NCCW declared itself solidly behind the decrees of the first and second sessions of the council, as reflected in its resolutions. The theme of the national convention in 1964 was "Vatican II and YOU." "Through all the conventions and conferences she attended, the bishops knew Catherine McCarthy as a solid citizen," piped in Margaret Mealey, who planned all the meetings during the McCarthy presidency. "One thing you learn through training and experience," said McCarthy (a former high school teacher) "is when to keep your mouth shut and listen. That was noted too."

I was curious as to why the NCCM (men's group) petered out, and I was told that apart from the fact that women are usually the driving force that keeps most things going, "the NCCW was organized right down to the parish, diocesan, national, and international organizations. Parish affiliations were our main stronghold," said Mealey. "Our mission," said McCarthy, "was to educate the Catholic woman from the parish level up to national and international level. I think the men operated more as an association. They didn't have a strong parish base. They had diocesan councils, and it was more for informing the men of what was happening, rather than for making things happen. One of the effects of Vatican II was a study of a NCCW and NCCM merger to become the National Council of Catholic Laity. But it didn't work." Mealey interjected, "Men are more interested in short-term projects. We at the NCCW always had continuing programs, and they sustain the organization."

When it was known that women would be admitted as auditors, Archbishop Leo Binz, episcopal chair of NCCW, contacted Rome, asking that the NCCW be admitted. Later the bishop's secretary, Msgr. Francis Hurley (later archbishop of Alaska), phoned McCarthy in San Francisco to say he got a cablegram inviting her as an auditor.

"After flying by Alitalia from New York, I registered at the Majestic Hotel," she recalled, "where a letter from Archbishop Binz awaited me." It read:

> October 22, 1964. Dear Mrs. McCarthy, I have received your cable message informing me that you will arrive at the Majestic Hotel. I am happy to welcome you to the Eternal City. I do not wholly trust the Roman mail, and so I do not send over your documentation. If this letter goes astray, the defect can be made up by telephone, but if your appointment is lost we would be in a bad way. . . .

You did not mention whether you would be alone. If there are others with you, we could have them at dinner also. The larger the number, the more important the advice or information we will get. If you want to come here for dinner, no telephone call will be necessary. If that's not possible, a telephone call just before or after the papal blessing will be sufficient to obtain the necessary documentation I have, which you will need. I renew my congratulations on the high honor you have received, and I look forward to seeing you on Sunday.

The letter demonstrated the good working relationship that existed between the bishop and McCarthy at the time. McCarthy got the precious documents that made her a citizen of the Vatican, and on October 26 she arrived at the council, a month after Monnet.

As Well Known as Any Prominent Cardinal

Early in the council proceedings, a bishop is said to have pointed to the larger than life marble statues of saintly founders and foundresses that decorate the higher niches in St. Peter's as proof that women were not excluded from the council. Two years later French **Suzanne Guillemin**, superior general of the more than forty-five thousand Daughters of Charity of St. Vincent de Paul, smiled up at her holy foundress, Louise de Marillac, as she made her way to the tribune of St. Andrew near the council presidency.[27] Given the scope of the Daughters' work and their international dispersion throughout five continents, Guillemin was an obvious choice for an auditor. She was already pioneering in the Sister Formation movement and led the Daughters of Charity in the revolutionary act of modifying their habit in September 1964, replacing the familiar coronet of "God's geese" with a simple blue veil, just in time to bring the "new look" to the council. Not only did this action cause a stir in the church; it even merited comment from the French Prime Minister Charles de Gaulle, as I will explain later.

When the *St. Louis Review* (October 29, 1965) printed an article, "The People of God of the Future," surmounted by a three-column photo of Léon-Josef Cardinal Suenens, author of the popular book *The Nun in the World*, talking to "a sister" in the auditors' box at the fourth session of the council, several letters to the editor queried why "the sister" was not named. She happened to be "the Superioress General of an international community numbering 45,000 Daughters of Charity, the largest body of religious women in the church." So wrote Margaret Kepler of the Archdiocesan School Office. Kepler continued: "There are fifteen houses staffed by 380 Daughters of Charity in the archdiocese of St. Louis. It would have taken a mere phone call to identify Ma Soeur Suzanne Guillemin, D.C. It's regrettable that no one could take enough time to inquire who the 'nun' was...Ma Soeur Guillemin is as well known in European circles as any prominent Cardinal; her one defect seems to be that she is a woman....May I suggest that if the picture is worth taking, the people are worth identifying" (November 4, 1965).

Kepler was correct in adverting to Guillemin's high profile in Europe. Jean Pihan, F.C., solicited eighteen monographs on "Religious in the Pastoral Context Today" by leading authorities in France in the 1960s. Suzanne Guillemin was the only woman published in the series. In his foreword to her collection of conferences, Pihan stated, "In the church at this time, Mother Guillemin has been 'the number one woman.' "[28]

A second letter came from James Lord, an editor, who extolled the Daughters of Charity as "nuns in the modern world" and Guillemin in particular as a twentieth-century religious, "a modern woman, cast in the mold of Pope John XXIII."

Both letters highlighted the irony of naming the theorist (Suenens) and leaving the practitioner (Guillemin) nameless when discussing a topic of the council that claimed to be predominantly *pastoral* in nature and that invited female and male auditors to supply the data of practical experience. Guillemin was living the "nun in the world" with her community, who were risking their lives for others. Although the Vietnam war was still going on, this danger did not deter her from visiting to express her solidarity with the 164 sisters in seventeen houses in Vietnam in 1963. She visited hospitals in Saigon, leper colonies, schools, fishing villages, mission outposts in the mountains, nurseries, and projects for underfed children. Passing through military installations, their car was fired on. "One shot would have reached Suzanne Guillemin directly if it had not been stopped by a stack of bread destined for the poor."[29] And who might think that the so-called "good sisters" would have nothing to contribute to the council?

On September 28, 1964, the day after her arrival in Rome, Guillemin wrote to her sisters about her first impressions of the council from the inside. "Seeing it is very different from hearing about it," she said.

> This very morning with beating heart I slipped in with the crowd of bishops, entering by the door of St. Martha's.... Mother de Valon and Mother Estrada with Miss Goldie of Australia were there already, and we soon became acquainted and united in our feelings of emotion. Many of the bishops came to greet us in passing. Ildebrando Cardinal Antoniutti came twice, the first time to tell us of his joy at the change we had made in our habit, the second time to bring me a humorous drawing on the flight of a coronet! All this was the exterior, and it soon disappeared when Mass began, answered by the two thousand and more bishops present. Words cannot express the impression given. This was already a taste of the celestial city: at any rate it was the church.... Tomorrow morning the new auditors must arrive a quarter of an hour in advance to take the oath, I suppose that of not revealing what is said at the council, so I shall have to limit my effusions.[30]

An Eloquent Condemnation of War

Paul VI, sensitive in many instances to the power of symbol, invited two Italian "war widows," intending by their symbolic presence "to honor the women who are, with their sorrow, an eloquent condemnation of war, and a symbol of the deepest hopes of humanity for a just and Christian peace." The widows were **Ida Grillo Marenghi Marenco**, a leader in Italian Catholic Action, and **Amalia Cordero Lanza di Montezemolo Dematteis**, president of the Spiritual Welfare Organization for Italian Armed Forces, a society of women (generally coming from military families), who devoted themselves to offering spiritual and material assistance to the military.

At her home in Tortona, in northern Italy, where five generations of her family have lived and three generations are currently living (Ida, her lawyer daughter with her lawyer husband, and their three children, plus ninety-four-year-old Gina, the woman who has been helping with running the home for eighty years), I met Iduccia Marenco ved. Grillo (Ida Marenco, the widow of Grillo).[31] Grillo is so small in stature that Msgr. Luigi Ligutti called her "Signora Zac-chea," after the biblical Zacchaeus, who was so small of stature that he had to climb a sycamore tree to see Jesus. Just as Zacchaeus was called down out of his tree to meet Jesus face to face, Grillo was called to be a conciliar auditor, an "expert in life," specifically from her point of view as a war widow. "Women are the ones who have to live with the reality of war and its aftermath in the loss of husbands, fathers, or sons," she told me.

When Grillo received her invitation to the council, she went to her local priest in Tortona. Together they went to the bishop, Francesco Rossi, who accompanied her to Rome and escorted her into St. Peter's for the first time. It was a personal boost to her to know that the pope wanted her symbolic presence as a woman at the council. She testified to the hardship of a young mother taking care of her baby and working outside the home to support both of them in the absence of her husband. "I could never have done it," she said, "if it were not for the help of two very courageous women, my mother and Gina here." (Gina came to help out when she was fifteen years old. Eighty years later she was still there and very much a part of this hospitable family, where she still insisted on putting on her white, starched apron and doing little chores.)

Grillo's fiancé was in the military. In 1938 he came home, and they got married. Three months later, he went with the armed forces to Africa. He was taken a war prisoner in World War II and was sent to India. He never came home, so he never saw his daughter, who was born the following November. In his letters, he said he was fine, but he had a tumor and did not want to worry the family about it. He died in November 1946, although his wife did not hear about it until January. She expected him home but got news of his death instead. His last letter arrived several months later.

After the war, Grillo was at the border to welcome the survivors, refugees, and war victims home. She was in a lay group that helped with bringing orphans to the beach and mountains and with provid-ing food in the schools. She became secretary for Catholic Action in Tortona and held this position for twenty years. The group collab-orated with the church in raising funds for postwar relief efforts, and they gave widows' assistance to UNICEF. Her active service to church and society was given public recognition when she was named an auditor. Her father was a lawyer and orchestral conduc-tor, and Ida herself played the violin. Her uncle was the first air force pilot to fly at night and take aerial views in 1912. For this he received several medals from the Italian president.

Ida Grillo had her own collection of medals and "trophies" by way of conciliar memorabilia. Foremost among them were a gilt-edged, leather-bound copy of the Vulgate translation of the New Testament and a special edition of Dante's *Divina Commedia* with colored illustrations, both gifts from Paul VI to all the council members. The significance of the Scriptures at the council was demonstrated in a major way by the daily enthronement of the Bible. In 1965, the seven hundredth anniversary of Dante's birth was commemorated. In keeping with the direction of the council and the opening up of the church to culture and society, the gifts were carefully chosen by the pope.

The council gave a boost to the local economy in Rome, and there were some breaks and special bargains offered to the conciliar participants. The women too got in on these, including discounts on trains and busses as well as on cigarettes and liquor.

There was no doubt in my mind as to how much Grillo learned, imbibed, and lived the spirit and content of Vatican II. She saw herself as a simple woman, like most of the worldwide church members for whom the council was intended. In typical deprecating fashion, she said,

> I have not very deep thoughts about the council because I never studied very much. I didn't go to university. I stopped about halfway through high school, as was customary for many young women at that time. It was a very different experience for me to have contact with women from religious communities at the council — those women in strange dress, etc., although they were friendly and cordial. One thing in my favor was that I had learned French at school, and during the council I was grateful to the teacher who had taught me because the language of communication among the auditors was French. When the auditors met each evening, they spoke French, and it was a definite advantage to me to be able to understand what was going on in the conversations. For instance, I was able to talk to the African layman Eusebe Adjakpley from Togo because he also spoke French.

Grillo lamented the fact that we could not communicate directly without an interpreter — "Di Tor Babel!" While I was in Tortona, she continued her routine of attending evening Mass on a daily basis, singing with all her heart, and taking up the collection. I got the grand tour of Tortona, "little Rome," as the residents called it because it is built on seven hills.

The other "war widow," **Amalia di Montezemolo**, in different circumstances also had to cope with the horrors of war and loss of a loved one. Her husband, Giuseppe Cordero Lanza di Montezemolo, volunteered for military service in World War I as a very young man. Later, as a civil engineer he joined the Italian Army as an officer of the Corps of Engineers and of the General Staff. It was as a major that he took part in the war in Spain (1937–38), gaining three further promotions on the field of battle. From 1940 to 1943 he worked at the Italian High Command, during which time he undertook numerous missions to the battle front, receiving many decorations for military valor. With the fall of the Fascist Regime and the German occupation of part of Italy, he formed the "Clandestine Military Front" as a movement of resistance against the Germans throughout occupied Italy. In January 1944, he was arrested by the German SS, imprisoned, and subjected to long periods of torture in order to extract information from him, but he never surrendered. He was shot on March 24, 1944, at the Ardeatine Caves, near Rome. "By the will of the Sovereign," he was posthumously decorated with the Gold Medal for Military Valor "on the field of battle," the highest decoration Italy grants for military bravery. Numerous military institutions, barracks, schools, and roads throughout Italy are named after him, and many articles and books have been published about him.

Marchesa Amalia di Montezemolo received a letter from H. R. Alexander, Commander-in-Chief at the Allied Headquarters in Italy, written July 29, 1944. It expressed profound admiration and gratitude for the invaluable and courageous work of her husband in Allied and Italian High Commands during the German occupation of Rome. "No one could have given more to his country," it continued. "We regret that he did not live to see the results of his loyalty and self-sacrifice. In him Italy has lost a great patriot and the Allies a true friend. We offer our sympathy on your own great personal loss."[32]

"My mother was essentially a 'woman of the home,' " wrote her son, Archbishop Andrea di Montezemolo, apostolic nuncio in Uruguay.

She had five children and dedicated her life to their education, to the promotion of family values, and the Catholic faith. After the death of my father, from 1945 onward, she was asked to head an organization called "The Society for the Spiritual Assistance to the Armed Forces of Italy," which depended on the military ordinary in Rome. Despite the difficulties of bringing up a family of five children on her own, all of whom were still minors, she immediately committed herself to building up this society. At first it existed only in Rome, but subsequently she founded new branches in many Italian cities. It was a society mainly of women (generally coming from military families), who devoted themselves to offering every form of spiritual and material assistance to all branches and ranks of the military. She was national president until about 1969, when she decided to pass this responsibility to younger hands. She retained the title of president emeritus. She was then awarded the cross "Pro Ecclesia et Pontifice" by the Holy See and was later named a "Dame of Honor and Devotion" by the Sovereign Military Order of Malta.

Montezemolo was greatly surprised on receiving Archbishop Pericle Felici's official letter informing her that Paul VI had named her as an "Uditrice" to the third session of Vatican II. "I do not know, nor did my mother ever discover who it was who had suggested her for such a nomination," continues her son. "Pope Paul VI knew well the story of my father and of our family, for it was he who in 1944, as 'Sostituto' of the Secretariat of State, had been concerned, unfortunately without success, with the possible freeing of my father from the hands of the Germans, as part of the efforts of the Holy See on behalf of political detainees and prisoners of war."

Speaking about his mother's invitation to Vatican II, Andrea di Montezemolo recalled:

> I was secretary of the apostolic internunciature in Tokyo, Japan, and I remember my astonishment on reading in *Osservatore Romano* that the Holy Father had named a number of lay "Uditori" to the next session of the Ecumenical Council. My wonder was turned to amazement when I read that among these there were also included women. However, my amazement was transformed to absolute surprise when I found my mother's name at the head of the list of women "uditrici." I recall having written to her at once to express my joyful surprise, but reminding her that St. Paul asserts that "women should remain silent in church," and that the task of the "uditori" appeared to be that of sim-

ply listening, or speaking only when asked to do so. I could only imagine the difficulty my mother must have encountered in accepting such a nomination, as she had always been reluctant in appearing and speaking in public. She replied telling me that her surprise was the greater before such an unexpected charge, which on the one hand was undoubtedly a great honor, but which on the other hand created expectations of her which, in all humility, she was not certain of being able to fulfil.

The archbishop's closing testimony sums up this war widow:

My mother left nothing in writing, only the profound memory, among those who knew her, of a simple, open woman, bound to her home, family, and church. A woman who was always seeking to do good, and who possessed a deep trust in God's help, even when the war and widowhood had left her in great difficulties of every kind.

Her two daughters, Adrianna de la Chiesa and Zolda Mancini, also bore this out. They said their mother never told them anything about what went on in the council because she felt she was bound to secrecy. "With her there was no compromise. We were not a talkative family, so we didn't push her on it. She was a very normal sweet woman, full of faith in God." Adrianna continued, "I remember when she got the word about being an auditor. She rang me, greatly surprised, and said, 'I don't know why they chose me because there are so many more women who could be chosen.' We decided it was mainly because she was a widow. Paul VI knew her and that she represented a normal mother of a family."[33]

The Payoff from Papal Connections

Constantina Baldinucci, born to Italian immigrants in France, was superior general of an Italian community based in Milan, the Sisters of Maria Bambina (the Child Mary) and president of the Italian Sisters Union. She attended a technical institute in Valturio, where she graduated with a diploma in accounting in 1924, the year before she entered the community. It was considered an unusual achievement for a woman in those days. Forty years later, the institute still remembered her, so that when her invitation to the council was announced, an Italian newspaper reported that "one of Valturio's foremost students had become a council auditor under the dome of St. Peter's."[34] She was well known to Cardinal Montini of Milan from his frequent visits to the sisters there. She recalled that on May 14, 1962, the feast of their holy foundress, Montini, tired after a heavy day of pastoral visitation, arrived at 9:00 p.m. with a live white lamb with a red collar for the sisters. When he was elected pope, Paul VI cabled Baldinucci saying he would remain the congregation's cardinal protector, and he requested that four sisters come to take care of his Vatican apartment.

The motherhouse of the Sisters of Maria Bambina on Via S. Sofia in Milan has an international flavor about it. It is a huge, spacious building with wide marble halls and steps, with maps, pictures, and artifacts that suggest worldwide contacts, interests, and missions. I got the sense of friendliness, hospitality, openness, and vitality, despite the diminishing numbers of novices.

I met Constantina Baldinucci in her room in the infirmary. Sadly, she had contracted Parkinson's disease about three years earlier so that her memory was not reliable. Helping to compensate for this were Sister Maria Clara Bianchi, Mother Baldinucci's secretary at the time of the council, and Sister Gemma, formerly a missionary in India, fluent in English, and generously acting as my translator. Bianchi was fluent in Latin and knew exactly what was going on at the council. With papal permission, she substituted for Baldinucci at the fourth session, when urgent community business needed the general's on-the-spot attention. Bianchi authored a book on the council, with special attention to Baldinucci's presence there.

The congregation was founded for works of charity, especially devoted to the poor — the materially poor, but also the spiritually poor, the handicapped, the sick, and those in moral danger, such as prostitutes. Their aim was to prevent this evil or help women get out of it. In recent years, they have opened a house in Rome for AIDS victims. The founder had drawn up her own rule for the congregation, but at the time a ruler in Lombardy would not allow any more new rules to be adopted, so she had to choose one that was already in existence. She chose that of St. Vincent de Paul because his charism was closest to what she was about. The sisters have great devotion to Maria Bambina.

Baldinucci was elected mother general in 1957 and served two six-year terms. She was the first general to visit the missions in India, Africa, South America, the United States, Spain, France, and England. She also visited Japan with a view to founding a mission, and there are now two houses there. She was both surprised and delighted with the unexpected invitation to be a council auditor. She had been in Rome September 10–14 visiting the community's novitiate. In fact, she was even present at the opening ceremony of the third conciliar session, although not in the official capacity of an auditor. From September 14 to 21, she had attended a course of exercises for superiors general in Rimini. She was back in Milan ready to continue her normal work routine, but providence changed her plans overnight when on September 23 her invitation came. All her activities now took on a much wider dimension. Following four intense days of work and advising on most urgent decisions, Baldinucci arrived in Rome on September 28, 1964. She was accompanied by her secretary, Sister Maria Clara Bianchi. Baldinucci had a decided advantage in being fluent in French, having taught it for years in the schools.

Baldinucci wrote the pope a note telling him that she was moved, joyful, and almost shocked by the invitation. "I feel vividly my smallness and lack of worthiness," she wrote, "in taking part in such a grandiose assembly of the teaching church and entering the conciliar hall — the hall par excellence of the Holy Spirit."[35]

Pioneering Women Religious
in Health Care and Education

Sabine de Valon was superior general of the Religious of the Sacred Heart and president of the Superiors General in Italy, the forerunner of the UISG (International Union of Superiors General) whom she represented, so she was well known in the Sacred Congregation for Religious. She was very intelligent and fluent in Latin and Italian. I was unable to make direct contact with Valon, who is now very ill and residing in Lyons. Repeated correspondence to her and her former secretary general, Françoise de Lambilly, brought no response. Valon lived "at the Trinità de Monti until spring of 1988, and up until the time she left she kept in contact with Vatican officials, probably SCRIS." Maureen Aggeler, R.S.C.J., wrote, "This period of our history has been carefully researched and sealed until its major players have died; it was a painful time for many."[36]

Valon was one of the founding members and a councilor of the

International Union of Superiors General (UISG). She saw it as "a funnel through which the Holy See could speak to religious and religious to the Holy See." Valon was very dependent on de Lambilly, a very gifted woman, who was also fluent in Latin. "But Mother de Valon was lost when Sister de Lambilly then went to be secretary general of the UISG, for her vision and leadership had been significant as the right hand of the superior general." Newspaper reports at the time of the council relate that Valon hailed women's role in the council as "moving from the waiting room into the living room." However, when it came to implementing changes in her own community, it was problematic for her, as will be seen in chapter 5, where I deal specifically with religious communities.

Valon visited the U.S. communities in California in the early 1960s. "She could not speak English, a real drawback for her, so she traveled with an assistant who could translate her French and who could visit with individual religious," said Aggeler.

Juliana Thomas was a sister of the Poor Handmaids of Jesus Christ, a community founded by Katherine Kasper in 1851 in the little peasant village of Dernbach, Germany, at a time when there was no church there locally and the people had to go to Mass in Virgus, a village a stone's throw away. It was there also that the first five sisters received the habit and were professed. I got a sense of the remoteness of the motherhouse in Dernbach, which I would have reached only with difficulty if the sisters had not been so kind as to meet me at the railway station in Darmstadt and get me back there in time to make my connecting train to Munich on the Feast of the Three Kings.[37]

Thomas was trained as a teacher, mainly at the sisters' Marienschule in Limburg (1922–35). She was a teacher in Düsseldorf, and she also had the task of being the special teacher for the handicapped children. She was the first general secretary of the Union of Major Superiors in Germany, a position she held for eleven years (1957–68). As such she was also a member of the standing committees of the Mother Generals' Conferences of the German Caritas Association, and this acquainted her with the problems of nursing care and gave her a bond with nursing sisters.[38]

It was in the capacity of secretary general that she was invited as an auditor to the council, September 21, 1964. She wrote, "The unexpected news coming from the motherhouse of the Vincentians in Paris that I was to come to Rome immediately reminded me of Habakkuk being grabbed by the head and lifted up by an angel and then dropped down in a different place."[39] Thomas had never been to Rome before, and in the course of the council she wrote frequently to her community about all the new experiences. She wrote about the gratitude and relief she felt on her arrival in Rome, when the Grey Sisters of St. Elizabeth met her at the airport and gave her accommodation for the duration of the council. They had a lodging house for pilgrims, which was kept free for twelve German bishops during the council. They also had a surgical clinic, and Thomas was given a lovely room there. It was only three minutes away from the Basilica of Santa Maria Maggiore. Thomas was known to several of the more powerful minds of the council from among the German bishops and theologians. The daily ride on the conciliar green bus gave her further opportunities to enter into the main conciliar discussions outside the official sessions. She was elated on her first day at the council when Fr. Friedrich Wulf, S.J., from Munich and Fr. H. H. Hirschmann, S.J., from Frankfurt came to greet her. Wulf remained the greatest part of the morning as her interpreter.

The sisters at Dernbach who knew Thomas said she was a very quiet person who did not talk much unless she was asked about her conciliar experience. She was never mother general of the order, so she did not go around to the houses talking about the changes, as other generals who were auditors did, but she kept the motherhouse in Dernbach updated on all the happenings in Rome. In 1977 on the feast of St. Martin, who is celebrated in Düsseldorf as the patron of the parish and community house there, the sisters had a pleasant evening together. They were also preparing for the beatification of their founder, and they were showing pictures of the churches in Rome, to acquaint the sisters going there with the buildings and history, so that their time in Rome would be more fruitful. Juliana Thomas relived the conciliar experience as she told them about her time as an auditor. She went to bed and died that night, July 11, 1977.

Besides Pilar Bellosillo, Spain got a second representative in Cuban-born **Cristina Estrada**. Her father was an army medical officer stationed in Havana at the time of her birth. Her mother did not work outside the home, nor did Christina ever hold a job before joining the community of the Handmaids of the Sacred Heart at an early age. It was not the thing for a girl of her social status to do in Spain at that time. As a sister, she taught in the schools in Spain and was school directress and local superior in some houses. She also held the position of third probation instructress, which meant she was in charge of sisters in an additional year before final profession. Estrada spent most of her life in community government. She was elected superior general in 1932, a position she held until she resigned in 1965. During that time she opened thirty-one new houses, almost one each year, and she visited the communities in the United States, Japan, and England. Her congregation's work is mostly in education "from university students in capital cities to the ragamuffins in Tokyo's 'rag-and-bones' area."[40] Even when Estrada resigned as general superior of her community in November 1964, her invitation to act as a council auditor was renewed on a personal basis, although she moved out of the generalate and resided in another house in Rome.

I was graciously received and given a hospitable cup of tea at the generalate of the Sister Handmaids in Rome, where Sister Concepción Ruz, aided by translator Sister Elena Bava, tried to construct some information for me on their former mother general, who had died in 1985.[41] Their recurring refrain was that "Christina was a very simple and holy woman." Some day they hope to have her canonized. A Jesuit priest present at her death spoke openly and claimed, "We are experiencing the death of a saint." She was well known to the Roman curia and to Pius XII more than John XXIII. In 1953 she took part in a commission of forty mothers general from all over the world and was one of the eight who formed the executive committee that collaborated in the work of preparation for the foundation of Regina Mundi, and a sister from her community was among the first to study there. "It was a bit of a surprise, however, that she was invited as an auditor, because women never went to a council before," said Bava.

It was difficult to say anything very substantial about Estrada's contribution to the council or what it meant in her life because "she was a very quiet, prudent woman." She took to heart the fact that the council members were supposed to maintain secrecy about everything that transpired on the council floor until it was made public by some official source. Consequently, the sisters learned about council happenings from the communications media, which was on the outside, rather than from their own general, who was inside.

Changes took place gradually in the community as they absorbed the conciliar directives. It was unusual for the mother general to resign, as Estrada did in 1965, because the appointment was intended to be for life. As I glanced through some of the community literature, I gained insight into the significance of what Estrada had done. The co-founders of the community in 1875, Marie Reparatrice nuns, as they were called, were very successful in attracting many members to the community, but they suffered much, and were eventually forced to resign. In 1886, Rome approved the new congregation, which was then called Handmaids of the Sacred Heart. The third general of the order, M. Purissima, was especially jealous of them and persecuted them in many ways, separating the two sisters in their later years. She had aspired to being general herself and engineered that. "She wasn't right in the head, putting it mildly," said Bava. As soon as she was elected, Purissima started looking for privileges and announced, "I intend to ask that the office of general in the Institute now be for life. Good. Everyone is in agreement."[42] One of the original founders objected, "I don't agree. We must never give up the holy freedom of the children of God." She was ignored.

By resigning, Estrada was going back to the original intention of founder Raphaela Mary, now a canonized saint, and opening up again the freedom for a new beginning in keeping with what the council was about in terms of renewal and recovering the spirit and original charism of the religious communities. The sisters who knew Estrada frequently referred to her as "holy and simple," terms also used about the original founders. It enabled rather than prevented them from doing great things, so that Raphaela Mary could exclaim, "This world of ours is like a huge church and I am in it like a priest who must offer a constant sacrifice and continual praise."[43] Estrada followed this model.

Women in a Different Rite

A third U.S. woman invited to the third session was **Claudia Feddish**, from a small Pennsylvanian town near Scranton. She was superior general of the Sisters of St. Basil the Great (1963–71), a congregation of Slavonic-speaking sisters of the Ukrainian Byzantine rite, with some 180 sisters then behind the Iron Curtain, including more than a third in Siberia. She took her appointment as a recognition of the Eastern rites. Soon afterward, congratulations began arriving from missionary sisters in a roundabout way, usually by an ordinary postcard sent to someone in a third country, and then readdressed to Mother Claudia in Rome. One cryptic message from Siberia read: "Dear Mother, we are happy that the White Father remembered us."[44] The present-day order of St. Basil the Great was founded in 359 by St. Basil the Great in Caesarea, Asia Minor. All monasteries were autonomous. The order spread to the Ukraine with the introduction of Christianity in about the year 988. It was established in the United States (from the Ukraine) in 1911. The two major motherhouses (in Uniontown, Pennsylvania, and Philadelphia) were autonomous. Each had parish missions with schools. In 1951, by decree of the Holy See, the order became pontifical with central government in Rome.[45]

Claudia Feddish taught in several parish schools in Pennsylvania and New Jersey. During that time, she also held the duty of local superior and supervisor of schools. She had been elected vicar general of the Sisters of St. Basil in Astoria, Long Island, New York, in 1954, and she also served as general econome during that time. When Mother Zenobia died in 1963, Claudia took over the direction of the order until the Second General Chapter was called, at which time she was elected superior general.

> Josyp Cardinal Slipyj, archbishop of the metropolitan see in Lviv, Ukraine, was arrested by the communists from Moscow in 1945 and sent to Siberia, where he spent eighteen years in forced labor. He was released through the intervention of Pope John XXIII and President Kennedy, with Norman Cousins as their intermediary with Khrushchev.... All Catholic bishops were arrested. All Ukrainian Catholic churches of the Byzantine rite were closed; the Orthodox (non-Catholic) faith was imposed. Catholic religious orders were suppressed. The Catholic Church of the Byzantine Rite operated underground... through its secretly ordained bishops, several priests, and many laypeople.
>
> When his Eminence Cardinal Slipyj came to Rome in 1963, Claudia was of great assistance to him. She helped him to open the University of St. Clement and the Stoudion by staffing these places with our sisters, and she also helped with her knowledge of English and the Ukrainian language.[46]

Jerome Maria Chimy knew Feddish well, since they were of the same rite and were often together. "She was a very personable character, lovable, and very kind," said Chimy.

In the Ukraine her Basilian community was mostly contemplative in the late nineteenth century and had only one high school for girls in their monastery. They never went out among the people teaching catechism, and the people were hungry for that. That was the main reason that our community, the Servants, was founded — to help the Basilian Fathers reach the people.

While Claudia was vicar (first councilor) in Rome, she was very friendly with our community and even came over to see how our archives were done, since they were new to centralization, and we were centralized from the beginning. She had trouble with her congregation while she was vicar. Someone in America apparently wanted to get even with her and sent a nasty letter about her to the curia. I got one; the fathers did; it went to the Congregation; and Slipyj got one. That was when she told me she would have to defend herself. She believed the letter came from sisters in her own community. She went back to the U.S. and confronted the sisters. Nobody knew for sure who wrote the letters, but they knew what was in them. Then a letter of apology was written. After that, everybody held her in high esteem for facing the sisters, and she was elected archimandre. On top of that came the honor of being nominated as an auditor.[47]

After the council, Feddish

called and officiated at the Special Chapter of 1969 (Sisters of St. Basil), which was held at the Stoudion in October 1969, in Castel Gondolfo.... It was during her administration that the Cloistered Monastery of Albano (San Basilio Magno) was united with the Order of the Sisters of St. Basil under the direction of the generalate.[48]

According to Chimy:

Claudia was very kind to Cardinal Slipyj when he was released from prison in 1963, and mind you he was a very difficult man. He was very much against Rome and spoke furiously about many things he said the Vatican did to his people. He somehow took over Claudia and had her under his thumb. He was the one who nominated her as an auditor. He equated me [Chimy] with Rome because of one incident when I said I wanted to consult the Congregation before taking over the economy of a house and farm he purchased for a minor seminary near Castel Gondo-lfo. He had no time for me after that, only for Claudia because her community did it instead — difficult work taking care of the cows, pigs, and chickens gratis. One thing that everyone knew was that Mother Claudia could get anything she wanted through Slipyj. When her term as general was over, she went to the Vatican, where Slipyj was given beautiful quarters, and she took over his economy there, while also teaching English to seminarians. Slipyj also got jobs for several sisters of her congregation in the university and in the Jesuit library, the Rusicum, where the oriental churches have their university. I must say for Claudia that she was very dedicated to her community and to the people at large. She didn't care about herself or her health or how tired she was. If there was anything to be done, she would just do it."

An interesting network developed from my trial-and-error approach to discovering the conciliar women. I had difficulty sorting out the community of Basilian sisters to which Feddish belonged. Then came the further challenge of finding **Jerome Maria Chimy**, who was listed in 1965 as being Ukrainian. Part of my strategy was to ask other auditors if they knew anything about the whereabouts of each other. Feddish's community provided me with a Canadian address for Chimy, and when I met her, she informed me about her friend, Feddish. By the time I rescheduled it, Jerome Maria had relocated in her native Alberta. I finally caught up with her, "the celebrity in residence," as I designated her, where she lives with her community, the Sister Servants of Mary Immaculate, who started the first Ukrainian hospital in Canada and now provide excellent hospital service to the people of Mundare, a farming area about two hours' drive northeast of Edmonton, a Ukrainian settlement, and the birthplace of Chimy's community in Canada.

Invitations to the fourth conciliar session included Canadian Jerome Maria Chimy, superior general of a Ukrainian community of Sister Servants of Mary Immaculate. She explained how this came about.

There was a great move among women of the Latin rite to have women as auditors at the council. The papers were full of their headlines and requests. We belong to the Ukrainian Byzantine rite, and our bishops began to think that Ukrainian sisters should also take part. Fr. Paul Minski contacted Cardinal Testa's secretary of the Sacred Congregation for Oriental Rites. Since there were only two Ukrainian congregations in the world, both should be represented. I was surprised when on November 25, 1964, I was in the office of our generalate there in Rome, and Cardinal Felici's secretary called to say that I would be receiving an invitation to be an auditor. His Eminence Gustavo Cardinal Testa, the secretary of Sacred Oriental Rites, visited our home on Via Cassia in Rome, bringing with him the joyous news. "I come to you," he said, "to bring congratulations to your superior general, Mother Jerome Chimy, and in the presence of all the sisters, I proclaim her an auditor of the Second Vatican Council. The official nomination from the Pontiff will be forwarded to the auditor at the appointed time."[49]

It came on February 25, 1965. Writing about the event, Sr. M. Christopher explained the community reaction:

> Our good holy mother church has valued the sufferings of our persecuted people and bestowed this great privilege upon the spiritual mother of our humble congregation. From among thousands of congregations only ten sisters were given the privilege of being auditors. Immediately the news of our newly appointed auditor appeared in every Ukrainian newspaper under the headline: "The second Ukrainian woman auditor of the XXI Ecumenical and Second Vatican Council — the superior general of the congregation of the Sister Servants of Mary Immaculate, Mother Jerome Chimy." The nomination was a recognition of the service our sisters have rendered to the church on the continents of North and South America, Europe (England, France, Germany, Poland), and in communist countries where amid persecution the sisters heroically bear witness to Christ.[50]

Chimy recalled, "On Tuesday, September 14, 1965, at 9:00 a.m., I entered the aula for the first time as an auditor."

The Sister Servants of Mary Immaculate were founded in the Ukraine in response to an apostolic need not being met by the contemplative Basilian community (Feddish's group). The Basilian Fathers did not know how to reach the people until a Jesuit student told them, "You need to get the sisters, who will go from house to house, helping the poor, teaching catechism and kindergarten, even helping with house cleaning and the children where mothers work outside the home, and even helping with deliveries in the role of mid-wives, like the Polish Sister Servants are doing. If you don't get those sisters, your church is lost." And so a new order was born, as Chimy explained.

In the Ukraine in the 1880s there was a large population, skilled in agriculture, but many had nothing to live for. Most were poor people without even an acre of land. In 1888, when the Canadian government's development agency offered Ukrainians a hundred acres of land for $10.00, there was a massive influx of immigrants, who had to work very hard to reclaim the wooded area with primitive tools and a lot of human muscle. The Latin rite church soon realized that they could not respond to the needs of the Byzantine Ukrainians. It was the *rite* more than the *language* that created the greatest problem. The Ukrainians could learn the language more or less, but they could not get used to the Latin rite. The Latin rite bishops took the initiative and sent Fr. Lacombe, "the Big Chief of the Prairies," to the Congregation of the Oriental Churches to ask for help. He was directed to go to the Ukraine and speak to the metropolitan to send priests to Canada. The Basilian order seemed most suitable, since most of the Ukrainian clergy were married and were afraid to leave their country and their riches and inconvenience their families by going to an unknown territory. The Basilians agreed to send four priests and two Brothers. They also were able to get four Sister Servants to accompany them, as they knew from experience in the Ukraine that they could not reach the people without the sisters. Jerome Maria Chimy comes from this stock and this tradition of pioneering women responding to the needs, primarily of Ukrainians but then also to the daughters and sons of other immigrant groups gradually integrating into Canadian life.

Mundare is but a few miles from Vegreville, which boasts of having the world's largest *Pysanka* (Easter egg), which measures 25.7 feet long, 18 feet wide, and 31 feet high. It is located at an angle and turns in the wind like a weathervane. It is a great work of art and technology and an impressive tribute to the early pioneers of the Vegreville community and the Royal Canadian Mounted Police Force. The giant Easter egg symbolizes the peace and security the Mounties had offered the area's pioneers and their descendants. Those familiar with Ukrainian culture will recognize the exquisite and intricate decoration of Easter eggs as a Ukrainian folk art that is world renowned.

Lest I be accused of getting carried away by an egg, I want to emphasize something that the church woke up to at the council — the importance of culture in understanding and nourishing a people's faith and developing its cultural expression, religion. Culture and religion were inseparable. The council embraced many enriching diversities, one of which was different rites. Viewing the egg was for me the culmination of a great experience of Ukrainian Catholic piety and proverbial hospitality. I attended Mass in the Ukrainian rite both in Ukrainian and in English.

The symbolism of the *Pysanka* is explained by the artist, Paul Sembaliuk. He used

> three colours — bronze, silver, and gold — to symbolize prosperity. Bronze is the predominant colour of the design and suggests the "good earth," the land on which our forefathers [and mothers] struggled for survival and existence. Five distinct symbols make up the design. The radiating gold stars on the end sections symbolize Life and Good Fortune. The three-pointed stars, in alternating gold and silver, symbolize the Trinity, representing the strong devotion to the faith of our ancestors. The band of silver circumscribing the *Pysanka,* with no beginning or end, symbolizes Eternity. On the central barrel section, gold and silver windmills with six vanes and points symbolize a Rich Harvest. The most prominent motif of the design — the silver wolf's teeth, which point to the centre from the silver band — symbolize the main message of Protection and Security afforded our pioneers by the R.C.M.P.[51]

When asked about the question of rite, Chimy explained how earlier on

> This was a big matter, even about the Ukraine, because we were not considered to be even Catholic and in union with Rome. We had to fight for it. We were called "Orthodox," and our community was called "Orthodox Sisters." Others would not receive our holy communion (administered by spoon with a host particle in wine) because they thought it was not a host. The bishops told the priests to do something about it by way of explaining to the people that we were Catholic, and they should not call us Orthodox. Now it is fine. The church's concern for humanity is our sisters' concern. In this cause, we belong to that special branch

of the church, known as the Eastern Rite. Our role is twofold;
(1) to the separated Eastern sisters and brothers, and (2) to the
Western sisters and brothers.

Continuing in the spirit of the early community, the sisters in
Mundare are trying to hold on to their rural hospital because they
realize how life-threatening it could be if the local people in crisis situations had to drive several hours for medical attention at a distant
hospital.

In nominating auditors an obvious attempt was made at geo-
graphical representation. **Marie de la Croix Khouzam**, superior
general of the Sisters of the Sacred Heart in Egypt, was invited as
chair of the Union of Teaching Sisters in Egypt. Looking back on her
long life she highlighted events that prepared her for being an auditor. After being educated by the Religious of the Sacred Heart, she
and two of her sisters entered the young congregation of the Egyptian Religious of the Sacred Heart, who had only seven professed
sisters and some novices and were scarcely sixteen years in existence.
Their Constitutions were barely developed and were not approved
until 1942.

Khouzam described herself as a teenager who

> had all the faults of the world — except that of lying — angry,
> coquettish, greedy, independent, intransigent, obstinate, daring,
> and dreaming of an ideal way beyond my abilities. But...I loved
> the Savior, and in a burst of total love, at age thirteen, I told my
> parents that I would never desire any spouse but Jesus Christ.
> According to myself, I was made for the absolute life of asceti-
> cism and contemplation. Then *in a divine way,* I would aspire to
> a life of prayer and solitude, I believed, under the cross by sac-
> rificing all my inclinations. I would drill as a recruit and become
> virtuous. After my first vows and during twenty-eight consecu-
> tive years of teaching eight hours a day and being the director of
> a school, I aspired to a total, absolute love, and I realized that
> *God had served me well and good in his way.*[52]

Khouzam was elected mother general in 1959, a position she held for
fifteen years. Her term of office spanned the most troublesome years
of the wars, "France-England-Israel" (1959–72), nationalization of
the Suez Canal, and the liberation of the Sinai from Israel.

The problems demanded an immediate response, and foreseeing the risk of nationalization that threatened the English and French properties, the apostolic nuncio advised them to transfer their schools, constructions, and movable and immovable properties to the Congregation of the Egyptian Religious of the Sacred Heart and register them with the publicity bureau before they left Egypt. Khouzam's community then assumed responsibility for four additional schools and two colleges.

> Aided by the nine lay professors in all our schools, we took over the direction of the schools and the responsibility of every area was assured by our sisters, as well as the Catechism courses and the morals courses given to Christians and Muslims together. How we felt we were realizing the words of the gospel, "You are the leaven in the dough"! How we were in the same way as the other religious institutions sought out, approved, and loved by the Islamic parents, who with full confidence entrusted their young daughters to us from age four onward like their own families, only God deserves the praise.
>
> Our institute was in charge of nine schools in Egypt and many centers of educational and missionary development in the villages of Upper Egypt. I think that's why I found myself nominated as president of the Union of Religious Educators in our country. It is also probably why I was chosen to represent at Vatican II the numerous Religious Institutes for the Education of Youth. Stephanos I Sidarous, then patriarch of the Catholic Coptic Church in Egypt, was happy to approve this initiative from Rome.[53]

Unfortunately, I was unable to visit Khouzam in Cairo. Apart from the expense of travel, increasing terrorist acts against tourists made it unsafe for me to travel there in summer of 1993.

Marie-Henriette Ghanem of the Sisters of the Sacred Hearts of Jesus and Mary was invited to the council as chair of the Assembly of Major Superiors of Lebanon. At that time she had already been a member of her community for more than forty years and had held governmental positions. Together with Olga Sara of the Society of Jesus Christ, she founded the Assembly of Major Superiors in Lebanon, and she was president until the end of the council. As president she was instrumental in the foundation of l'ISSR (the Higher Institute of Religious Sciences) as part of the Faculty of Theology of the Jesuit University of St. Joseph in Beyrouth, to provide a solid theological formation in various branches for religious and others. Ghanem's invitation to the council arrived after July 31, 1964, the date when her second term as superior general expired.[54] She regretted that all the pictures taken of her and others during the conciliar era were destroyed during a bombardment of the Maison Notre Dame during the war years.

Regretfully, I was not able to accept the warm invitations I received both from Henriette Ghanem and her superior general, Antoinette Bassil, to go to visit in Beyrouth. I discovered that travel from the U.S. to Lebanon had been suspended. My option was to use my European passport and Irish homeland base as a point of departure and return. However, in the summer of 1993, war broke out again in Lebanon, and my family had grave reservations about the safety factor of traveling there, so I had to settle for written communication.

Women in the Work Place

During the fourth session, Juliana Thomas was joined by another German laywoman, **Gertrud Ehrle**, a founding member and for many years president of the German Catholic Women's League and a board member of WUCWO. With a background in social work and a doctorate in sociology, Ehrle was a practical feminist in terms of her work and lifelong dedication to the cause of women in the workplace. She initiated and established the Helfta-Colleg and Helfta-Seminar to further international development efforts for young women, especially in Africa, India, and Korea. She was co-founder of the Mothers' Recovery Work, obtaining help for families after the Second World War. In the ruins of the central office in Cologne she welcomed the first Catholic women's foreign delegation. Thus she performed an extraordinary work of peace even before the politicians could do anything about it. In 1984, a year before her death, she was awarded the Elly Heuss-Knapp Medal for distinguished service in the foundation and continuation of the German mothers' recovery work. She was also a holder of the first-class Federal Distinguished Cross and the papal distinction Pro Ecclesiae et Pontifice. In 1951 she issued an informative volume, *Licht über dem Abgrund* (Light above the Abyss), a record of the experience of Christian women from 1933 to 1945. With her remarkable record

of public service, the surprising thing is not that Dr. Ehrle was a conciliar auditor but that it took so long to get her there. Ehrle was a
niece of curial Franz Cardinal Ehrle, S.J., Vatican librarian and former colleague of Msgr. Ambrosio Achille Ratti, later Pope Pius XI.
Gertrud Ehrle was friendly with the Jesuits and also with Augustin
Cardinal Bea, who was anxious that she be invited to the council.[55]

Helga Sourek, Ehrle's translator from 1967 onward, spoke of her
as "a very open, kind-hearted woman, who was proud of all the
things she had done for the Frauenbund; she was someone I respected and liked very much, especially because of her interest in
international relations."[56] As a young woman, Sourek first met Ehrle
through the international relations of the Catholic Youth Movement.
Years later after she was married and living in Cologne, still working with youth, she met Ehrle again and was greeted with a new
mission: "Helga, I have a very important task for you," Ehrle said.
"You are no longer working with the youth. You must now come
to work with the International Union of Catholic Women." Sourek
continued: "There was a general assembly of WUCWO in Belgium
in 1967, and there my career as interpreter for Gertrud Ehrle began.
It was more than interpreting; it was also listening and speaking to
her." Although Sourek did not know Ehrle while she was an auditor, she frequently heard her refer to "when I was an auditor at the
council."

> She never spoke in a boasting way about anything she did, al-
> though one couldn't say she was a modest woman, but she was
> proud to have been at the council, proud in a way, *as a woman*
> being there. Women's affairs were always so important for her,
> perhaps not in the modern way of a feminist theologian's ap-
> proach, but to do something for women and in the name of
> women. She counted among her dearest friends women like Pi-
> lar Bellosillo, who shared the conciliar experience with her. She
> got her doctorate late in life, but she never flaunted the fact that
> she was "Dr." while someone else was less educated. She always
> treated people with respect and was never condescending.[57]

Ehrle came from a very respected family in Ravensburg, and
among her forebears were bishops, auxiliary bishops, and priests,
so her family was also connected to the church and monastic life.
They were well known, and a bishop from Westphalia may have recommended her for nomination as an auditor. At the time she was

president of the Katolischer Deutcher Frauenbund (German Catholic Women's League), a position she held for about twenty-seven years — the longest mandate in its history. She had been in the league before the war, and she and Maria Prümm held it together during the Nazi period. "She did an important bulletin on how to stand up against the Nazis, and this always impressed me very much," admitted Sourek. "She was one of those women who very early on saw what was behind the propaganda and never fell into it."

When she became president of the Frauenbund after the war, she immediately went into action to develop ways for women to link together internationally and to communicate and have friendly bonds and exchange ideas. This was one of her leading ideas. Her concern was not just spiritual; her great task was also to work, for example, with architects in the construction of an international students' residence in Cologne for girls coming from foreign countries. She said development aid will never succeed if we cannot get education for the girls and women. "I must have heard her repeat it one hundred times," said Sourek.

> She would say, "Helga, all that we have to do in development aid is education and once again education for women." She had a wholistic approach to women's education in the sense that she realized their need for an atmosphere where foreign women could feel at home, get educated, and as a kind of multiplier bring these ideas back to their home countries. This was what the Helfta-Colleg and Helfta-Seminar were all about.

However, her efforts were confined mostly to educated women, in the hope that they would bring education to those women who were deprived, but all the contacts she chose were not as trustworthy as she believed, or they were not capable of doing the task at hand. Sourek explains:

> Both Ehrle and Prümm had strong ideas of faith, religion, devotion to God, and the idea of going out to spread the gospel in the whole world. They were convinced that the future of the Frauenbund had to be religious. Ehrle's earlier book, *Licht über dem Abgrund* explained her religious idea for the Frauenbund, that all the women filled with faith and love for God are like a light above the terrible darkness of the abyss of life with its tragedies and atrocities. The Frauenbund's magazine, *Die Christliche Frau*

(The Christian Woman), had a completely different shape to what it has now. It had long twenty-page articles of theological, philosophical, or other kinds of reflections that would appeal only to intellectuals. There were no one-page pieces. The articles appeared as "edited by the Zentrale" (the organization). In reality, they were the work of Ehrle and Prümm, although their names never appeared. The fact was that *they were the Zentrale,* and they identified so much with it that it was their life. The sad thing was that when they were old and no longer in control, they were like old fossils, not knowing how to bow out and let new blood take over.

Drawing further on her personal memories of this greatly admired woman, Sourek is candid in her appraisal.

Her style was not giving great speeches; it was conversational. She was not at all gifted rhetorically. Her gift was addressing people with personal, friendly remarks that made one feel like a human being. She had a way of winning people over and getting them to implement her ideas. Later in life, even people who liked her, found her cajoling style off-putting.

Sourek summed up Ehrle's six main ideas:

(1) the Katolische Frauenbund was really her child. It was the whole focus of her life, and she did everything for it; (2) WUCWO — having international relations among women; (3) to do something for the Third World; (4) to further the ecumenical movement in practical ways; (5) commitment to political questions; (6) to give religious congregations more importance in WUCWO.

She always regretted "that the church, with all these men, never paid attention to this highly qualified potential it had in women religious."

Ehrle was politically minded and very committed to the Deutsche Frauensrat, which is a confederation of all women's organizations, Catholics, trade unions, etc. Right from the beginning, after the war, she was a member and longtime president of this and mentioned its work as a kind of practical ecumenism. She was made a Knight of the Holy Sepulcher, and she used to smile when she recalled being among all those men and being proud that she was allowed to wear the long robe that went with it. Sourek explained:

She may have been smiling because of her outlook on dress. If ever there was a prize given for the worst dressed woman, Ehrle would have gotten it! She always looked dowdy, and nobody seemed to care that she wore the same thing over and over, and sometimes she would mock herself and joke about it. She was not gifted in speaking, but she could relate very personally to people. She was not gifted in style, but she could admire what other women wore.

Ehrle was indefatigable in her efforts for the cause of women. It was her life. When she finally let go and died, she was given the glorious funeral and recognition she deserved. Sourek went alone to the grave after the ceremony and admitted the personal sadness she felt. "All the wreaths and remembrances were from the many associations she served so well. Only one little wreath was from a cousin of a cousin. I felt very sad for her that this remote connection was the only family she had apart from her work." It was the choice a single woman like Ehrle made at the time as the only way to accomplish her goal in life for the cause of women. Her presence as an auditor at the council was linked to her sense of the worldwide church. "She always had a very strong sense that the church was international, that women must stand together, the women of the whole world, and that it can best be done by having faith in God, a faith that links us all together."

Representing Young Women and Girls

At age thirty-two **Anne-Marie Roeloffzen**, a lawyer graduated from the University of Nijmegen, was one of the youngest auditors at the council. Living in the Netherlands, she had been working since 1959 with the World Federation of Catholic Young Women and Girls (WFCYWG) and was its general secretary. This position brought her into direct contact with Maria (Rie) Vendrik, former president of the WFCYWG and board member of WUCWO, who was invited to the council, not as an auditor, but as an expert (*peritus*) to follow the work of the commission on "The Church in the Modern World." Some of the auditors recalled, "She was around so much that we considered her one of us." Vendrik was a teacher and head of a girls school. She was founder of the Catholic Young Women's Organization, a federation of all the Catholic young women's movements in the Netherlands (Girl Guides, YCS, YCW, etc.), and she was its national president for ten years. For four years she was president of the International Catholic Organizations (ICO). From 1964 until her retirement around 1974 she worked for Catholic Action in the Netherlands. Roeloffzen commented, "Rie Vendrik was an inspired and inspiring woman. Her main aim was to obtain equal rights for women, especially in the field of education and work. She made studies of women in many situations in life (as working woman, as widow, etc.)."[58] This was the wealth of experience and expertise Vendrik brought to the council as a *peritus* in her own right.

Representation of women from Latin America was still lacking until the fourth session of the council. Then Argentinean **Margarita Moyano Llerena**, president of the WFCYWG, was added to the list. The WFCYWG was headquartered in Brussels, where Moyano worked for fifteen years, at Lumen Vitae and Pro Mundi Vita, international Catholic organizations, and at Taizé, in stimulating youth meetings. As a younger female auditor, thirty-eight-year-old Moyano joined two men (Eusebe Adjakpley and Juan Velásquez) as the group that received the concluding conciliar message, "To Youth," on December 8, 1965. Horton commented that "according to the European theory of youth, not one of the recipients appeared to be less than forty years of age."[59] In 1974, she returned home and went to work in the rural advancement of poor areas in northern Argentina. For four years she worked for the Instituto de Cultura Popular.[60]

Women in Rural Life

In time for the final conciliar session, Uruguayan **Gladys Parentelli** was invited as vice-president of the female branch of the International Movement of Catholic Agricultural and Rural Youth (MIJARC), based in Louvain and with members from sixty-five national movements. Obviously, this gave public recognition to the movement's significant apostolate among rural youth, bringing to them the richness of Christ's message to transform their personal, familial, social, and professional lives. Paul VI said as much when he received MIJARC in a private audience on Friday, October 10, 1964. At his request, they named three potential auditors — Parentelli and two men. The pope selected the thirty-year-old Parentelli. Until then, the Latin American presence of women was totally lacking.

Parentelli's initial reaction was that being an auditor was an additional responsibility at a time when she was heavily involved in rural youth organizations, which entailed a lot of travel. "I felt like a Joan of Arc, a person who is taking care of a mission that God had given me, and I didn't know where I'd get the energy to complete it."[61] She recounted one of her first surprises when she got her passport. "They had changed my name, and I was no longer Gladys, but Claudia. They 'latinized' my name because it seems that Gladys is not a Catholic name, so it didn't fit the Vatican mentality."

Parentelli returned to Uruguay in 1967. She has lived in Caracas, Venezuela, since 1976, and she currently serves as documentarian for the embassy of European communities in Caracas.

One Married Couple

This detective project on the women of Vatican II has taught me that if at first you do not succeed, try again, and again, and again. My first visit to Mexico City took place in August 1989. Unfortunately, due to communication problems, I was unable to meet **Luz-Marie Alvarez-Icaza**, despite a prearranged interview in Cuernavaca with Betsie Hollants acting as translator. Hollants provided me with a new dimension of life surrounding the council, which I could otherwise have missed. Five years later, I succeeded in meeting the Icazas.[62]

I got a wonderful welcome at the Alvarez-Icaza residence. Luz-Marie gave me a pressing invitation to return a few days later. "You must meet my husband," she said. "He has such a good memory for the details." She was right.

Of the twenty-three women auditors, nineteen were single, three were widows, and one was married. This was not surprising, given that most women in the 1950s and 1960s were homemakers, and it was mostly the single women who were active in international lay apostolate groups. Mexican Luz-Marie Alvarez-Icaza and her husband, José, were the only married couple invited to the council, and the fourth and last session at that. Until I met the Icazas I thought they were both invited simultaneously as a couple. That was not the case. Luz-Marie explained:

It was at the end of 1964, and I was pregnant with our twelfth child, Emilio. The original invitation was just to my husband. José told the apostolic delegate, Msgr. Raimundo, that he and his wife were both presidents of the Christian Family Movement, and both should be included in the invitation. The church is definitely man-oriented, and preference is usually given to the man. Our case was harder to resolve because we were a *couple*. Each of us got a separate invitation, but we always worked together. I was the only married woman invited.

José elaborated further on politics operative with Luigi Raimundo. As José remonstrated with the nuncio on behalf of his wife, the bishop said he understood Mrs. Icaza was a great lady, "but what would she do? She doesn't represent anything internationally. She hasn't written a book. She hasn't high standing in church or society." José replied, "That's precisely why she must go. She's the mother of a family. She has the biggest job of passing on the faith to the family."

"Right," said the nuncio. "How could we have forgotten that? How wonderful! The first married couple is going to the council because of me."

The CFM did not begin in Mexico as a movement but as several families who got together as a group and created working teams. Fr. Pedro Richards, a Passionist priest and founder in Argentina and Uruguay, went to Mexico to observe the groups there. Through him they became the CFM in Mexico.

José gave up his work as a civil engineer to devote himself totally to the CFM. He traveled around to all the meetings, while Luz-Marie created the family. "I had little children; I had children on the way; I had children to take care of, and sometimes I was nursing, so I generally had to stay home," she explained.

The CFM's aim was to try to live a Christian family life, to live more fully the sacrament of matrimony. The couples wanted this to affect their children. Through the parents' example, they wanted the children to be inspired to become good Christians. The families also projected their view into the surrounding community. After a few years the Icazas realized that there was not sufficient interaction with the community around them. Some people were strong and effective in their own family or circle, but they did not see the need for involvement in wider social issues. Luz-Marie explained:

Some things we fought for and wanted to see change were the connections between rich and poor families. We wanted to work toward a society that was more just and solidly connected or unified. The CFM began with higher class families. We tried to include people from farming classes, Indians, because we knew that they were a part of our society, knowing that to be effective at all, the movement had to affect all classes of society. After two years as presidents of the Mexican CFM, both of us were invited to become co-presidents of the Latin American groupings, and that is probably why we were invited to the council. It was not for personal merits but what we represented.

Most people reading *Gaudium et Spes* today remark the change that has taken place in the understanding of marriage and family, that is, if they remember the old pre–Vatican II approach and use it as a basis for comparison. Few, if any, besides the conciliar auditors, know the role that one Mexican couple played in giving the document a face-lift and a focus on the couple's love as the core of the sacrament. The Icazas were that couple, experts in married life, and their names deserve to be spoken and preserved wherever and whenever the document is read or invoked.

While completing the final revisions of this text, I read Robert McClory's book *Turning Point,* which recounts the inside story of the papal commission on birth control, mostly from the perspective of Patty Crowley, who with her husband, Pat, was a member of that commission.[63] Patty was one of the four women invited to the commission and then only to its fourth and fifth meetings in March 1965 and June 1966. Like the Alvarez-Icazas, the Crowleys were active leaders in the CFM. They collected international data in similar ways, and some of Patty Crowley's input to the birth control commission was similar to what Luz-Marie Alvarez-Icaza gave in the *Gaudium et Spes* commissions in the fall of 1965. I presume the language barrier had something to do with the fact that the Alvarez-Icazas never mentioned the Crowleys to me, nor did Robert McClory mention the Mexican couple in his book. Bernard Häring, a member of the commission and a *peritus* at Vatican II, had an opportunity to be part of both worlds and served as a key link between them. He recognized Patty Crowley's significance on the commission and thought she deserved some inclusion in my book, although she was not a conciliar auditor.

Missing in Action

It was difficult to track down conciliar auditors at the best of times. In the case of the deceased, it was even more difficult, but not impossible. The problem was compounded when the person's country of origin did not coincide with where she lived during the council. The easiest scenario was when dealing with women religious, since most communities preserve archives, and some living members remembered the deceased. Likewise with families to some extent. Most of the conciliar women were single, and that presented its own kind of problem regarding information about the deceased. Fortunately, most of the women founded or belonged to well-known organizations, so they left behind a living memorial legacy.

Baroness Hedwig Skoda is the only female conciliar auditor whose current whereabouts — dead or alive — I have not yet been able to establish. She was listed among the auditors as being from Czechoslovakia. I heard from Gertrud Heinzelmann that she was founder and president of Nouvelles équipes internationales de Renaissance chrétienne, which no longer exists. Some bishop with clout must have known her and recognized her prominence or she would never have been nominated. Because she came only to the final conciliar session, the other auditors, already bonded into a cohesive group, had less opportunity to get to know her through meetings and working groups, although some remember seeing her.

All I know about Skoda is that she came from a rich family in the automobile industry in Czechoslovakia. She studied at the University of Zurich, completing her doctoral dissertation in 1944. She had a French address during the council, but I got no response from writing there. She bought a cherry tree farm in southern France, which did not work out well. She may have returned to Switzerland. She appears to have founded a pension for women in the southern Swiss Canton Tessin/Ticino.[64]

In an interview conducted by Suzanne Cita-Malard about the question of Christian women and politics, Skoda carried a folder of grievances and complaints that appear to have been well founded. She claimed that it was the socialists and communists, not the church, that put women on an equal footing with men. She gave a practical example:

In Switzerland, women vote only in three cantons where there is a Protestant majority — Geneva, Vaud, and Neuchâtel. The church in our home has never aided women in obtaining the right to vote. It has hindered it. However, femininity leaves a permanent stamp on the life of the church by the far greater number of women than men who are among the churchgoers, by their involvement in Catholic Action, and by the work of female religious communities.[65]

As part of her ongoing "sleuthing," Rosemary Goldie found an invitation sent by Edwige de Skoda from her central Swiss office to Vittorino Veronese, secretary of the Committee for Laity Congresses. She invited him to take part in the Sixth International Theological Week of the International Teams of Christian Renaissance in Holland in August 1955. Skoda was president of the "Teams," which were founded in Germany in 1950. The members were from different fields of professional or international activity and aimed at a "Christian reconstruction" of society that would recognize Christ as "Center of the World and of universal history." Goldie concluded: "This would explain, I think, Hedwig Skoda's appointment as auditor. On our lists, as you know, she is simply identified as from Czechoslovakia. She would have been one of the very many exiles enjoying the hospitality of Switzerland."[66]

Conclusion

Marie Louise Monnet drew attention to the whole world, the independent social milieux, as God's created realm where grace is at work and the church's mission is in progress and needs to be recognized. Until Vatican II, most official church representatives focused too narrowly on the sacralized realm of specifically church matters. As a kind of afterthought, they realized how they had forgotten about the laity, so lay *men* were invited to the council. The banquet hall still was not full. Their eyes were opened further, and it dawned on them, "We forgot the other *half of humanity, women.*" When looking at the scant outlines I have given of the experiences and accomplishments of the twenty-three conciliar women, one realizes how impoverished the clerical church has been without them. Most bishops were surprised and taken off guard when the conciliar women arrived. The real surprise was not that twenty-three women of their caliber could be found in the whole world. They were but a sampling or symbolic presence of all the available qualified women who could have far outnumbered the bishops, if the truth were told. Add to that the groundswell of women involved in the sacred trust of birthing and rearing children, and true ecclesiogenesis comes to light, as evidenced even in one couple.

CHAPTER THREE

FLOWERS HAVE AT LAST BLOOMED IN OUR LAND

═══❖═══

The New Springtime

Women are tired of being treated as a joke. Whether they are ro-manticized, pedestalized, or trivialized, it all amounts to the same thing — they are not taken seriously as human beings on equal footing with men. The women of Vatican II became keenly aware of this, as did some bishops, although not without effort and residual ambiguity. My main focus in this chapter is on how the women were received and how they experienced the council from the inside.

Carmelite Donal Lamont practically brought down the house with applause (even when applause was supposedly out of order) with the oratorical flourish of his now famous "Dry bones" speech at a cru-cial moment in the discussion on the missionary text *Ad Gentes*.[1] He was an Irish bishop in Rhodesia at the time, the first bishop in a new diocese, with all the problems of racial discrimination. Before Vat-ican II came at all, he insisted that girls get the same educational rights and opportunities as boys, and general access to education came in 1940. Lamont once took home a child who was about to be sold into slavery, and she was reared on the mission. The bishop was later deported with many other missionaries.

In reply to my query about his general impressions of the council and its direction, he warned that I was working on too large a can-vas. On the question of women, he summed up the truth for many bishops. "It would be an egregious error to think that bishops came to the council determined to keep women out. We were all formed in the straitjacket mentality of Vatican I," he said.

95

With no previous experience of women's involvement in church structures, it never occurred to us that they should be there. However, under the guidance of the Spirit, a new awakening took place — like spring coming to the Arctic, thawing the barque of Peter out of its ice-locked moorings and setting it afloat with a new sail. Some jump ship when things begin to change because they think all is falling apart. Many of us welcomed new possibilities and exclaimed, "thank God our time is now." At Vatican I there were no African bishops at all. Women's coming to the council was part of the new "signs of the times."[2]

When pushed further about women's actual contribution, Lamont had nothing to say. Working as he was for the education of women and bettering their everyday situation in a polygamous situation in Africa, he was not affected specifically by the presence of a few bourgeois women in a predominantly male, clerical gathering in Rome.

Even bishops and *periti* who "were nice" to the women, whom they considered their friends in court, were not aware that the women were making any lasting impact. Writing a few months after the council's closing, Goldie remarked, "It is doubtful ... whether all the Bishops who gave a kindly welcome to the women 'auditors' on their appearance in St. Peter's attached real importance to their coming."[3] Léon-Josef Cardinal Suenens, renowned for making the first conciliar intervention calling for the missing "half of humanity" during the second session, admitted that "at the council time attention was concentrated as such on our Christian duties as baptized people, and the specific role of the women was not on the order of the day. . . . In fact, I insisted on their presence in the council, but my own attention was concentrated on the apostolic renewal in our active religious congregations."[4] Canadian theologian Gregory Baum, often referred to by conciliar women as "stellar" because of his press conferences and theological updates, confessed twenty-five years later,

> I am ashamed to say that during the council I was a male chauvinist pig, untouched by the woman's movement, and hence I simply do not know what happened in regard to women at, during, and around the council. I have no idea. It does show you that the paradigms we have in the imagination are research-guiding; they determine what we see and what we do

not see, unless something altogether drastic happens to raise our consciousness.[5]

Tom Stransky, noted for his work for ecumenism through the Secretariat for Christian Unity, was often referred to by Mary Luke Tobin as an auditor's ally. He sent me one of Goldie's articles, adding, "I am surprised you can get a book-length manuscript out of the topic."[6]

When asked about her remembrance of how women were received in the council, Tobin reflected,

> There was none of the "pedestal" mentality. I would say there was something else — either we were ignored or trivialized. Some bishops thought it was a good idea that we were there. There were three categories: (1) A minority of "good guys" really appreciated our being there (Archbishop Thomas D. Roberts, S.J., from England and some of our own bishops) and displayed a respectful sense of support. (2) The majority acted indifferently. Some appeared scared and shied away from even meeting us. (3) Then some clearly disapproved of our being there and avoided us totally.[7]

Parentelli noted that Cardinal Felici, responsible for oversight of the whole council proceedings, had the reputation of being a "woman-hater," who never spoke to a woman. "Later we realized that was the truth when we, as auditors, sat near where he was working, but he never greeted us nor even looked at us."[8]

Baldinucci, a resolute, soft-spoken woman, regretted that bishops did not see the problems of religious women as important. She asked one bishop what he thought of *Perfectae Caritatis*, the Decree on the Appropriate Renewal of the Religious Life, He replied, "It is surely well done." "He hadn't even read it!" That lack of interest angered her. From her own consultations with Cardinal Montini and later when he was Paul VI, she knew the pope's mind. She was not appointed as a "decoration by the vicar of Christ." She represented the Italian sisters of the federation and their important work for the good of the whole church, which should have concerned bishops.

Capturing Baldinucci's sentiments and experience, Maria Clara Bianchi (Baldinucci's secretary during the council and her substitute as an auditor during the fourth session) highlighted and analyzed the significance of the women's presence.

For the first time in history women found themselves admitted to assist in council works. By contrast, we can remember the Council of Saragossa, which declared it most inopportune to have women know Sacred Scripture directly. This affirmation was reemphasized practically in 1713, with the condemnation of Quesnel's "proposition" that declared the reading of Scripture necessary, even for fools and women! Their presence [at Vatican II] was not a negative silence but a seed that was developing. Paul VI wanted them to be *locutores* (speakers) everywhere else, since they were to spread the evangelical message widely so that it could penetrate the world. With this gesture, the pope intended women to enter the complete vision of God's design for salvation.... He didn't want to limit them to building their own personal spirituality, but he wanted them to feel that even in their own work the grand scheme of the apostolate of the church was inserted.... It really meant a new sense of responsibility invested in women, of fuller participation in the life of the church, especially in the liturgy and social charity, and renewed apostolates at the service of others.

Some commentators who were deeper into things of the church and were more mature knew how to see in a few female auditors who occupied the tribune of St. Andrew in St. Peter's that they were representing the multitude of invisible sisters, silent as they were, but working hard and striving to do what the New Testament women, Tabitha, Lydia, and Prisca, did in Jerusalem and Rome. They were there to help the apostles, to pray, suffer, work, and educate in the faith, within the home, school, and all the other surroundings of modern society.[9]

Baldinucci, in summing up the council, noted that "a world is dying, and a new one is being created with the wealth of contributions of interest to all people. Nothing higher or more majestic could be thought of on this earth about this assembly in which the protagonist is the Holy Spirit itself."

Grillo expressed similar connections. "During the council, it was like the time of Christ and the early church when women did the same thing as the bishops. We read the same documents, discussed them, and gave our input to the commissions." Grillo continued:

At the beginning I was confused, but after working in close proximity to the council, I realized that something was going to change. The church isn't only the hierarchy, but every baptized person must have some responsible role, and we have a lot of problems to solve. It was important to involve the laity from the point of view of service, not of prestige. The hierarchy or magisterium were an important point of guidance for the introduction of the laity into the work of the church.[10]

Speaking particularly about women, Grillo interpreted Paul VI's inclusion of them as wanting women's symbolic representation "because women must know how they are important for the church and how their mission is important for humanity and Christianity. The fact that women were coming into their own was a 'sign of the times,' and one way of showing that was by having them there at the council." Her overall experience was a sense of unity and taking part in a reality much bigger than herself. "Some things have changed since then in women's position in the church, slowly and often in silence. Certainly women are going to take more space in their service of the church and the world." Grillo, like the other women, grasped readily enough the importance of their role, but the council fathers faced a more difficult adjustment.

Bishops and theologians had to overcome years of misogynistic seminary education and church practice in order to be civil to the women. Eva Fleischner, a journalist for a small but significant publication, *Grail Notes,* made headlines during the second session because of how she was publicly affronted in St. Peter's. The occasion was an ecumenical Mass to which the journalists were invited. Fleischner was the only female in the tribune with the male journalists. When it came time to receive communion, she followed the others down the main aisle. "A Swiss guard in Vatican uniform put up his hands. I didn't know what he meant, so I kept coming toward him. He pushed me back and physically prevented me from going to communion," she recounted.[11] Naturally, her journalist peers publicized the discriminatory molestation. The explanation given was ridiculous and an embarrassment to the Vatican. However, instead of an apology being issued, no more journalists were invited to the conciliar Mass.

Rome was not built in a day; neither can its bulwark of chauvinism be expected to collapse overnight. However, by degrees the walls began to crumble, and Pope Paul VI was the one to dislodge the first stone by inviting female auditors to the third session. He had to proceed cautiously because of opposition, especially from the Roman curia and some Italian bishops. He invited a small but significant number of women to attend "sessions of interest to women," and he emphasized the symbolic nature of their presence. The women could not imagine what might not be "of interest to women" in their own church, and all seventeen of the earlycomers to the third session decided to miss out on nothing. No curtailment whatever was placed on their attendance.

Many bishops stopped by the tribune of St. Andrew on a daily basis to greet the auditors, either out of genuine interest to see if they could be helpful or curiously to gawk at this new species: council mother. Half jokingly, a bearded archbishop exclaimed that hitherto the only place he felt safe was in the hallowed male enclave of St. Peter's, but now the women had invaded even that.[12]

Twenty-five years later, Tobin recalled as an affront to women how an eminent *peritus,* Henri de Lubac, regaled his colleagues with a French quip about the women, which he put in the mouth of the majestic baroque statue of St. Andrew that dominated the auditors' tribune. "Mon Dieu, les femmes!..." In essence it amounted to Andrew's saying, "My God, have we come to this? — letting in women!"[13] However, in her 1965 article, Tobin, like most women then, appears to have gone along with the joke, stating that the comment was made "to the delighted surprise of all those viewing the latest arrivals at the third session." She continued: "In reality, we women, fifteen in number, rubbing elbows with distinguished *periti* and leaning over the tribune to shake hands with friendly bishops, could not have received a more positive welcome."

The auditors were the only ones receiving communion during the conciliar Mass, so they had no breakfast and had to look for the first opportunity to retrieve something from the coffee bar after Mass, while the order of the day was being announced. Presumably, the bishops said their private Masses and came to work fortified with breakfast. Reliving the scene, McCarthy stated convincingly, "Believe me, one felt humble and microscopic with the tiers of seats on both sides the full length of St. Peter's, and the eyes and mind of the world on you, as it were." It was progress from the second session when the women were no longer excluded from communion. Bellosillo remembered, however, seeing an elderly bishop cover his eyes when the women walked past to and from communion. "He was scandalized to see women walking down the aisle in St. Peter's, and he could not bear to look at such a desecration. It was all so new," she said. It would not have been possible if Cardinal Suenens had not intervened with the pope. Parentelli said she always went to communion "with no headcovering and short sleeves, as I was accustomed to do in the cathedral of St. Joseph or in the university chapel at Louvain. Here it was considered unseeemly so that when official photos of the council were taken, I was never pictured in those put out for all to see, and to buy a complete set, I had to go to the Vatican files and ask for copies."[14]

What God Has Joined,
Let Not the Bishops Pull Asunder

Segregation at the coffee bar — the place of communal eating and drinking — is highly symbolic of the deepest rift within the Roman Catholic Church: male and female relations and how they are played out in the Eucharist with its male-only presiders. Every auditor I spoke to had something to say about the bars. Eva Jung-Inglessis, wife of one of the first male conciliar auditors, Emile Inglessis, was a conciliar journalist in her own right. Sometimes she was allowed in to the council as an "auditor's wife." Her version of the coffee bar saga is that

> when the women came, there was a great dilemma. They were entitled to free refreshments like everyone else, but the council fathers did not want to admit the women to the bars — not because they didn't like women — but because it was so overcrowded that very close contact was unavoidable, and you couldn't have women squeezed in between bishops, etc. So they decided to open a third bar *just for the women.* It was under the tomb of Pope Clement XIII, where two marble lions guarded the entrance so that no man was allowed to enter. So Emile (my husband) and I talked to each other through the doorway because he could not come in.[15]

The lions were a spectacular monument, as Juliana Thomas, orienting herself to the floor plan of St. Peter's and looking for a landmark for the women's coffee bar, noted the "two powerful, marble lions, one sleeping and the other awake...ready to pounce."[16] Between the lions, two or three steps led downward into the brightly lit room, decorated with white and yellow silk, the papal colors, and flowers on the table. Nothing alcoholic was served, just coffee, hot milk, and baked goods, and every council member could have a free breakfast. (The accounts of Thomas and Inglessis were practically identical on this.)

Tobin recalled her first day at the council. Her fellow Americans and co-auditors, James Norris and Martin Work, led her to the coffee bar and introduced her to several bishops. The next day a separate coffee bar was set up for the female auditors behind the Porta Rezzonico, the door behind the main altar to the right end of the basilica. "There we could munch our Italian cookie and have our cup of coffee in obscurity behind the red velvet curtains. That gives you a good picture of what was happening," said Tobin, "and how unworthy it was." Goldie reminisced, "I still often meet the same *san petrino* [the name given to the whole corps of men responsible for the general maintenance of St. Peter's] who was our waiter. He was then very young, and he performed his task with great zeal and courtesy." Parentelli referred to him as "another type of clown, this time dressed in a black frockcoat." Her earlier comments pertained to the Swiss guards. "I saw that those men, so tall, with those clownish uniforms (colored yellow, orange, and blue), although they were very proper, didn't quite fit the formality of the occasion."[17]

The women called their segregated area "Bar-None" to distinguish it from the episcopal "Bar-Jonah" or "Bar-Abbas." Some bishops who tolerated women's presence in the formal context of the aula found it too close for comfort to be rubbing shoulders with them over coffee and relating to them as peers.

Grillo remembered how she and Amalia di Montezemolo wandered into the wrong bar, "but they gave us coffee anyhow," she said. Obviously, the male auditors who had come a year earlier fit in quite easily and could mingle with the bishops during break time. Not so the women. The greatest barrier was and continues to be male-female relations, rather than the clergy-laity divide.

At a later date (after the Icazas achieved the desegregation of the women's bar), the women could invite others to join them, but not many Fathers ventured into their *salotta*. The segregation, while not fully observed, was regrettable because it narrowed the opportunities for the women to communicate their ideas. Much of the politicking went on there, as what was spoken into an episcopal ear later got voiced in the aula. The women depended on episcopal spokespersons since they were only listeners in the aula.

Luz-Marie Alvarez-Icaza saw the women's coffee bar as "coquettish and special for women," while the male auditors could still attend the bishops' bar. She remembered how after the solemn opening of the fourth conciliar session a bishop who was a great joker, perhaps the bishop of Cuernavaca, Sergio Méndez Arceo, asked her husband, "If you don't want to separate now, how are you going to decide whether to go with the women or the men for coffee?" Luz-Marie refused to go to the bishops' bar, so José accompanied her to the women's, and they brought along a male Protestant observer who was more open to women. The women did open the door to the two men. After that first day, they invited other men friends to join them, and people looked at them in amazement. After a few days, a Swiss guard appeared at the entrance and would not permit the men to enter the women's coffee bar. The idea was considered scandalous, but the scandal continued to grow as José insisted that Archbishop Felici, conciliar president, permit the couple to have coffee together. Felici was in a solemn session, and he just motioned for the Swiss guard to withdraw and let them do whatever they wanted. He could not understand why he would be interrupted from an important matter for such a trivial thing as drinking coffee. But José insisted, "It is not trivial. This is very important because you are discussing at this moment the changing front of the world today — the theme of the church in the modern world in *Gaudium et Spes,* while it is being played out here in front of your eyes." After that, they could come and go as they pleased.

The Alvarez-Icazas saw the irony of discussing the modern world while ignoring it in practice. "Never would it have occurred to the council fathers," said José,

> that in a restaurant, at work, etc., I would never have to be alone with the men and Luz-Ma with the women. This shows how archaic the actual mentality of the church was. It was a protection for priestly celibacy, and they were imposing it on the laity. It was precisely because of that Luz-Ma's participation was so important in the council's mixed commission, with cardinals, bishops, ten laypeople, and just one couple. Not only that. On weekends there were no conciliar sessions, so we went to Mass at St. Charles Borromeo Church, near where we lived. Our old-

est daughter held my arm in church. An Italian priest who was hearing confessions was scandalized and gave an exclamation of horror at the sexuality of it. "Without arms!" he said. We sent in a protest that I couldn't hold my daughter's arm in church, and I couldn't be with my wife in the coffee bar. We did it so that there would be a document about relations between married people.

While the Mexican wife and husband got separate invitations to the council, they made a point of always acting as a couple. José continued.

We created a real ruckus the first time we entered the council. We should have come from the back, but we made an intentional "mistake" and walked through the main door, arm-in-arm, just as the solemn session was about to begin. Bishops were astonished. They thought we were lost tourists. When we were half way up the center aisle, the bell rang, indicating that all council members should go to their places. A purple cloud came toward us as the bishops scurried to take their places, and we got bumped from all sides. Then we realized the danger of going against the tide — the hierarchy of the church! With this incident and many others, we became a notorious couple. The other auditors went to Mass and communion in single file. We always went together arm-in-arm. The Swiss guards tried to separate us but with no success. One old Irishman, Frank Duff (founder of the Legion of Mary), knelt down for communion between us one day. There was Luz-Ma, Frank, and I. The pope gave communion first to Luz-Ma, smiled, skipped over Frank, and came to me, making a gesture that he knew we were together; then he went back to Frank.[18]

Separating Myth from Reality

The climate improved for female journalists with the presence of even a few female auditors. Canadian Bonnie Brennan was in Rome during the third and fourth sessions of the council as a radio producer, registered as a member of the Vatican press corps. She was executive director of the National Catholic Communications Center, an office sponsored by the Canadian Catholic Conference. Her task was to produce radio programs for use in Canada to help inform Canadian Catholics about the council. Like other journalists, she lived in a hotel and worked out of the Vatican Press Hall. Like other radio producers, she recorded either at Radio Vatican or on location with her portable recorder. She attended daily press briefings, press panels, and press conferences, and conducted interviews.

Brennan reminded me of the need to sort out fact from myth. She gave the straightforward facts of her own story — one that was later highly embellished.

> Guest passes were available to bishops for important visitors. These were usually issued for visiting priests. Bernard Daly, a lay journalist, was director of the Information Service of the Canadian Catholic Conference at the time. This was a print service for Canadian Catholic papers. He was in Rome for all four sessions of the council. During the fourth session, Bernard asked the bishops to try to get a visitor's pass for him. I supported this request but did not make a similar one for myself.
>
> A request was sent to Cardinal Felice's office asking that passes be prepared for both Mr. Bernard Daly and Miss Bonnie Brennan, describing our work in print and in radio, and that we were staff of the Canadian bishops. The request was sent over the signature of several (approximately 12) Canadian bishops.
>
> The passes were issued. They were valid for either one or two weeks.... They were issued for Reverendissimo Sacerdotal Bernard Daly and Reverendissimo Sacerdotal Bonnie Brennan, i.e., Father Bernard Daly and Father Bonnie Brennan.
>
> We both entered the aula on the next Monday morning and sat with the lay auditors. On the second morning, the guard at the tribunal challenged my pass. One of the Canadian bishops argued with him and insisted on sending both passes to the Cardinal. Bernard Daly might have been able to remain uninvolved if this had not been the case. We were given seats in the special guests' area until coffee break. At that point, Archbishop Krol was sent to tell us that we were permitted to stay for the rest of the morning, but that our passes had been revoked because journalists were not permitted to attend the sessions.[19]

So much for the facts. Brennan continues her own hermeneutic.

> The press focused on the "novelty" factor of a woman being asked to leave and having been issued a pass as "Father."

The false stories and myths began to build, and some people spread them. I've heard people say I was "disguised as a priest," i.e., wore a cassock. One rumor even said I had hidden in the church overnight. Some got the title wrong and said the pass was made out for a monsignor or a bishop. Even when I have told people these were not true, they have persisted, insisting they had been told it by someone who had been there! One Roman paper, which also happened to support the Italian Communist Party, covered the Associated Press story about me. Someone then started the rumor that this was the only story about the council the communist papers carried. This was not true either.

Brennan developed her analysis and drew helpful conclusions:

If there is a lesson in any of this, it comes from focusing on the essentials, not the rumors and myths. The essentials are:

1. Two lay employees working as reporters in Rome;

2. One asks for a pass. To be fair, the bishops ask for equal treatment; i.e., two passes;

3. Both passes were revoked because both were journalists;

4. It was the news media and human gossip, *not* the official church that differentiated between the two people and focused on the fact that one was a woman.

Brennan continued:

I can tell you that as a woman *journalist,* I did not feel I was treated any better or any worse than male journalists by bishops, or *periti,* or other Vatican clerics. In fact, I found much less male chauvinism among the clergy than I did among the male population of Rome as a whole or the male population of the press corps.

I did find some "paternalism" among the clergy, but it has to be remembered that I was twenty-nine and thirty at the time and far away from home. The kindness shown and the fatherliness was appreciated. It is only looking back from the 1980s that I would even begin to see it as a form of paternalism. I believe it is important to be realistic about the time period and not judge 1960s people and actions with 1990s measuring tapes.

Renowned Irish journalist and reporter on the council and subsequent synods Seán Mac Réamoinn remembered the women as a novelty at first, making headlines. "When that wore off, only someone who had nothing to report would look to the women for a story." Mac Réamoinn, however, emphasized that it was his *perception* that nothing much was going on with the women, so he left room for a deeper reality.[20] This lack of perceived importance of the women — just like their regular presence in church — accounts for the total lack of response I received to my letters written to key U.S. bishops of Vatican II. Charles Buswell of Colorado was an exception. He replied and remembered Tobin.

Fly from the Public Gaze

The training of the women religious conditioned them to flee from the public eye. Baldinucci, for instance, despite her intelligence, training, and vast experience as chairperson of the Nursing Sisters of Italy (FIRO) and president of the Italian Federation of about 130,000 religious, hated to be interviewed. She defended herself by explaining: "Having spent our lives in the shadow of the convent, or hospital, or anonymity of a mission, it wasn't easy for us to give interviews, meet journalists, and speak about ourselves as we were waylaid by photographers and reporters outside the council aula." Speaking about her experience as an auditor, she said, "it was like being part of the heavenly Jerusalem." A German reporter found Juliana Thomas, "the only German female auditor at the council" (this was during the third session before Gertrud Ehrle came), in the front seat of the German bishops' bus on the way back from St. Peter's. She is referred to as *eine zierliche Ordensfrau,* (delicate or dainty nun). When asked about her earliest impressions, the sixty-six-year-old woman, surrounded by a busload of bishops and theologians, gave a rather typical response from a first-timer in Rome and plunged into the strange environment of high-level clergy. "It is the goodness and fatherliness of the cardinals and bishops without exception. No radio or television could reproduce the atmosphere of love in the spirit of Christ. One has to experience it."[21]

On her very first day at the council, a bishop from South Africa came looking for the Dernbach sister but did not recognize her changed habit. As a child, he had attended kindergarten in the sisters' school. Another chance meeting with a bishop on a bus revealed that he had been restored to health in one of the sisters' hospitals.

Later on, Thomas included more content in her letters regarding topics under discussion in the aula and the public briefings in the afternoons, for example, regarding the progress of Schema 13. New horizons also opened for her, as she came in contact with "members of the whole world in a small circle." She concluded, "We sisters cannot cut ourselves off when we are invited to such time-consuming meetings. We are often the first to withdraw after the opening greeting." She referred specifically to a meeting with St. Joan's International Alliance, where she met Swiss lawyer Dr. Gertrud Heinzelmann. "She is very much for the ordination of women, and she has become well known for her book on the subject. She stood before me like a 'red flag' and said she wanted just to unleash the discussion on this question."[22] Another new experience for Thomas was the ecumenical dimension: she encountered the Quaker Douglas Steere from the U.S., Brother Roger from Taizé, and Vitaly Borowoy from the Moscow patriarchate and a member of the World Council of Churches, who hopefully stated, "At Vatican Council III, we will all be one."[23] This nun was being exposed to the modern world.

Baldinucci finally agreed to a seven-minute interview with Suzanne Cita-Malard on the Catholic weekly program *Art and Faith,* on Montecarlo Radio, October 14, 1964. During another interview at her convent in Milan, two little African children the community had befriended rushed into the room and hugged Mother Baldinucci. The reporter had no camera but dearly wanted to capture this unusual sight. Baldinucci hesitated, lest it be attracting too much personal attention to herself. One of the sisters got a camera and flash, only to discover she had no film, so Baldinucci was relieved to be let off the hook. Some women took to heart the secrecy they were expected to maintain regarding conciliar discussions. Cristina Estrada took it literally, even in dealing with her own community, as did Amalia di Montezemolo in regard to her family. Her two daughters heard nothing about the proceedings. Suzanne Guillemin mentioned taking an oath of secrecy, but Goldie remembered nothing about it.

Forget the Flowers

When Marie-Louise Monnet crossed the threshold of St. Peter's all-male enclave and took her place as the first female conciliar auditor in history, Archbishop Denis Hurley of Durban, South Africa, gave her a welcoming acknowledgment: "Flowers have at last bloomed in our land." His well-intentioned florid greeting was hardly appropriate for this stolid founder of MIAMSI, an organization now of international proportions. Reminiscent of Thérèse of Lisieux, one could appropriately say, "Little flower indeed! Little rod of iron!"

Right through the council the women had to remind bishops and theologians that they were just ordinary human beings, and they wanted to be treated as such. Tobin remembered how during the commission's work on *Gaudium et Spes*, Yves Congar read a flowery piece he had written, and to his surprise there was no response from the women. "Rosemary," he said, "you don't like it?"

"No," she replied, "you can cut out all the references to women as flowers and light, etc. We don't need any of that grandiose stuff that has no basis in women's reality. All we want is to be treated as full human beings, accorded the same equality as men."

In their enthusiasm to acknowledge the women auditors' presence, several bishops specifically mentioned them in the opening addresses of their interventions. Some appellatives included "carissimae sorores" (dearest sisters), "sorores admirandae" (admirable sisters), or even "pulcherrimae auditrices" (most beautiful female auditors).[24] Well-intentioned as they were, they betrayed their own social conditioning of entrapping all women in the beauty myth. It was a struggle for most to get past that. Some never did. Goldie admitted that "by the end of the council the women were gratified to see that their presence was taken for granted, and their contribution was taken seriously."

A related myth posing a challenge to the women themselves as well as the clergy was that of the "good sisters" — who looked like adult dolls in the dress of another age. It was difficult to discover the real person of the individual sister and take her seriously when she was seen in the mass-produced habit that suggested she was a carbon copy of all her other dresslikes, leaving her little personal identity beyond "one of the sisters." The bishops too had to get beyond the myth in order to hear the different voices and concerns coming from individual sister auditors. Only then did real communication take place, and the sisters' voices were relayed and amplified by caring bishops.

For better or worse, laywomen in their secular dress presented less of an aura than the women religious. As women they were threatening to most clergy, but they lacked the habit barrier. There was no dress code for the conciliar women, although some frequently wore black or other dark colors and dressed professionally as they would for going to an office. Roeloffzen remarked that some of the laywomen looked more nunlike than the sisters. All wore the black mantilla customary for church attire in those days when head covering was still required of women. McCarthy paid tribute to the maturity of the U.S. bishops in relating to her — the only woman on their bus each morning. She explained the arrangement.

> The American hierarchy leased a fleet of attractive blue and white buses. Each was numbered and had an assignment of stopping at a given group of hotels. The first stop for the no. 4 bus was the Majestic Hotel, where Bishop Frederick Freking and I were staying. The bus was quite full by the time it reached us each morning at 8:15. Bishop Freking introduced me the first morning, and I got on. The bus proceeded to the Flora Hotel and on and on until it reached St. Peter's, the greatest church in Christendom. I think it's a great tribute to the bishops that they could continue to laugh and talk and let their hair down without feeling they had to be watching their words in the presence of a woman.

The bus driver was more chauvinistic, however, as McCarthy explained:

> One day when Bishop Freking wasn't there, the driver gave me a tirade in Italian and refused to let me on the bus. I don't know if he was a substitute driver that day. He thought he was just picking up a bishop, and I was on the bishop's coattails every other day. Anyhow, nothing would convince him that a woman was legitimately going to the council with the bishops. He drove off without me, and I had to take a cab.[25]

Through Their Eyes

When asked for concrete images of the council, various women were forthcoming with descriptions that recreate the scene for post-conciliar people. Goldie recalled one of her first impressions after entering the Porta de Santa Marta (St. Martha's door), which opened directly onto the Blessed Sacrament chapel. (This was the door assigned to the auditors.) She saw there several bishops kneeling in prayer. This brought home to her that "the council is in the first place the prayer of the bishops." Within the aula itself, "it was a curious mixture of quasi liturgical solemnity and familial simplicity, especially when the bishops leave their places to go to the bar."[26]

Parentelli commented on the continual motion going on during the sessions, as bishops got bored or tired sitting on the hard bleachers and moved around or went to the coffee bar. Her overall impression was that not many people were listening to what the speakers were saying in Latin. Since the auditors and cardinals entered through the same door, Parentelli had several opportunities to observe the cardinals' entrance.

> They usually arrived in very impressive black Cadillacs, or limousines like those certain U.S. presidents used. The license plates were engraved with the letters SCV (which means *Sacra Città Vaticana*), but there were jokes about what it *really* meant. The Italians said it stood for *Se Cristo Vedesse* (if Christ could see) the luxury that surrounded these representatives of the church he founded. Something else that impressed me was to see close up and hear the rustle of the silk robes, a set of very old cardinals, some obviously sick or ailing...like a realistic Italian movie. It showed with a certain amount of disillusionment in what hands was the church Jesus founded. In some cases, the cardinals were so crippled that their chauffeurs or bodyguards had to help them get out of the car and take them to their seats. A lengthy session was almost impossible for some of them to sit through.[27]

Goldie described a morning in St. Peter's square.

> When the council fathers arrive for the general congregation, many of them are like school boys of 30 or so in a bus; others are on foot walking up the Via de la Conciliazone; others still are driving a *deux chevaux* (a very popular French car), laden with

French bishops already discussing with their theologians. Then there is the other spectacle at midday when the fathers coming out of the council transform the square into a kind of multi-colored garden of varied flowers with all shades of violet and red, set in relief by the black, grey, or brown of the friars and non-Catholic observers and some rare layperson or sister.[28]

Mass preceded the council meeting daily at 9:00 a.m. Ruth Wallace, not an auditor, but part of a team working with Cardinal Suenens on renewal of religious life, gave her personal observations on "woman's 'place' during the council."

There were many dramatic displays of patriarchal symbolism. An unforgettable sight, for instance, was the daily convergence of hundreds of bishops from all over the world dressed in their colorful regalia at the doors of St. Peter's Church. No layperson could be seen among them because the front entrance was re-served solely for the voting members of the council. Women who were not auditors participated in the council itself only by at-tending the Mass celebrated before each day's Council session. However, they were instructed to leave immediately after the lit-urgy, because only bishops, periti, auditors, and staff could be present for the council deliberations. (There were some mornings when we felt we were literally being shoved out of St. Peter's, like uninvited guests at a party, because the ushers pointed to the door while announcing in very loud and insistent voices, "Exeunt omnes," indicating that we were to exit immediately.)[29]

McCarthy gave a glimpse of the inside:

I entered through the massive bronze doors to a scene very dif-ferent from that which most visitors to St. Peter's cherish. The main aisle was blocked. I walked to the left behind stadium-like bleachers, where cardinals, archbishops, and bishops were seated in order of rank. The same gleaming marble, mosaic, and gold, and the gorgeous sixteenth-century tapestries provided a worthy background for the council's deliberations. The auditors were most fortunate because their box was next to the cardinals. Directly in front of the main altar was a long table of the cardinal presidents and a shorter table in front of that for the moderators. At each session, the pope's secretary, Archbishop Felici made the announcements of the day. Directly opposite the auditors were the Protestant observers, numbering about double that of the auditors. Intently, they followed all the proceedings, and as we met in the aula, discussed the events of the day.[30]

From Novelty to Normality

"How quickly we adjust to revolution!" wrote Douglas Horton.

> Last year Catherine McCarthy was in Rome on civil rights work, and there was the possibility that she might be an auditor. Now she is here in her own auditor's seat.... Last year the observers' wives and a few other women sat in a little huddle in the corner of the room; this year they are spread, in great numbers, throughout the audience. Two months ago no women had even been seen at a business session of the council. Today the women are not only in the auditors' tribune but also are to be seen every day wandering about in the apse and transept, just like the men, and apparently able to consume just as much coffee.[31]

As the council geared into action, Goldie noted aspects of the world-church and the new Pentecost as Latin was spoken in diverse tongues. In 1962, bishops generally mentioned this as the most impressive factor of the council, as they experienced concretely for the first time the catholicity of the church in Indian, African, Canadian, Brazilian, Chinese, and other bishops from all over the world. By the council's end in 1965, this diversity was taken for granted as all the bishops had discovered and accepted what international "globe-trotters" like Goldie had already experienced for more than a decade.

McCarthy described the general flow of a conciliar workday:

> The formal session began after Mass. All talks of the council were in Latin. Poor Cardinal Cushing couldn't take it at all. "I can't understand a word they're saying," he said, "so I came home." The auditors were far better off than the bishops because we had theologians translating and summarizing for us. Both Sr. Mary Luke and I had our interpreter, as did all seven national groups. When we went for coffee, our interpreter got a break. Instantaneous translation was not installed at St. Peter's, but IBM machines were there for counting the bishops' votes. At 12:15 or 12:30 the council closed each day. At 1:00 at Salvatorean

House nearby a Holy Cross priest, Fr. Edward L. Heston, C.S.C., gave a concise, staccato news briefing. At 3:00 p.m. at the USO, the press was permitted to ask questions concerning the morning session. Theologians, scientists, doctors, and *periti* answered the questions. The auditors' meetings were usually held around 6:30 p.m., mostly in French. A talk was given concerning a topic under discussion in the council. The auditors made suggestions, which were passed on to the various commissions. A day at the council was long but exciting and exhilarating. History was being made, *aggiornamento* was taking place, making the church more relevant to the twentieth century. Both women and men were injecting new vitality into the people of God.[32]

Several auditors commented on their good fortune in being assigned to plush velvet seats, while church dignitaries balanced on hard bleachers. Guests are generally given better seats than family members, so the Protestant observers also sat in comfort. McCarthy commented: "Maybe that was the only place left for us, but we were *next to the cardinals.* There couldn't have been a more important spot. Women could use that to gain recognition in their own countries, saying, look where women were at that important gathering of the church."

A Blinding Light

Like Goldie and other women accustomed to living internationally, attending and addressing large gatherings, Bellosillo took her attendance at the council in stride. Belonging to international movements expanded her horizons beyond the Iberian peninsula, putting her in touch with the church of central Europe. She had, therefore, a decided advantage over the bishops, including those of her native Spain, and she embraced the council with great expectation. "We were already reading Congar, and we knew several of the theologians of the council. I lived the council from the outside for two years before being invited as an auditor," she explained. She and members of WUCWO elaborated notes that they sent to the commissions, and they answered questions and responded to consultations on particular topics, especially concerning women, the family, and the lay apostolate. In this way she was well in touch with the major

themes and thrust of the council and its deliberations, so incorpo-
rating herself into the assembly and its commissions was an easy
transition.

> Still, I was not prepared for the blinding light of the Spirit that
> confronted me in new experiences and discoveries and frequently
> kept me awake at night as I tried to process all that was going
> on in the council and in my own head. I recognized that this was
> a historical moment in which new ways had to be found for the
> church and the world. It was not just a matter of participating in
> the council but of comprehending the new quality of conscious-
> ness which the church was acquiring at the time and which the
> world was living. Being an auditor was not an event that was
> over and done with a quarter of a century ago. Paul VI's invi-
> tation was a call to commitment that altered the course of my
> life forever. It's a reality I have lived with a mixture of pain and
> enthusiasm every day of my life since that initial experience.[33]

Strong testimony from this eagle-eyed woman who led WUCWO for
thirteen years!

Bellosillo was sensitive to the fact that her participation was not
just a personal privilege but a commitment on behalf of the 36 million women of WUCWO and indeed all women everywhere. Her
main concern was to pass on to the organizations everything the
council gave her. This was in keeping with the mind of the pope,
who, receiving the auditors in audience, told them they were selected
as "experts in life" from within the Catholic organizations because
they shared the life of many Christians throughout the world.

Miceli saw her conciliar experience as longlasting:

> It was really a turning point in my life. It left a deeper impression
> on me than a retreat, because after the council I just couldn't be
> the same as before. It was not just an impersonal stimulus to take
> part in the activities of the church but an inner conversion and
> change of mentality. Being called to take part in the council was
> a "gift" from the church and a special "grace" from God which
> deeply marked my life. An experience of this kind cannot be
> forgotten. It is still a bright light on my way toward the ultimate
> goal, which I await with fear, but also with such joy![34]

Monnet's reaction was similar. "This stamped me so profoundly
that I can say that it oriented irreversibly the final years of my apos-

tolic life: my nomination by the Holy Father as an auditor to the council."[35] Writing about her first day in council as the first woman to arrive, she remembered, "It was *the* event of the day, which merited for me a visit to the tribune of St. Andrew by several bishops, including the young bishop of Cracow, who had to give me a message from the Polish women. I was profoundly touched, and I was happy to be able to return the visit a little later, November 17, 1964, to Archbishop Karol Wojtyla, at his residence in the Polish Institute, close to the Palace of Justice."[36] Little did she realize at the time that she was trying to proselytize a future pope about the independent milieux. Her immediate concern was how she could follow all the morning sessions in Latin. Others had the same concern, so Fr. Jean M. Tillard, O.P., translated for the Francophones, while Canadian Sulpician Edouard Gagnon rendered the same service for the Spaniards.

Bishops Moved to Tears

Comments from all the female auditors revealed their intense involvement in the progress of the council. All the ups and downs were also their ups and downs. Five days after Vatican II closed its final session, Guillemin addressed the seminary sisters back at Rue du Bac, Paris.[37] Her intention was to give impressions of the final days of the council. She talked at length:

> The council has ended on a note of joy, and the participants have returned again to their normal work, but there is also a note of sadness because it is being said, "The council has come to an end, and for us there will never be another."

Addressing her young audience, she continued:

> You perhaps, dear Sisters, will see a new council. Perhaps even one or other of you will participate in it, for at the next council women will most certainly be admitted in a far greater number than now, and their role will assume a greater importance. Our presence has been rather meaningful for us, symbolic perhaps; it has however certainly borne fruit. These last days were filled with joy, a joy, I might say, that gradually grew to a climax as the last schemas were taking shape, and the last difficulties were overcome.

She referred particularly to "Black Friday," at the end of the third session when the Declaration on Religious Freedom failed to pass, but now in 1965, the hurdles had been overcome, and the new text was approved.

Reports from Rome generally focused on the fanfare of the outdoor closing of the council on December 8, 1965. Without taking from that, Guillemin felt that the final acts of the council on December 7 were far more important. Seven documents were promulgated. Besides, there was a spectacular ceremony of far-reaching historical import. Paul VI had hinted that the reciprocal anathemas between the churches of Istanbul and Rome were about to be lifted. Guillemin described the proceedings in detail.

> When the day of the ceremony arrived, we saw to the side at the foot of the altar of the confession of St. Peter a delegation of Orthodox priests representing Patriarch Athenagoras, and in their midst was the Latin bishop of Constantinople. At a stipulated time in the ceremony, the Latin bishop of Istanbul arose from his usual tribune and began to read in French the text of the common declaration of his holiness Paul VI and Patriarch Athenagoras amidst such thunderous applause that he was unable to continue. This lasted several minutes. Truly it could be said that the heart of the entire Catholic Church could be felt beating under the vaulted roof of St. Peter's. The two names of the universal head of the Catholic Church, the pope, and the head of the Orthodox church of Istanbul were united. In this proclamation the Holy Father made a great act of humility in recognizing before the entire world — before all separated Christians and all people — the errors of the past.

She explained the unfortunate historical facts that led to the divisions of more than a thousand years.

> When the Latin patriarch had eventually finished reading the declaration, he returned to his place. On arriving there beside Athenagoras's delegate, they embraced one another. The thunderous applause broke out anew. The ceremony continued. The decree of *anathema* was lifted. Cardinal Bea read the decree for the Holy Father, while Athenagoras's delegate mounted the altar of the Confession beside the papal throne. He was a fine tall priest with typical oriental beard and the same headdress you

saw on Bishop Sidarous, CM, patriarch of Alexander. He wore a large black and purple cope embroidered in gold — it was splendid. He listened majestically and dignified to the reading of the decree, then approached the Holy Father, who had descended at least one step from his throne to embrace him, amidst fresh applause from the entire assembly. He then descended, but he was a practical man and with the decree in his hand he looked around at those who were searching for the container in order to put the document away. He then returned to his place, going the long way around by the Confession, to the tremendous applause of everyone... I am telling you the little details which were not pointed out in the newspapers because each sees things in her own way.

What struck me most after the reconciliation of the two churches was the final ceremony — the asking pardon for offences committed during the council by all the conciliar fathers. In spite of the presence of thousands of persons everyone was truly recollected and silent, seeking union with God. After some moments of silent prayer the Sovereign Pontiff arose to sing the prayer of pardon: "By the infusion of the Holy Spirit, may you have a safe return to your flock... and may the divine light of our Lord go before you." The Cardinal Deacon sang, "Arise," and the Holy Father concluded, "May the peace of our Lord be with you," to which all replied, "Amen." All the Fathers embraced and we too embraced one another, the auditors, the religious, the priests, etc.

Our two experts, who had hardly ever left us, did not embrace, and someone said they should. They looked at each other and said, "It's hardly worth the trouble because we always had the same opinion," and they too embraced. I met several French bishops and they were crying. Msgr. Rhodain said to me, "Don't speak, I can't talk," so overcome were they all. Never in our life had we lived a moment such as this. There was a tremendous consciousness of the mystical body; it was magnificent.

With less exuberance but no less appreciation for profoundly moving conciliar experiences, Khouzam recalled three major high points. First was

Paul VI taking from his head the triple tiara, studded with precious stones and gold metal, and donating it to the poor people of India. Second, the most Holy Father on his knees at the feet of Msgr. Meliton, delegate of Patriarch Athenagoras, during the celebration of the Eucharist, a staggering, historic gesture of reconciliation and of pardon — he kissed his feet. And finally, Pope Paul VI and the patriarch of the Orthodox Church of Constantinople, Athenagoras, giving each other the ineffable sign of peace during the Eucharistic celebration.[38]

Moyano observed that "a page of history was turned by this gesture... With tear-filled eyes, we asked ourselves, why should *we* be witnesses of this unique moment? Roads had been opened, and the renovation now seemed like an official orientation of the church in its conciliar texts."[39]

While looking forward to the 1994 Synod on Religious Life, Ghanem looked back to Vatican II as

> a council that contributed to a great opening up of the understanding of the church, of the apostolate, of dialogue, of reconciliation among people in spite of their differences, of ecumenism, etc. The role of the laity was particularly felt and put to practical application in Lebanon. The council was a unique occasion of fusing the different categories of people present — council fathers, experts, non-Catholic observers, lay female and male auditors, women religious auditors, etc. Very instructive, friendly, and recreational gatherings were often organized at the level of all. They permitted fruitful exchanges and friendships that have withstood the erosion of time. The conferences outside the meetings in the Aula often threw light on many questions and served to disperse a lot of prejudice.[40]

Many of the auditors commented on the wonderful liturgies during the council. Of great significance was the experience of different rites. Chimy served as spokesperson for what others echoed:

> Yes, we even had the Ukrainian rite. I was at the Coptic rite before that. With the drums and all, you got some insight into their mentality. It still was Catholic and universal while being theirs. Ghanem and Khouzam were of the Coptic rite. You can't have uniformity — everybody in the same language and the same rite. You have to respect differences. All want to celebrate and go to God in their own way. The council leaders wanted to give us the experience of liturgies in a different language and rite.

You know, I don't think that the Latin rite, even the pope, considered us of the Ukrainian rite to be Catholics and in union with Rome until just lately. When the Ukrainian bishops were able to have their own rite there at the council, it was an eye opener for everyone. We were all Catholics together. It was hard for our people always to be a minority, and there was always that inferiority complex that survived through the years. It was high time for it to change. Bringing the rite into St. Peter's clearly suggested that the Ukrainian rite is on a par with the others.[41]

Of Interest to Women

Little of the council discussions pertained specifically to women, and yet all the female auditors considered *everything* of interest to them, having a bearing on their lives, and therefore as being their business, so they showed up for everything — Mass, formal conciliar sessions, press briefings, special lectures, social gatherings, as well as their own auditors' meetings. The events the women remembered as particularly noteworthy were usually general conciliar highlights, while some had predominantly personal meaning.

Goldie demonstrated both. "Paul VI's pilgrimage to the Holy Land was a practical return to the sources of Christian and ecclesial life. The longing for unity was made manifest with paternal love in the ecumenical embrace on the Mount of Olives with the Patriarch Athenagoras." McCarthy claimed that Msgr. Luigi Ligutti, "the rural life man from Iowa," was responsible for telling the pope, "You must go to the Holy Land; you're never the same once you've been there." The pope took his advice, apparently, and said McCarthy, "that was the beginning of the traveling popes because until then, they never left the Vatican except for their summer residence." Goldie was impressed by another symbolic gesture and travel:

> The call to the true mission of the church to evangelize the poor with the poor Christ, to bring light, hope, and salvation to those who are seeking, to those who are suffering. This call, which was already heard or seen in the symbolic gift, the giving away of the tiara, took on new accents which could be heard even by those who do not yet know Christ, in the meeting at Bombay, when Paul VI attended the international Eucharistic Congress.

Goldie continued:

> When I wrote those lines in March 1965, I had not yet expe-
> rienced one of the most deeply felt, most significant moments
> of the council years. That was in the late morning of Octo-
> ber 5, 1965. In the aula, the fathers were discussing international
> problems, war and peace, but those listening to the various inter-
> ventions were very distracted. Lo and behold, the main doors of
> the basilica opened, and Paul VI came in. He was coming di-
> rectly from Fumicino airport on his way back from New York.
> He had taken to the United Nations on behalf of the whole coun-
> cil on the feast of St. Francis his insistent message of peace. He
> repeated, "The people must stand together, one with the other,
> not one above the other, and never one against the other, but
> one for the other." In this way, *Gaudium et Spes* was a living
> experience before it became a document."[42]

Moyano remembered how "just before the fourth session opened,
there was a penitential procession in the streets of Rome, with
Paul VI at the head and more than two thousand bishops in two
unending lines, reciting and singing the penitential psalms, far away
from the rows of decorated windows and from the people. The next
day, when the session opened, the Veni Sancte Spiritus sounded in
St. Peter's like a cry of petition."[43]

In keeping with her concern for the church of the poor, Moyano
was impressed by the action of a group that became known as the
"Bishops of the Catacombs." Since the first conciliar session they got
together every year to reflect on the topic "the church of the poor,"
and they often went to pray at the catacombs. "Before the closing
of Vatican II, those anonymous pastors told all their peers what they
modestly called their 'project' — in reality it was a binding promise
of poverty of life . . . renunciation of all possessions, a wish to be addressed simply as Padre Obispo. They wished to avoid every privilege
and every alliance with the powerful. Finally, they did everything to
fight for justice by way of a ministry of service."[44] One can see here
the spirit that later took hold in liberation theology.

Women called forth to receive special conciliar messages were
deeply touched by that experience. McCarthy was taken by surprise
when, before the promulgation of *Apostolicam Actuositatem,* she
was told that she, Bellosillo, and Monnet, with three men, were cho-

sen to receive a Latin copy of the document from the pope. Reliving her excitement, she described what happened.

> I looked myself over and thanked God I was respectably dressed that day. I wondered how I could make it up the steps in St. Peter's to the main altar. As I knelt down at the Holy Father's feet, I attempted to express my gratitude on behalf of all the women. He was whispering into my ear about his wonderful trip to the UN in New York. It was breath-taking. Bishop Hugh Donohue, a darling who was always our good supporter, told the story of when I turned around to come down — I don't know he could see so well — but he said he detected a tear on my cheek. That experience and receiving holy communion so many times from the hand of the Holy Father were such a blessing.[45]

Bellosillo noted how the incident caused some bishops to murmur, "Incredible! Incredible!" "Women climbing up to the papal throne was unheard-of audacity," she said. It was almost as bad as the Pharisees murmuring because Jesus let the so-called "sinful" woman minister to him with the sacramental acts of washing his feet, drying them with her hair, and anointing him with the alabaster box of rich ointment.

Monnet recalled two great joys afforded her during the final conciliar session. "November 18, 1965, the Decree on the Apostolate of the Laity, voted almost unanimously by the council fathers (2,305 voices for, 2 against), was promulgated by the Holy Father. He decided to present it symbolically to six auditors. I had the honor of being part of that group, along with M. de Habicht, Eusebe Adjakpley from Togo, ... John Chen from Hong Kong, Pilar Bellosillo, ... and Mrs. McCarthy." Next came "December 8, 1965, the closing day, when the council addressed itself to the world by means of 'messages' proclaimed by a cardinal and received by a delegation of three laypersons. ... I was one of those chosen, the others being Laura Segni, wife of the past president of Italy, and Luz-Marie Alvarez-Icaza, mother of a Mexican family."[46]

Goldie, in her usual low-key fashion, added,

> One last memory concerned me directly. On November 20, 1964, the Holy Father received an audience of the auditors, men and women, together with the parish priests who had been invited during the third session. It was on that occasion ... that I

experienced one of the dearest memories of my life. The pope, recognizing me in the group, greeted me with a smile, saying, "Ah, *nostra collaboratrice!*" our co-worker.[47]

I might add, reminiscent of an earlier Paul of Tarsus, greeting his co-working women, Prisca, Phoebe, Chloe, and others.

Lucienne Salle, not an auditor but a young woman involved in the youth movement, came to Rome during the council. I wondered how she felt about happenings that were so exciting to the middle-aged and older auditors. "It was fantastic," she said. "We could visit every bishop, and they were open, friendly, and free. Sometimes I meet people of my own generation who are not happy with the church and harbor much resentment. It was that experience in Rome that gave me a new view of the church as nothing else could."[48]

Salle thanked Monnet for getting her to Rome:

> I was there for some time during the council, and then Marie Louise sent me to Rome for the Lay Congress in 1967. We were organizing the Youth Movement. Monnet came, and she said, "No, no, no, no. It's too French. You must internationalize. Do not stay in France. The place to go is Rome." For her, Rome was the center of the Christian Movement. If you wanted to be universal, you had to stay in close contact with Rome, so she sent me on ahead of her. Finally she came to live there in 1969, within walking distance of Piazza San Calisto, where the MIAMSI office was set up. She would have ended her days there, but ill health necessitated going to the Little Sisters of the Poor back in France.

In the preceding pages of this chapter, I have deliberately focused on the women's experiences, which are all too often overlooked or trivialized in the church and consequently in life in general. The various anecdotes capture the mood of the council and some highlights. Now it is time to move on to the women's real work, when they rolled up their sleeves to remake several of the major documents.

CHAPTER FOUR

EXPERTS IN LIFE

═══ ❖ ═══

Bringing the World to the Council

Twenty-three women could never *represent* the women of the world
with their specific and diverse concerns. The pope who appointed
them knew this, so he called them a "symbolic witness" of women's
presence. Those aware of the transforming power of symbols will
recognize that this was not a mere token or empty gesture. The
women took to heart the responsibility of their privileged position,
despite its limitations.

With the male auditors, the women were to "bring the world to
the council and the council to the world." As part of the lay presence, some joked that they were "specimens of humanity like the
creatures who were brought into Noah's Ark."[1] As a group, the
women symbolized the female face of the church hitherto eclipsed
by the patriarchal, hierarchical, clerical dominance in all sectors
of leadership, legislation, and sacramental administration. Their
presence expressed, however timidly, the conviction that such structures — propped up by women's silent, invisible cooperation — had
to change. Women must be rendered visible and given recognition
for their unacknowledged contribution to the church's mission in
the world.

Reporters admired how this body of efficient women brought organization to the auditors' tribune. They heralded their coming as a
revolution in an extraordinarily practical sense. Most, if not all, had
some knowledge of Latin and French from high school or college,
and that was helpful, for much of the commission work and most of
the auditors' own meetings were conducted in French. They wanted
to be fully informed about the conciliar discussions, however, and
lest they miss out on anything, they organized themselves into lan-

124

guage groups with *periti* as translators in the aula, since they shared the same tribune.

Apart from their "passive" symbolic power of presence, the women also played a more active role, primarily in the working commissions that wrote and amended the documents. Their input was most notable in *Gaudium et Spes*.[2] It was the last document to be written, updated, and promulgated, so it benefitted from four years of development of conciliar thought. Besides, it was the only text that originated on the council floor, so it had the advantage of starting from scratch and was not the cut-and-pasted product of a preconciliar text. Women and laymen were included in drafting this document from the beginning, whereas all the other texts were, in the words of Canadian Bishop Alexander Carter of Sault Sainte Marie, "conceived in the original sin of clericalism."

Two of the most notable groups involved in lobbying the bishops during the council were the Catholic Worker and Pax Christi. Their representatives from the U.S., **Dorothy Day** and **Eileen Egan**, were not invited as auditors. Egan said she came to Rome for the discussion of *Gaudium et Spes* that pertained to war and peace during the month of October in 1965. She lobbied bishops and found those from Canada, New Zealand, and Africa most encouraging.[3] Dorothy Day joined women from five continents in a ten-day water fast to pray for the council members in their deliberations. Egan wrote in suggestions on *Gaudium et Spes* and communicated them to the commissions through U.S. auditor Jim Norris.

Häring the Daring

Thanks to Bishop Emilio Guano, the chair, and Bernard Häring, secretary, women played a significant role as full voting members of the mixed commission for *Gaudium et Spes*. The initiative came directly from Häring, recognized by many today as "the greatest moral theologian of the twentieth century," who admits that "sometimes I have to be a troublemaker."[4] Those who know him realize that his courageous action in regard to the women, as in other things, is rooted in his conviction that responsibility and discernment form the basis for obedience in the church, while the old concept of "blind obedience" is "stupid."[5] Häring learned this hard lesson in service as a medical orderly during the war, when he was condemned to death as a traitor to the German army for leading three hundred men to safety in Stalingrad. The Russian advance came before his sentence could be carried out; otherwise, he would not be alive today. Several of his family members died. The same man disobeyed laws by praying and saying Mass several times for the soldiers of different Christian denominations.[6] As Häring easily admits, he stared death in the face twice — during the war and since with throat cancer — so he is not easily cowed by anyone trying to club him with a stupid exercise of authority. He is a man of courage and conviction who loves the church. He is no knee-jerk liberal. He does right because it is the right, intelligent thing to do. His action regarding women at the council was the obvious, sensible, righteous thing to do.

Häring himself gave me firsthand information on manoeuvres behind the scenes.

The auditrices had no great impact; it was a more symbolical act to allow them to "listen." But the proposal made by Cardinal Suenens stirred up a great displeasure among conservative bishops, especially Italians. It took courage for Pope Paul VI to decide to invite auditrices. However, they had the opportunity to speak privately to the bishops and Major Superiors who participated in the council.

Then, efforts were made to get religious women invited for the commission on religious. Refusal!! A historical remark of Card. Antoniutti: "You may try again at the fourth Vatican Council." After that debacle, I spoke to Bishop Guano, who headed the subcommission elected for the drafting of *Gaudium et Spes* (where I had the role of coordinating secretary). There were just appointed a few bishops (Helder Camara, Wojtyla, etc.) from the East European countries and from the Third World, after a smart intervention of Cardinal Bea to get this started. He had in the aula declared: "Although the commission has 60 bishops, it is not truly representative, since most important parts of the world in view of its future are not fully represented." Paul VI approved our list, and Bishop Guano was happy. I said to him: "This step, important as it is does not change much, since 55 percent of the world Catholics have no representation whatever."

Response of Guano: "What do you mean?"

My response: "*The world of women.* I think we should get them into our commission if they have no place even in the commission for the religious, although they are approximately 80 percent of the religious."

Guano was practical and understood me fully. So he asked immediately: "Whom would you like to invite?" I had a list prepared. On the top of the list Rosemary Goldie (an Australian lady, outstanding in the field of lay apostolate). Guano remarked: "This list is quite good. These are women of the church of today." Then we added a few more names. I did really not know what Bishop Guano now had in mind. I think that he thought that I would try to get up unto the pope. But I just decided to write to all these women, inviting them to come for the session in Ariccia [January 31–February 6, 1965], and they all came.

Justly proud and amazed at his accomplishment, Häring continued:

Maybe not even Guano knew what had entitled me to invite these gracious ladies. Alfredo Cardinal Ottaviani — considered almost blind — saw then of course. He made no trouble. He did not inquire how this surprising presence came about, and nobody had the courage to tell them they should not be there. So, in a very relaxed atmosphere, they participated just as the men did, talked frankly, and were listened to. This in the doctrinal, mixed commission for the major document, *Gaudium et Spes,* was something quite different from "auditrices," listening women. The ladies in the commission made excellent contributions in preparing the text and in understanding a little bit better the world today.[7]

The "ladies" were **Bellosillo, Goldie, Guillemin, Tobin, Monnet,** and **Vendrik.** Häring said: "I did not appoint, nor request appointment. I just took it into my own head to invite them for active participation." Also in the commission were thirty council fathers, forty-nine *periti,* and ten laymen. Goldie found herself at one point in a subcommission with Yves Congar and Karol Wojtyla.[8] With a twinkle in her eye, she added, "I was a voting member of the commission, while Wojtyla was not, although he talked a lot — he was one of the extras brought in to give input from Eastern Europe." Bellosillo, Goldie, and Tobin were invited to a meeting in Rome the following week to complete the work done in Ariccia. Other women participated in the ten subcommissions that reworked the text in the fall, while it was being publicly discussed. This would never have happened without Häring's initiative.

The Door-Hinge between Doctrine and Action

Bellosillo noted a very important (*muy importante*) conciliar development exemplified in the preparation of *Gaudium et Spes*. Paul VI had called the female and male auditors "experts in life":

> not in theology or any other specific area but *in life*. We were being treated as such for the first time in the consultations that shaped the documents. *The council fathers listened to the laity.* They wanted to know the experience lived by Christians in the new situations created by modern life because there was as yet no church teaching about them. This *inductive method* was new. It was both exciting and gratifying to be part of this magisterium of the laity in practice.[9]

The fathers respected what the laity said and maintained three of their suggested amendments, even when they themselves were not in agreement. Here "the magisterium of the laity prevailed in an area of their exclusive competence." Bellosillo appreciated when bishops and pastors trusted the laity to act responsibly and courageously in concrete situations where the church had no immediate solutions and free investigation was valid and necessary.

Bellosillo stated that naturally the laity worked on the topic of lay apostolate because it was about their duty and responsibility for the church's mission. There was at least one woman and one man on each of the commissions, so that their input could be pervasive. The decree *Apostolicam Actuositatem,* while on a different level from the four main dogmatic constitutions, fulfilled an important function in two ways. (1) It was the practical application of the richness of the two major constitutions on the church (*Lumen Gentium* and *Gaudium et Spes*). (2) It was the door-hinge between the doctrinal principles of *Lumen Gentium* and the action of the laity opened up in *Gaudium et Spes*.

Bellosillo further commented on the methodological evolution of the decree. "Frequently during the discussions of lofty theological ideas and principles, the council fathers asked the laity, 'How do you live it? How do you answer the call of *Gaudium et Spes* in the world?' In general it deals with the apostolic activity of the baptized as a consequence of their Christian vocation. *The laity translate conciliar doctrine into life.*"

Because the lay auditors, women and men, worked together in compiling joint responses to the conciliar texts, the *women's* specific contributions cannot be easily isolated. In some instances, individual women's suggested interventions are available. Such is the case in regard to three different texts, including a letter (not dated) to the bishops, submitted by Monnet on *Apostolicam Actuositatem*, bearing the stamp of her consuming interest in the independent social milieux. Obviously, she read the document carefully and responded to each section. Overall, she cautioned against rigidity and recommended a more flexible and pastoral style. I highlight a few significant points. She expressed grave reservations about chapter 6, Formation for the Apostolate. "If one speaks of the spirituality of the laity, it is more important to talk about what is specific in regard to the *life* of the laity than on a spiritual plane... The lay apostle may pray in the metro, but she can exercise her spirituality as a lay apostle by associating in the life of the people she encounters in the metro."[10] A year later, she was still not satisfied with the section on formation because it did not respond to the needs and actual realities. She wrote:

> *I very eagerly desire* that this chapter not be treated from an individualistic perspective and that it be less in a scholarly style. This must be the occasion for bringing into relief the double aspect of the quality required for a modern apostle: a profoundly interior bearing of the person, supported, guided, and aided by the active and collective support of a militant team. *The formation must not be considered as a preliminary postulate to an apostolic action,* but *it must appear as closely linked to the exercise of the apostolic action, whose natural fruit it is.* Putting the SEE, JUDGE, ACT to work in different stages of attention to the whole of life could give rise to the need for a spiritual deepening at the same time that it guides the steps of that formation. The reexamination of life would assuredly stamp and prolong it.[11]

In a letter addressed to the council fathers and drafted as a proposal for the auditors' intervention in regard to *Apostolicam Actuositatem*, Monnet traced the development of lay involvement and recognition in the work of the church. A key point was that people of all ages and social conditions, women and men, adults, youth, and children, have come to recognize the need to live the Christian message daily in the midst of their profane lives. The work of the council will be the church's response to the world. This is where the schema on the lay apostolate is especially important. Referring to the conciliar achievements in terms of religious liberty and establishing relations with Jews and non-Christians, she concluded that "the laity are at the heart of those problems and are full of concern for them." She continued:

> Your assembly has been a good example for the laity of seeking the truth and showing us in numerous gropings, even confrontations, that it is necessary always to have a profound sense of listening to others and of the necessity of prayer. Paul VI said recently: "It is by the common effort of all the baptized that the council will bear fruit. That is why we have seen that the laity are represented at the council by choosing men and women totally dedicated to the apostolate."

Practically all of Monnet's ideas were incorporated into the somewhat longer text that Patrick Keegan of England delivered on behalf of all the auditors. I include one sample paragraph:

> The lay apostolate cannot be an isolated entity in the church. It reaches its fulness in close collaboration with all the other members of the church. By its very nature it demands a constant and regular exchange between the hierarchy and the laity. It is for us lay people to bring to our pastors our experience of the needs of the world in which we live, and to seek from them guidance in our endeavor to respond to these needs. In simple terms, there must be the "family dialogue" of which our Holy Father Pope Paul has spoken so frequently and emphasized in his recent letter *Ecclesiam Suam....* While there is a distinction within the church between hierarchy and laity, this distinction implies no distance. This debate in the council has done much to bind us together inseparably in the single mission of the church. (October 13, 1964)

Neither Monnet nor any other conciliar woman was permitted to speak in the council. The same week as Keegan's speech, a French paper bore the headlines of Bishop Alfred Ancel of Lyons and Monnet sharing a platform as they spoke to a group of African bishops on the schema pertaining to the Church in the Modern World. Monnet mentioned three signs of the times: the promotion of the working class, the place of women in the world, and the independence of peoples, and she expanded further on the second point, emphasizing "that the woman is equal in dignity to man and that she should be free in her choice of vocation." The reporter noted the significance of the fact that *a woman was telling bishops,* "You must have great faith in the possibilities of the council!"[12]

In the final drafting of *Apostolicam Actuositatem,* the general commission added a *modus,* or amendment, that mentioned women specifically. Walter Abbott, general editor of the most widely used English translation of the documents of Vatican II, included a footnote (26), drawing attention to this fact as "one of the few places in all of the council documents where special attention is given to the contribution of women to the mission of the church." He continued: "It is interesting to note that by the time the council ended twelve laywomen and ten religious women were present as 'auditrices.' Mrs. Joseph McCarthy and Sister Mary Luke, S.L., joined James Norris and Martin Work as official representatives from the United States." This is the only place where Abbott mentions the women. In his appended list of "Important Dates of Vatican II," he noted the arrival of Protestant observers but not the lay auditors, not even the historical event of women coming for the first time ever to a council.

The Smell of Prophecy

The women auditors were sought outside the council aula, as invitations, interviews, and meetings filled the few free moments they had between sessions. A few days after Goldie became an auditor, she was invited to address a meeting of French-speaking bishops from Africa about the Decree on the Apostolate of the Laity. She shared a panel with Msgr. Achille Glorieux, secretary of the conciliar commission, and Roberto Tucci, S.J.

"I commented positively on various aspects of the schema, different forms the lay apostolate could take, concerning also the associations and international work," she said. "Finally, I picked up on some criticisms which had already been expressed by others and which were summed up by a Canadian bishop when he said, 'This schema was conceived in the original sin of clericalism.' But only the criticisms made their way into the daily press, and with them repercussions which I discovered many years later."

She explained how in August 1978, when John Paul I was elected to the papacy, the *Avvenire,* a Catholic daily paper, published various writings of the new pope. Among them was a letter from the council father Albino Luciani, bishop of Vittorio Veneto and future Pope John Paul I, to chaplains of the women's and young women's association of Italian Catholic Action. Commenting on the appointment of women auditors, he related it to feminine prophecy in the Bible. Luciani said,

> It will not pass through any of your minds that these few references I make to prophecy indicate any sympathy for a church of charisms as opposed to the hierarchical church, to the detriment of authority and in favor of an exaggerated independence on the part of the laity. And none of you will feel it as a blow to the heart, as did a parish priest the other day when he read in the paper that Rosemary Goldie, auditor at the council, had become a speaker expressing before a group of bishops some reserve with regard to the schema on the laity and wishing that it should be less paternalistic, less clerical, and less juridical. "The end will be," the parish priest said, "that for these good women Catholic Action will be no more the collaboration of the laity in the apostolate of the hierarchy, but the collaboration of the hierarchy in the apostolate of the laity." I reassured the parish priest that the laity refuse paternalism, but they accept and honor spiritual paternity in priests. They like and ask to be guided in spiritual matters, but they judge it to be an exaggeration, that is clericalism, that absolutely everything in the church should start from the bishops and priests. Finally, they would like that . . . we stress a little less the rights and powers, being too juridical, and remember a little more that we are all one family practicing charity, fraternity, and service.[13]

Thus spoke a pope in the making, one with the ability to listen, learn from others, cooperate with them, had he been given more than the thirty-two days of papacy that endeared him to the world, as did "good Pope John." Surprised and delighted at her new discovery, Goldie exclaimed, "I did not know that I had such an authoritative defender and one who was so paternally sympathetic." This pope had also about him a "smell of prophecy," as

Eva Jung-Inglessis suggested in an anecdote surrounding the conclave that elected him. Apparently, journalist Frances Magillacuddy sent a communication to the cardinals in conclave, asking them not to forget the women. When the new Pope John Paul I made his first appearance on the balcony, his first words were, "My dear *Sisters* and Brothers," the first time ever women took precedence over men, that is, if they were mentioned at all in the solemn addresses that began with "brethren."

Family Expectations

Since the vast majority of human beings get married at least once and the Roman Catholic Church talks about the sacredness of marriage, it is amazing that there was only one married couple invited to Vatican II, and that only after some maneuvering on the part of the Mexican nuncio and a husband who held out for his wife's equal rights. If one conscientious couple could accomplish as much as they did in the final conciliar session, how much more could be gained by a concerted effort to include and listen to the experience of a wide circle of married people, their perception of family problems, and how the church could help handle them.

When the Alvarez-Icazas were named as auditors toward the end of 1964, they had about nine months to prepare themselves for attending the fourth and final session of the council. They listed qualities an auditor should have because, mistakenly, they expected to have something to do when they went to Rome in September 1965. "But in reality," José recounted, "we were only listeners, sitting on a red velvet covered bench, hearing things we didn't understand, and having no opportunity to respond." Without realizing how literal their role as *auditors* was to be taken, they prepared themselves for active participation. Among the eighteen qualities of an auditor they listed were the following: (1) have a knowledge of theology; (2) know the history of the church; (3) know Latin; (4) know the council fathers. "We discovered that we had none of the eighteen qualities," José admitted, "so before going to Rome we went to the Christian Family Movement in Mexico and formed teams — one for each of the eighteen specialties — and twenty-five people went to Rome with us to help us out. We made a good showing at representing all the married couples of the world. We met with friends and decided to visit thirty-six countries to gather input and be better prepared." They sent out questionnaires posing four questions:

1. What do you think of the council in relation to family life?

2. What do you think of the council in other respects?

3. With regard to the present position of the church, what do you think is most adequate for the needs of the world today?

4. What do you think should be reformed or changed in the church?

They received forty thousand responses. They classified them into eighteen different groups. When they arrived in Rome, there were more than twenty-five hundred bishops, five hundred *periti,* and all the world was talking. It was difficult to be heard with their modest opinions — one Mexican couple. The French asked why a French couple was not chosen, since they have very devoted families. Others asked why not an American couple. "We saw that people were sad because we were *only a Mexican couple,* so we couldn't represent them," said José.

A summary of their findings appeared as a press release from the CCCC (Centrum Coordinationis Communicationum de Concilio). Their preface read:

> In a world made up of families, or let us say, of men and women who have children, it is very rare to find spiritual instruction directed specifically to them. Although the church has always attached great importance to the family, there are thousands of dioceses where there is not even one priest specifically devoted to promoting the spiritual welfare and the apostolate of the family. Millions of men and women who have received the sacrament of marriage and its particular graces do not profit from it because they are unaware of the dignity of their sacrament and...there is nobody to explain it to them. In the meantime, the family, the cell at the base of civilized society and of the church in the world, is disintegrating...and is deteriorating rapidly.

Aware of the limitations to what one couple could accomplish at the council, they tried to bear witness to the prayer, study, hospitality, economic cooperation, and work of thousands of families who express their faith in the church and in the council. They synthesized the results under seventeen major topics.

1. *Lay Apostolate:* The majority felt that the work of the laity needed stimulation. New forms of the apostolate should be encouraged to meet the needs of the modern world. Laity should be authorized to organize their own apostolic structures, renouncing paternalism.

2. *The Bible, Revelation, and Tradition:* The results of the council concerning revelation and tradition should be adequately explained. Private reading of the Holy Scriptures should no longer be seen as "dangerous."

3. *The Council:* A great number of people and institutions have prayed for the council and rendered thanks for it. Many are of the opinion that it should deal with urgent problems, such as family breakup, education of children, birth control, and the spirituality of the family.

4. *Birth Control:* Some proposed methods should be allowed (minority opposed). Some pronouncement should be made to end the confusion. Not only births, but marriages should be controlled.

5. *Ecumenism:* Many spoke of the need to change attitudes among Christians themselves.

6. *Spirituality of the Family:* The life of grace in the family should be safeguarded and appreciated. It should be stated that the family is a road that leads its members to God. Couples need better preparation to live their sacrament. There should be more understanding between parents and children. Family morality needs reform.

7. *The Structure of the Church:* Luxury in the church should be abandoned. A new general plan should be worked out concerning the economic activity of the church and the unequal division of wealth. Female religious communities should be reformed.

8. *The Formation of Priests and Members of Secular Institutions:* The formation of priests, monks, nuns, and members of secular institutes should be reformed. Catholic schools should be given aid to accommodate those without resources. An effort should be made to understand the faithful, and clerical despotism should end once and for all. Preaching should be improved. Christian authenticity should be promoted.

9. *Jews and Non-Catholics:* Help should be given to promote union with other religions.

10. *The Liturgy and the Sacraments:* Mass in the vernacular is appreciated. Sermons should be more concrete, complete, and shorter. Religious orders (vows, etc.) should be reformed.

11. *Means of Social Communication:* Christians need to partake in the means of communication by offering constructive criticism.

12. *Misery and Development:* The moral conditions of the poor constitute a problem that the church is pledged to resolve. Paternalistic aid that degrades the individual should end. We should have a *Christian* interest in those who are miserable and ignorant.

13. *The Missions:* Realistic information about the missions is needed. Missionaries should relate their experiences more often by means of broadcasts. A just and adequate sum should be allotted to each mission to help eliminate economic problems.

14. *The Christian Family Movement:* The Christian Family Movement should open its doors to the lower socio-economic levels. It should be closer to the hierarchy.

15. *The Church and the Political World:* The church should not mix in politics. Laypeople with the necessary liberty and personality could be utilized to improve relations between church and state.

16. *Sociology and the Family:* More attention should be paid to all family problems and spirituality.

17. *Subjects:* Coeducational schools help form more rounded personalities. Bishops and priests should approach the people. The children of unfit parents should be taken away from them. Give more dispensations to priests.

Although the Alvarez-Icazas did not conduct a technical inquiry, their fact-finding survey was a valuable concrete resource for a pastoral council that was trying to address the needs of the church at large and family life in particular.

Everyone Is Family

Both Luz-Marie and José noted the invaluable assistance they received from Betsie Hollants. "The first thing you do in Rome," she said, "is get in touch with the press — the IDOC (a Dominican priest, Allfin Von Cesau) and the CCCC (Padre Tonna). Say, 'We have opinions of forty thousand couples of the world, and it will be a great piece of news.'" Hollants herself was a Belgian newspaper editor for years. Inside the council the persistent couple tried their best to introduce different ideas in such a way that the council fathers would become informed about the place of Catholic married couples and the importance of the findings they brought from all over the world. They gave presentations to IDOC, the CCCC, St. Peter's College, Propagation of the Faith, Domus Mariae, the Brazilian bishops, and many other groups in various houses. They remembered Betsie Hollants's advice: "Don't go to a religious house, and don't go to a hotel. Rent a house, bring two of your daughters with you, and live your family life there. Never give a talk in your house because at home there are never formal talks. Announce that you are setting up the 'Casa Familia' (Family House) in Rome. Tell all the council fathers that when they are tired and want to rest or have a personal need, come to see you." Hollants invited lots of people to her apartment in Rome, and she sent many over to the Icazas' and vice versa.

Luz-Marie explained how she changed as a result of the Christian Family Movement. Family life in Mexico was a closed circle. It was within the family of a given class, and the families were very close. Because the CFM had its center in Mexico, and Luz-Marie and José were its co-presidents, all kinds of people came to their house. They received everybody. The children were taught to meet people, talk to everyone, and be hospitable. When Luz-Marie was growing up, she was afraid of everyone outside the family circle.

Changes were taking place also in other families in CFM as they experienced many different people, and their children became part of the life they lived. One day a man came to the Icaza residence while the parents were not home. The hospitable children said, "Come in, Uncle." They took him all around the house and showed him everything. Retelling the story, Luz-Marie said, "We're sure he came to rob us, but he was so surrounded by children that he couldn't rob anything, and he left the house running." Hospitality won the day.

The house the Icazas rented in Rome had many rooms so that twenty people could live there. It belonged to a man who had been appointed ambassador to Spain. It was large but cheap and suited their needs. Two station wagons came with it, and it cost no more than $5.00 per day. They did their own shopping and cooking and felt very much a part of the social and cultural life, as they talked to everyone — the butcher, the baker, etc.

The house was always full, mainly because the council fathers had already spent four years in Rome with no place where they could relax. The archbishop of Mexico, Miguel Darío Miranda came. He sat silently in an armchair with his eyes closed, and nobody interrupted him. The girls sang and talked to everyone about everything. Then the archbishop would open his eyes and ask what they were talking about. One day he announced, "On September 29, the feast of St. Michael, I'll come to your house for a banquet. I'll pay for it. It's my feast day, and I want to eat pheasant." So they got the pheasant and found out how to cook it, hanging it up for a few days to let it age. Those who lived in the house didn't eat any of it, but the archbishop enjoyed his feast. Another day an American theologian arrived with a tear in his shirt, and someone sewed it for him.

The auxiliary bishop of New Delhi, Angelo Fernandes, ordained in 1959, gave the Icazas' oldest daughter, Lupita, his pectoral cross. She still has it. After wearing it a few times she decided it was too precious, so she decided to put it in a frame in the bedroom of her son Stefano. Lupita was just fourteen years old when she was in Rome, and she was small for her age. Besides a big dining table there was a small (*piccolo*) table alongside it. Lupita always ended up at the small table and was served last. Noticing this, Bishop Fernandes sat at the small table one day, and then Lupita was on the first serving round. Some day she hopes to travel to India to visit Fernandes.

The Icazas always tried to maintain their family spirit in Rome. In one hundred days more than a thousand council fathers visited — about one-third of the entire council. There was always someone to be served. Seminarians came too and complained about the mistakes in the seminary system. Through their hospitality the Mexican couple and their friends created a climate of trust and facilitated honest exchange among bishops who hitherto were strangers to them and to one another.

The Dignity of the Human Being

Bellosillo participated in five subcommissions for *Gaudium et Spes:*
(1) human dignity, especially of women; (2) the dignity of marriage
and family; (3) safeguarding peace; (4) construction of the community of nations; (5) culture in relation to women. She was most
involved in no. 1 and no. 2, so she elaborated on the general thrust
of their discussions. They synthesized well the common threads of
the conciliar women's input.

Cardinal Cento presided over the Mixed Commission for *Gaudium et Spes.* Its membership of about sixteen fathers included Karol
Wojtyla (the future Pope John Paul II), Archbishop Marcus McGrath
of Panama, Msgr. Thils (who is currently helpful to Pilar's women-
church group), Tobin, Goldie, and Spanish Joaquín Ruiz Ramírez. In
the commission, lay experts could ask for the floor and speak — the
only place where women could do so. Based on the doctrine of equality of human beings — men and women — found in Genesis, they laid
the foundations for human equality. Afterward, some of the Fathers,
wanting to pay tribute to women whom they greatly admired, went
overboard in Bellosillo's estimation, and she asked for the floor to
set them straight. She warned of the dangers involved in employing
a different, romantic language to speak of woman — comparing her
to flowers, sunlight, etc. "That imagery has nothing to do with the
reality women live," she said. "This kind of language detached from
life puts woman on a pedestal instead of on the same level as man.
By doing so, you demonstrate that in reality you consider *man* the
human being, but not woman. This does woman a disservice because
it does not take seriously her equal dignity and humanity."

This intervention came as a surprise to many of the fathers, and
they took it to heart in writing the final text. Principles and foundations were laid. That was as far as they could go at the time.
Their actual concrete implementation was not spelled out. Bellosillo
explained how "the question of women's ordination, for example,
which was being advocated by St. Joan's Alliance, was light years
away in terms of that particular commission with its advocacy stance
for the human dignity and equality of both women and men at the
most basic level — creation in the image of God." She regretted that
in this area, as in several others where progress was made at the
council, regression became the order of the day in the church of the
1980s. One can now add, unfortunately, also in the 1990s.

The Dignity of Marriage and Family

One of the immediate implications following from acceptance of the dignity and equality of women with men is seen in the conjugal relationships of marriage. This was obvious to Bellosillo, who worked on both subcommissions (human dignity and equality, and marriage and family). The idea of woman being created to be man's helpmate in procreation dominated traditional Catholic theology up to the council. She was not considered his equal but his helper, at his service sexually as in other things. Procreation was emphasized as the primary end of marriage, to which the happiness of the couple was secondary. "Once human dignity is seen as referring equally to woman and man, the traditional doctrines have to change," concluded Bellosillo, "because it is against woman's dignity to be considered only as a functionary of man, especially from a sexual point of view." She was gratified that mutuality and the specifically human character of love's sexual expression, ignored in the past, was recognized and incorporated into the renewed theology of marriage set forth in *Gaudium et Spes,* especially no. 14 (dealing with the human make-up) and no. 49 (on conjugal love).

Recognition of the importance of women's presence in making the connection between the rethought equal dignity of all persons and the interplay of male-female relations in marriage led experts like Häring to be instrumental in getting women's input. Bellosillo explained that she has never been married, so she could not speak about marriage from personal experience. However, as president of WUCWO she knew that the vast majority of its members were married women who lived with the problems of marriage and family. In these areas lay expertise was both sought by the council fathers and forthcoming from the auditors as problems of love and procreation, birth control, demography, freedom, and responsibility came together in this topic. It sparked world interest and expectation, as numerous communications received by the Fathers and articles in the press and specialized magazines demonstrated. One document in particular was noteworthy. It was a fifteen-page text on family problems written by 152 Catholic laity — doctors, biologists, gynecologists, psychotherapists, sociologists, etc., from fifteen European countries, America, Africa, Australia, and India. It was obvious that laity had to be present in commissions dealing with these issues. The auditors created a subcommission, under the leadership of the

Icaza wife-and-husband team. They were in dialogue with the other commissions.

Unclogging the Pipeline

Bellosillo noted how at first the council fathers shied away from discussing the problems of marriage, especially in relation to birth control, although they were sympathetic and aware of the difficulties married people encountered. Yet they were not prepared to do anything to help alleviate their burdens. The old fear of sex muzzled this group of celibates, and Maximos IV admitted, "We act and react with the complex of old bachelors!"

Eventually, as Bellosillo explained, the problems came to the surface in an open debate. "It was like unclogging a pipeline, as many things said previously in small groups came rushing out into the open. Recognizing and naming the problem meant that it was no longer viewed as an untouchable problem but as material for reflection and investigation by the church."[14]

Paul VI said the question of birth control and conjugal morality needed to be studied in depth. The church's moral doctrine was to be reviewed, not with a view to changing moral principles, but to adapting them to human life. Bellosillo underlined "the important element of discovery involved in finding the divine law in the midst of human problems. It is not ready-made and immediately obvious." Cardinal Suenens brought up the point that the twofold purpose of matrimony — conjugal love and procreation — is based on two scriptural indicatives: be fertile and be two in one flesh. Paul-Emile Cardinal Léger of Canada concluded his intervention by asking the council to proclaim without fear that both ends of marriage are saintly and good, so that experts can better determine the obligations of fecundity and love.

During the final drafting of Schema 13 (previously Schema 17), the Alvarez-Icazas were very influential. Their presence at the commission table never went unobserved. Many tensions surrounded the question of birth control, and all the laity participating in the commission's work were very concerned. The problem was that in the schema there should be no formulations that would give the impression that the question of birth limitation was already decided, since it was under study in the pope's special commission and he reserved the right to make the final judgment. Therefore, the laity and some bishops wanted the question left open-ended.

Auditors coming out of the heated debate as to how the question of birth control was to be treated felt frustrated on November 25, 1965. Yet, encouraged by Häring, they drafted a letter to the pope. It was signed by as many auditors — women and men — as could be reached to beat the time deadline. They delivered it directly to Maurice Cardinal Roy from Canada, who later became first president of the new council of the laity.

Goldie was among the signers and testified that according to the report on the commission's work, published the next day in the Catholic daily paper, *L'Avvenire d'Italia* (the future of Italy), the letter was not without effect on the positive development of the discussion.

> This commentary on the council by one of the most competent journalists, Vanier Vivaldi, and the fact that it was published in the Catholic daily paper meant that *it was meant to be published* because nothing was published without first being screened by the secretary of state. The reporter said that this intervention, corresponding to the specific role of laypeople in the church, particularly their role in relation to the council, seems to have met with "serene evaluation," so it was not rejected.[15]

Motherhood for the Bishops

Little by little the council fathers became interested and asked the Icazas to talk about family life, since they were the only people there prepared to do so. At first they were not included in the Mixed Commission, so they wrote their ideas and gave them to the commission. Their ideas were passed on to the subcommission. Then the president of the subcommission on family life — part of Schema 13 (the Church in the Modern World) — invited them to give their views and to speak of their own experiences as members of the CFM, not only in Mexico, but also in their own lives and family. The meeting was at the Belgian College, with cardinals, bishops, theologians, and other important people. The Icazas told them that what was written about the Christian family was poorly done. After that the subcommission began to listen to them.

They were invited to a plenary session of the Mixed Commission, where the reports from all the subcommissions were read.

Bishop Michael Browne from Galway was very conservative and opposed the commission's work. He insisted that there be no doctrinal changes. He wanted the traditional church teaching on matrimony to be kept — the primary and secondary ends of marriage, etc. Bishops and experts tried to talk to him, but he remained unconvinced. When the reporting bishops read their conclusions, to their surprise Luz-Marie laughed. She said:

> I kept telling my husband, "Why don't you speak up?" And my husband said, "No. Here it's important that *you* speak." I was not accustomed to speaking in public, and I didn't feel prepared to do that, but the Holy Spirit sent down a strong ray, and I spoke. I raised my hand to indicate that I wished to speak, thinking that nobody would see me or let me talk. But Cardinal Ottaviani's secretary — Ottaviani was blind — saw my hand, spoke to the cardinal, and the cardinal said yes, I should be recognized and given an opportunity to speak.
>
> I spoke in Spanish because I felt better prepared for that. I said, "I'm just imagining the face Catholic couples of the world are going to make when they find out what you think about family life." I didn't think it was correct to be treating the sacrament of matrimony in the traditional ways it was taught. It was a legal document that viewed marriage only as a contract. It talked only about obligations and responsibilities. It was a canonical presentation. My question was, why did they put so much emphasis on concupiscence and sin because there were many mothers who had their children as an act of love? I said, "Since I am the only married woman here, I feel I have the responsibility of saying that when we have had intercourse, giving life to our children, it wasn't an act of concupiscence but an act of love, and I believe this is true of most Christian mothers who conceive a child. With all respect, I tell you that when your mothers conceived you, it was also in love." This wasn't just a thought I had, but I was sure that many Christian mothers felt the same way. Many of the fathers looked with wide eyes because they were surprised. At first not all of them understood what I said because I spoke in Spanish, so they had to have my words translated. When they understood, first they turned red, and then they laughed. But at the end they listened, and all twenty-four of the cardinals present came to me later saying, "We never thought of that; you have

spoken the truth." They acknowledged that the end of Christian marriage is love. Even Cardinal Ottaviani and Bishop Browne admitted that it was an act of love, not of concupiscence. When Bishop Méndez Arceo heard this, he came running to our house shouting, "Luz-Ma, you have just created motherhood for the bishops!" At the end of the council, they said thanks again, and when Bishop Browne came to say goodbye, he said, "I remember who you are."

Since the Icazas were not satisfied with the text on marriage, the commissions asked them if they could come up with something better. They replied, "Of course we can." "When?" "Tomorrow." They went back to the house, took out all the documents they had brought to Rome, and put something together for the next meeting. José acknowledged, "It wasn't the best text in the world, but it was a lot better and closer to married people's experience than the one the bishops wrote." He calculated that the average number of years bishops had been out of touch with Catholic families was forty, since most of them were at least in their fifties, and they had gone to the seminary when they were very young.

An Attempt to Muzzle the Laity

The following day, as promised, the couple presented their document to the subcommission on family life, and they approved it. Then it was passed on to the Mixed Commission. All of a sudden, the auditors — who were supposed to be listening, not talking — became *locutores* (speakers) in that high-level commission. When they discussed birth control there, it was directly related to family living. Then one day in the Mixed Commission, someone read a letter from the pope, asking that the laity should not participate in the discussion because this was such a difficult topic. The laity sent a letter to the pope, saying, "We cannot believe that you invited us to the council, and then you deliberately tie our hands and tongues." The Icazas, Habicht, Bellosillo, Goldie, and some others signed it. Next day word came from the pope, "Let the laypeople speak." José remarked, "We believed that the first letter never came from the pope at all."

After Luz-Marie's spectacular intervention in the commission, the couple were contacted for a press conference. José proudly told how

Luz-Ma, who is a very humble, discreet woman, in no way given to showing off in public, was interviewed before the world. Rightly so, because she was extraordinarily eloquent in that discussion. From that moment onward, I became the husband of Luz-Marie Alvarez-Icaza! I had no prominent place at all. Cardinals wanted to talk to Luz-Marie, and they would tell her, "Tomorrow there will be a difficult session. Don't miss it. We need you there."

At the closing conciliar ceremony, Luz-Marie was one of the three women to receive the special message addressed to women. As she approached the papal throne to receive the message, she got dust in her eye and dislodged her contact lens. People thought she was crying because she was so moved, and Patrick Keegan whispered to her, "Courage!" She was moved, but not to tears.

Parentelli related how the auditors wanted to make a critical intervention in the aula when Schema 13 was being discussed, but they were told there was no time. Instead, they were asked to give input on *Ad Gentes*. Parentelli was part of the committee of four chosen to prepare a text, after they overcame the first obstacle — a Latin document — and had it translated into French. The night before it was due for presentation, they informed Cardinal Suenens, the intermediary between auditors and the council secretariat. Suenens wanted to read the text.

He was considered very progressive, and he said that in no way could we criticize a schema. That was a right reserved to the council fathers. So the morning we hoped it would be read, we were faced with the fact that it only contained thanks for being permitted to be present at the council. It was read by the Rwandan auditor [Adjakpley], dressed in his native garb. We were unpleasantly surprised and humiliated for the lack of respect — all of which meant that our work was for nothing! We asked what had happened, and it was then that our representative told us that the text he had just read had been drafted by Cardinal Suenens and that *he* had decided that the reader would be the Rwandan — maybe because he was the only African auditor, and he wanted to show that they were treating the Africans just like everybody else.[16]

When questioned about her reaction to this, Parentelli continued:

> I was very disconcerted and disappointed at the church or the
> ugly face of the church that I was coming to know. I remem-
> ber that on one occasion I was wandering through the streets of
> Rome thinking about all this. All of a sudden I was at the edge
> of the Tiber River, which looked back at me from its riverbed
> of murky water. It seemed a voice said to me that I could re-
> solve all this if I'd just throw myself in. My disillusionment had
> reached a point that led me to decide not to stay in Rome wast-
> ing my time and to return to Louvain to continue my job there.
> Although I should have known that was a time of learning sit-
> uations of every type, especially about the methods of the curia,
> nevertheless I did go back to Louvain and didn't return to attend
> the council, which closed that same year.[17]

The Icazas maintained an open-door policy in their family house
in Rome. "Regardless of what people were saying, we felt that we
were all one and in this together," said Luz-Marie. In the atmosphere of openness they created, people felt free to say what they were
thinking. That did not mean that the conciliar days were easy. The
Icazas brought the two older teenage girls, Luz-Marie and Lupita,
with them because they did not want to leave them at home. As ado-
lescents, they were at a turning point in their lives. They learned a lot
about the church, the differences among the people of the world, but
also the similarities. Farming out ten children, including a six-month
old baby, could have been a big problem, as Luz-Marie recalled with
gratitude, "God provided and gave us the right people with whom
we could leave our children. Some stayed here in the house with
people who were highly thought of and trusted — members of the
CFM and other friends. Others went to different places. Emilio, the
baby, went first with one good friend, then another."

It was not easy to become so deeply involved in conciliar discussions while wondering how the children were doing back in Mexico,
as Luz-Marie clearly remembered. "A few times in Rome," she said,

> I went through a crisis period because I couldn't see what was
> happening to my children at home or how that was less impor-
> tant than what we were doing in Rome. I felt that especially
> when there were misunderstandings between us and the conser-
> vative Mexican bishops. They didn't like that we as laypeople

had the opportunity to express ideas that sometimes differed from theirs. But at the end they came around and agreed with us. Overall, they were proud and happy we were there, but there were some difficult times. The house we rented was on the Via de la Croce — the Way of the Cross — near the Spanish Steps. It joined another street, Calle de la Boca Leone — the Lion's Mouth. When we had difficulties with the bishops, our friends said, "It's very typical because of the two streets where you live — between the Way of the Cross and the Lion's Mouth."[18]

Unfinished Business

The council confronted the demographic problem, and for the first time its many aspects were discussed, as the experts sought to discover the meaning of a truly human fecundity. They realized that there was more at stake than just bringing children into the world. The task was to really "create" them, rear, educate, and provide for them. An argument set forth was that if God has put gaps of infertility in human procreation, how can humans intervene somehow in God's way by determining and fixing those periods of infertility? Bellosillo recalled how a Canadian ex-Dominican, married and father of ten or twelve children, was invited to Rome as an expert to speak to the commission regarding fertility, on the basis of his studies of many different species of animals in Canada. Unfortunately, the man died suddenly in the hotel the night before he was due to return home.

Tobin remembered Bishop Roberts talking about the earlier days of child mortality when parents had to produce more and more children in the hope that a reasonable number would survive. Roberts referred to his experience of walking through cemeteries in India and seeing one tombstone after another raised in memory of young children. He concluded that today when scientific progress should be able to prevent much of the infant mortality due to preventable or curable childhood diseases, greater attention needs to be paid to responsible regulation of births, lest overpopulation of the world's poorest countries lead to the plague of famine and disease that could wipe out whole generations of children. The wisdom of his words rings true as the specters of famine and war loom large in the 1980s and 1990s in Ethiopia and Somalia, with Sudan and other African countries threatening to follow.

So important was the issue of birth control that Paul VI set up a commission with several experts, theologians, and laity to study the question. Among them was Patricia Crowley of Chicago, who made significant contributions. The first meeting took place in 1964, while the council was still in session, and comprised three numerically equal groups representing different positions: natural family planning, the pill, and acceptance of the pill under certain conditions. The third group believed that if the birth control pill were accepted, there would be no objection to other methods of birth control. Shaking her head and reliving her disappointment, Bellosillo commented, "Then came *Humanae Vitae* in 1968, disregarding the commission majority's findings." More recent information revealed that the pope, like most of the originally conservative committee members, had come around to accepting the majority position, and the out-of-town committee members went home. But Ottaviani stayed and got to work on the pope. A Franciscan, Fr. Lio, advisor to the "old watchdog of the Vatican," as Ottaviani was called, told some of his confrères, who then told Häring, "that two audiences with the pope organized by Ottaviani were sufficient to reconvert the pope, who had already been seduced by the commission."[19] Häring, who was also living in Rome and knew the lobbying was going on, tried to see the pope, but neither he nor anyone else from the majority position ever gained access to Paul VI.

Bellosillo produced a clipping from a Spanish paper of January 1989, in which Häring made headlines. As a member of the original pontifical commission and because of his ongoing study and pastoral concern for those leaving the church because of unsatisfactory teaching on the question, he wrote to Pope John Paul II, reminding him of this problematic carryover from the unfinished business of Vatican II. Bellosillo repeated emphatically, "Church authorities need to listen again to the 'experts in life.' Answers of 'no, no, no,' are not sufficient for the complex situations in which married people continue to struggle."

Galileo's Ghost

When scientists and council members were debating the question of birth control, Galileo's specter was felt stalking the council. A group of commission workers for *Gaudium et Spes,* including several women, signed a petition asking that the church's condemnation of the great sixteenth–seventeenth century genius be lifted and that he be reinstated as a church member in good standing, albeit three hundred years too late. Goldie gave eyewitness testimony.[20]

In the context of discussing the connection rather than dichotomy between science and faith, since both come from the same God, the final draft of *Gaudium et Spes* 36 captured the seriousness of the Galileo affair with its strong language: "Consequently, we cannot but deplore certain habits of mind, sometimes found too often among Christians, which do not sufficiently attend to the rightful independence of science."[21]

The petition and discussion reflected an astute perception on the part of council members that science had still not been accepted as a partner in dialogue in its own right when it came to church teaching, as the birth control debate demonstrated (cf. *GS* 36). It was not until the 1990s, when the white heat of the 1960s had cooled that Galileo was reinstated without much fanfare.

Should the Council Speak about Women?

Given the sexist language of the 1960s, women were expected to find themselves in the so-called generic term "men." Conciliar texts contain very few explicit references to women — perhaps fourteen in all. This was the result of deliberate and significant action on the part of the female auditors. They wanted to avoid anything that would define woman's role in a rigid or poetic way that would ultimately be limiting. This was a real threat as evidenced elsewhere in this text. Their presupposition was that all women in the Roman Catholic Church are laity, not clerics, despite distinctions between "secular" and "religious" women.

The schema on the lay apostolate distributed to the council fathers in 1963 contained two articles respectively on men (*De Viris*) and on women (*De Mulieribus*). Fortunately, they were deleted when the schema was revised. Savoring the fruit of her work, Goldie pointed out that "only toward the end of *Apostolicam Actuositatem,* after mature reflection, did the Fathers insert in the decree a very general statement, which we find in 9: 'Since in our days women take an ever more active part in the whole life of society, it is of great importance that there should be an increasingly wider participation also in the various fields of the apostolate of the church.' "

During the work on Schema 13, Claude Dupuy, archbishop of Albi in France, asked Goldie, "Should the council speak about women?" Aware of the many implications, the female auditors wanted to speak with one voice on this question. After consultation with Bellosillo, Goldie replied in writing to Dupuy:

> Yes, the council should speak about women, on condition that women are not isolated as a problem apart, as it were on the fringe of society and the modern world, or as if real problems that women experience were their exclusive concern.
>
> 1. It seems to me to be necessary to make clear that society is made up of men and women, a fact not without importance for the mission of the church in the world.
>
> 2. It would be necessary to stress some aspects that concern women more directly, but always showing that these problems are aspects of an overall human evolution which concerns both men and women.

Goldie affirmed that related areas pertained to the integral human vocation, dignity of the human person, the dignity of marriage and family, and economic and social life.[22]

Goldie highlighted a few places where concrete evidence of women's input occurs in the final texts. "Women are employed in almost every area of life. It is appropriate that they should be able to assume their full proper role in accordance with their own nature. Everyone should acknowledge and favor the proper and necessary participation of women in cultural life" (GS 60). Archbishop Frotz voiced this on behalf of the auditors. Goldie linked it directly to perita Maria Vendrik, who gave a talk on women and culture at the ICO conference in Vienna.[23]

Because some women participated in the discussions and amendments of Gaudium et Spes, their input there was more extensive than elsewhere, especially section 29. "With respect to the fundamental rights of the person, every type of discrimination, whether social or cultural, whether based on sex, race, color, social condition, language, or religion, is to be overcome and eradicated as contrary to God's intent" [my emphasis]. Later in the same document (60), in explaining the right to culture, the same theme recurs.

The imperative is found as an indicative in *Lumen Gentium* 32, in the context of establishing the equality and dignity of *all human beings,* made in the image of God. "Hence there is in Christ and in the church *no inequality* [my emphasis] on the basis of race or nationality, social condition, or sex, because 'there is neither Jew nor Greek; there is neither slave nor free[person]; there is neither male nor female. For you are all one in Christ Jesus' (Gal. 3:28)." Elsewhere, e.g., in *Ad Gentes* 12, there is an obvious omission of reference to sexual discrimination in a document that has more specific references to women than elsewhere, possibly because of the preponderance of women involved in missionary work. The same telling omission, with less excusable reason, occurs in the Final Report from the special 1985 synod commemorating Vatican II and purporting to continue its direction.

Another almost hidden reference to women, which reflected Goldie's concerns, occurs in *Apostolicam Actuositatem* 32: "Furthermore, centers of documentation and study not only in theology but also in anthropology, psychology, sociology, and methodology should be established for all fields of the apostolate, for the better development of the natural capacities of the laymen and laywomen, whether they be young persons or adults."

Parentelli still has her copy of the original Schema 13 document, whose complete title was "Schema of the Pastoral Constitution in the World of Our Times." "I had analyzed this text and underlined all aspects that seemed to be an advance of the church's doctrine. It wasn't a surprise when I read the final draft and found that all those passages had been taken out."[24]

From the Mouths of Bishops

The first substantial intervention in the aula about women came from Canadian Bishop Gerard-Marie Coderre of St.-Jean-de-Quebec on October 28, 1964. He acted as spokesperson for more than forty bishops and a lay consultation of women and men in his diocese. "God has given woman her own personality, she has therefore a specific and necessary role in the community as well as in the church, which she has not hitherto been able to fulfil. We are living in a time of universal evolution and women have gradually realized their own dignity and their God-given state, which is not one of inferiority. The church must accept this new situation and promote it."

The auditors greeted his intervention with a murmur of assent. Soon afterward he received a thank-you letter, bearing the signatures of the women auditors. It read: "The women auditors have found in your words ideas and truths which for some time we have been hoping to have expressed in this aula, and which on various occasions we have taken the liberty of expressing on our own part and in our own way, perhaps less theologically, when speaking to bishops and *periti* who are working on this schema."[25]

The next day, Augustinus Frotz, auxiliary bishop of Cologne, expressed his agreement with Coderre and spoke of the changing social situation in which modern women expect to be treated as equal partners with men in intellectual and cultural life. He stressed the need for a new pastoral approach in the church to meet the changes taking place in women's lives. He concluded: "These women have to be treated as 'adult' daughters of the church, and therefore they deserve to be called with their sex and not dealt with simply as 'sons of the church' or 'brothers,' as has happened until now." During the last session, on October 4, 1965, Frotz again made an important statement on women's contribution to cultural life, which is reflected in *Gaudium et Spes* 60. "Women are now employed in almost every area of life. It is appropriate that they should be able to assume their full proper role in accordance with their own nature. Everyone should acknowledge and favor the proper and necessary participation of women in cultural life." Frotz further expounded on the fact that "many women go through a state of human and religious crisis never seen before. Women need, therefore, the pastoral care of the church, which cannot ignore this problem coming from every part of the world, and on this problem the church must focus its attention and state clearly its opinion."

Frotz suggested further that "the modern world be reminded of the development and of the decline of people and that the increase or the loss of human cultures depends in greater measure on the place that is given to women in the consciousness and the attitude of the people; therefore, the civil society and the church must really safeguard the dignity of women."[26] In other words, "the rising of the women means the rising of the race."

Bishops Malula, N'Kongolo, Yago, and Zoghby pleaded the case of the African woman. Malula of Leopoldville, speaking on the church in the world today, said that progress was evident in the abolition of slavery and the achievement of woman's emancipation, but in Africa much will have to be changed before women are granted the same dignity accorded to men. "The church should call on all people to aid the completion of the great work of civilization by promoting the woman to full human dignity and complete responsibility. The church itself should give an example by abandoning its distrust of women and according them a larger share in the common task."

N'Kongolo of Bakwanga-Congo said the difficulties of African marriage customs, the absence of free consent, and the indissolubility of marriage should be specifically mentioned in the schema because "in Africa thousands of women are forced into polygamous relations without consent." Yago of Abidjan, Ivory Coast, asked the council to "insist on recognition of the dignity of the African woman; polygamy, forced marriage, and the abuse of the dowry system should be condemned." Zoghby of Nubie, Egypt, also added his voice to these concerns, stating that "Christian men" are also guilty of polygamy in many countries, and "this tradition does great damage to the dignity of woman and to her promotion." Stiepan Bauerlein of Djakove, Yugoslavia, stood for equal treatment regardless of race, sex, or social status. "Theoretical recognition of equality is useless," he said, "if not translated into action."

Lack of time prevented Atlanta's Archbishop Paul Hallinan from making his intervention in the aula. Instead, he released it to the press, too late unfortunately, to be incorporated into the final form of *Gaudium et Spes*. Hallinan was the only American bishop to speak publicly for the cause of women, and he went further than others in specifying practical ways for implementing doctrines of woman's dignity and full human equality. His text included several main points: "That the complementary role of woman as equal partner of man be given proper recognition in the schema on the Church in the Modern World." He questioned whether in this regard the church "has given the leadership that Christ, by word and example, clearly showed he expected of [it]. . . . In proclaiming the equality of man and woman, the church must act as well as speak by fraternal [*sic*] testimony, not only in abstract doctrine; . . . Every opportunity should be given to women, both religious and lay, to offer their special talents to the service of the church, and the role of 'auditrices' in the present council must be only the beginning."

He further specified the following recommendations as being in keeping with Paul VI's statement that "women must come closer to the altar" (see above p. 14):

1. That in liturgical functions women should be permitted to act as lectors and acolytes (Mass servers);

2. That women, after proper study and formation be allowed to serve as deaconesses in proclaiming the Word of God and in providing those sacraments which deacons do, especially solemn baptism and the distribution of the Eucharist (Holy Communion);

3. That women should also be encouraged to become teachers and consultants in theology when they have attained competence in this field;

4. That women be included in whatever instrumentality is established for the post-conciliar implementation of the lay apostolate;

5. That women religious be fully represented and consulted, at least in all matters concerning their interests, in the Congregation for Religious and in the commission for the revision of Canon Law.[27]

Picking up on *Gaudium et Spes*'s idea of the community between woman and man, the Atlanta bishop said it should be "one of harmony, mutual respect, love, and responsibility.... We must not continue to perpetuate the secondary place accorded to women in the church of the twentieth century; we must not continue to be latecomers in the social, political, and economic development that has today reached climactic conditions." He continued to explain how in our society women in many places and in many respects still bear the marks of inequality, such as in working conditions, wages, and hours of work, in marriage, property laws, and other areas.

Hallinan came closer to home in talking about the church, whose history indeed has been a struggle to free women from the old place of inferiority:

[Despite] its great women saints, its dedicated virgins, its defense of woman in the family, a few women theologians, but especially the unique honor given to God's only perfect creature, Mary Our Lady ... the church has been slow in denouncing the degradation

of women in slavery, and in claiming for them the right of suffrage and economic equality. Particularly, the church has been
slow to offer to women, in the selection of their vocation, any
choice but that of mother or nun. In fact, among the saints, there
are only three groups: martyrs, virgins, and a vague, negative
category called "neither virgins nor martyrs."[28]

Goldie explained how Hallinan intended women's increased contribution to be included under "the help which the church receives from
the modern world" (GS 44).[29] In 1995, Hallinan would be labeled a
"radical feminist."

I doubt that such statements would have been possible without
the presence of the conciliar women. Bishops who took time to listen
to women were more attuned to their real issues. Augustinus Frotz,
who had contact with Gertrud Ehrle and the German Women's
League, could not remain untouched by Ehrle's strong personality,
informed positions, and persuasive arguments.[30] Thirty years ago
both pope and council recognized the church's need to respond to
the new emergence of women as a "sign of the times." They made
a groping beginning, indicating that the tide was turning in women's
favor, and the church needed to swim with it or be swept away to
irrelevance.

In "Random Notes" from Rome, Robert Emmet Tracy, bishop
of Baton Rouge, summed up the response to his fellow bishop's
statement.

> One of the most notable interventions on the Church in the
> Modern World was not given on the floor of the Aula at all.
> It was a written intervention on the role of women in the church
> entered by Archbishop Hallinan of Atlanta. The ladies here —
> lay and religious — say that the intervention stated their position
> to perfection. It included everything that any feminist could ar-
> gue for: active participation in liturgical functions; full education
> in theology with a view to consultation; a voice in the shaping
> of the new apostolate of the laity; representation in force on
> all bodies that seriously affect, by their decisions, the status and
> interests of women, and so on.
>
> The Archbishop can expect to be the target of interest of
> grateful women everywhere, and a positive hero to the feminists.
> (In addition, he should also do right well in getting religious sis-
> ters for his schools.) Most important, he alerted the Fathers to

156 EXPERTS IN LIFE

the fact that the Church, in the past, has not really taken much of a lead in the emancipation of women from obvious discrimination and injustice. If the Church in the Modern World text can only manage to say something significant on this question, then the other Fathers will be able to join the Archbishop as he takes the bows at home-plate on Ladies' Day at the council.[31]

I read Tracy as favorably disposed to learning new insights from Hallinan and being convinced of the need for advancement of women in the church. However, his presentation lacks seriousness in dealing with issues that women deemed *very serious*. The message conveyed is that *women are basically a joke*. Tracy was writing for the diverse audience at home in the U.S., and perhaps he had to feel his way in breaking the news of a new revolution in the making. "Ladies' Day at the council" conjured up for me Ladies' Day at the races, when the emphasis was on dress, big hats, and flowers — in other words, something eye-catching, a pleasant but passing attraction, but at the end of the day *nothing very serious or lasting*. I know that commissions were working overtime to finish the documents before December 8, 1965, but Hallinan's text came in October. It would seem that something so important could still be incorporated into the final text, seeing that Paul VI was known to be still penciling through texts the night before they were promulgated. Was Hallinan too far ahead of the council in the *specifics,* when something more general and symbolic was less likely to disturb the conservative minority?

The most traditional speech about women was given by Bishop Luigi Carli of Segni, Italy, who used the old "rib" theory of the Genesis text to affirm the primary and secondary goals of marriage as procreation and reciprocal love, respectively. Woman was created as man's helper in generation by supplying what he lacked.[32]

At the United Nations but *Not* in the Church

Regardless of what was said by the bishops and whatever progress and understanding seemed to be made in regard to woman's position, their actions in key areas suggested that very little of importance had changed, when one could have hoped for more prophetic action.

The female auditors were on a par with their male counterparts (except in the coffee-bars), but old prejudices prevailed when it came to speaking in the aula. The laymen spoke on six different occasions in St. Peter's, while women were denied this equal opportunity, despite two petitions to the pope from the joint group of auditors. They requested that Bellosillo be permitted to address the council, first in giving the auditors' response to the discussion on *Gaudium et Spes* and later at the end of the fourth session as a member of the Spanish-language group, to express gratitude for the privileged presence of the women and men as auditors. Both petitions were ignored.

It was considered premature for a woman's voice to be heard in St. Peter's. Some auditors appear to have internalized this belief. When questioned by Ralph Wiltgen, S.V.D., on November 19, 1964, about whether a woman would soon be speaking in the council, Goldie said, "It seems premature."

Expert economist Barbara Ward was not allowed to deliver her prepared address on world hunger and poverty. Instead, James Norris read it in impeccable Latin. Miceli quipped that it was not until the 1971 synod that *bishops were sufficiently mature to hear women speak in the aula.* Ward was vindicated at that synod and so impressed the bishops that Donal Lamont still remembered her twenty years later and declared, "They broke the mold when they made her."

Roeloffzen admitted that "the church has given the world a startling headline in being the first Christian body ever to admit women to its deliberations... [and] there has been an explosion of encouragement to the laity, but especially in reference to the help women can give in making the Christian message heard throughout the world. Now and again this new infusion of spirit and hope that is burgeoning out into a new springtime for the laity receives a freezing kind of check. It is puzzling to the lay observers." Part of the puzzle was the discrepancy between theory and practice. The church proclaimed women's equality and dignity but refused to let women speak in council for no apparent reason, when laymen were permitted to do so. Roeloffzen observed that "the real conservatives are a very small group," and she did not understand why the larger "working majority do not make their influence prevail." In other words, she had problems with Roman church politics. This young Dutch lawyer could not understand the irony that "a woman's voice may be heard at the United Nations, but not, so far, in the hall of the Vatican Council." She noted how "to date all the significant interventions at the council have been made by bishops working for the church in distant lands. They have a livelier sense of reality where the world's needs are concerned. They want to make the church's message more effective by bringing it up to date."[33]

The women entered fully into the spirit of the council, making its joys and sorrows their own. Tobin recalled the depression of "black Friday" at the end of the third session, when *Dignitatis Humanae* failed to be promulgated because of strong political feelings and a mixture of residual rancor and ambiguity in Jewish-Christian relationships.

Time Out

McCarthy spoke from her own experience of overload during the prolonged conciliar workdays:

> Every now and then during the council, when the voting, corrections, amendments, and *modi,* etc. got so overwhelming that the printers could not keep up with the paperwork, a recess was declared. On one of those recesses, Archbishop Hakim of Israel (the one who complained that nothing was said in *De Ecclesia* about women, "as if they didn't exist") planned a trip to the Holy Land. The guide was exceptional. No matter where we went, he had the biblical references, and it was just as if we were living in that time. Refreshed, we returned to continue our work right to the end.[34]

Douglas Horton, a U.S. Protestant observer at the council, also recounted outings arranged for the observers and some of the experiences the wives encountered in visiting monastic cloisters where women were explicitly prohibited.

Papal Audiences

Part of the Roman scene during the council and one of the ways the pope got to know various people and express his interest in their concerns was through the much cherished papal audience. Pictures recorded an audience when the pope met with all the auditors — women and men — together with a group of parish priests invited during the third conciliar session. Goldie appreciated being called

Paul VI's "co-worker," as already indicated. Moving somewhat from the sublime to the ridiculous, she also recalled a less decorous incident during an audience and picture-taking session with John XXIII. Because she was so small of stature, someone pushed her forward into the front row, and she almost fell at the papal feet. A little startled, John exclaimed, *"la piccatina!"* the little bit of a thing," and her friends did not let her live it down. Joking aside, this powerful little woman was known to most of the council as "a walking encyclopedia of information, especially about the laity all over the world." Because of her fluency in Latin, English, and French, she wrote the first English translation of *Gaudium et Spes* that was put in the hands of the commission.

The day the council ended the auditors asked for a papal audience. The Icazas wrote the pope a note, which they enclosed with their compilation of the responses from their world survey. It said:

> Holy Father, here we are representing 40,000 couples of the world. We are waiting to hear from the council. We have divided our ideas into 18 chapters. The one on Mary is included in *Lumen Gentium*. The other seventeen chapters represent the themes of *Gaudium et Spes*. They are the same main themes as came from the responses to our four-part questionnaire. We have the pleasure of saying to you that everything the people asked us to say was spoken about, discussed, and accepted in the council.

The pope was delighted. José spoke up about that final audience:

> The most solemn moments often take place in ridiculous situations. When we were supposed to give our document to the pope, the secretary hadn't finished typing it. [It consisted of the complete text that is briefly outlined earlier on in this chapter.] I asked Luz-Ma to go on to the audience, and I would follow later when it was finished. She said she would wait for me. At the last minute, I came dashing along past the Swiss guards and the nobility of the Vatican court with their stiff, high collars. When I was going up the steps, I caught my shoe on the step, and the sole split open at the toe. I went to the audience, shuffling along as best I could. Luz-Ma nudged me, saying, "Clown, what are you doing?" She hadn't seen my shoe. So we both, with the two girls, went up and offered our document to the pope. Each audi-

tor had an opportunity to speak personally to the pope. We were the last because I was so late in getting there.[35]

McCarthy remembered one time when just the women were there with the pope in a small reception room. Remembering how her fellow auditor Ehrle "was always packing bag and baggage around with her — camera, camera, camera" — she was amused when Paul VI also caught on. "You with your fotografia," he said. On the closing day, Baldinucci was called back from the airport in Rome as she was about to return to Milan because the pope wanted to see her. She thought he would pass up on her appointment because of his busy schedule, but no. His old friend from Milan was just as important as any of the world's bishops in the papal eyes.

Mutual Appreciation

After the promulgation of the decree *Apostolicam Actuositatem*, the lay auditors sent a letter of thanks and appreciation to Cardinal Cento, president of the Lay Apostolate Commission, for the part he played in consulting laity and including their views in the document that pertained specifically to them, as well as in other conciliar texts. Cento replied: "I make no secret of the fact that this work will leave with me one of the happiest memories of my life. For the first time lay people — other than Kings or their Ambassadors — were present at a Council; they were present, not passively, but in an active manner for they had made an effective contribution to the preparation of our schema."[36]

Goldie added her own comments on both the significance and the time-conditioned limitations of the lay input. It may now seem limited and little more than symbolical, but it marked a milestone. Paul VI called them *experts* on the life and apostolate of the People of God (to *Concilium de Laicis* on March 20, 1970). "*Periti* from this category will surely be present from the initial stages of 'Vatican III.'"[37] The Rubicon had been crossed, and the only logical way was to go forward.

Auditors en route to their daily session at Vatican Council II. (From left) Jerome Maria Chimy, S.S.M.I. (Canada); Catherine McCarthy (U.S.A.); Ida Grillo (Italy); Juliana Thomas, A.D.J. (Germany); Pilar Bellosillo (Spain); Marie de la Croix Khouzam, R.E.S.C. (Egypt); Suzanne Guillemin, D.C. (France); Anne-Marie Roeloffzen (Belgium).

Auditors, like guests, enjoy the best seats in the house in St. Andrew's Tribune. (Top left) Catherine McCarthy, president of NCCW; Mary Luke Tobin, S.L., president of the U.S.A.'s LCWR; Jim Norris (U.S.A.); Dr. Gertrud Ehrle, president of the German Women's League; (Bottom left) Anne-Marie Roeloffzen, general secretary of WFCYWG; Cristina Estrada, ACJ (Spain); Pilar Bellosillo, president of WUCWO; Jerome Maria Chimy, S.S.M.I., Ukrainian Byzantine rite (Canada), superior general of the Sister Servants of Mary Immaculate.

Attending a special service of beatification of Ugandan Martyrs and enjoying front row seats are (from left) Ida Grillo, war widow; Jim Norris; Constantina Baldinucci, S.C.; Suzanne Guillemin, D.C.; Henriette Ghanem, S.S.C.C., Coptic rite and chair of the Assembly of Major Superiors of Lebanon; and Juliana Thomas, A.D.J., general secretary of the Union

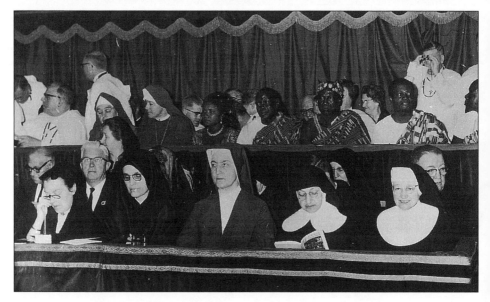

Mary Luke Tobin, S.L. meets Pope Paul VI, as Bishop Guano looks on. Constantina Baldinucci, S.C., president of the Italian Sisters' Union and Marie de la Croix Khouzam, R.E.S.C., Coptic rite and chair of the Union of the Teaching Sisters of Egypt, wait their turn.

Doing business over coffee in Tribuna SB 52 are (from left) chaplain to the International YCW; Alda Miceli (Italy), international president of Secular Institutes; Anne-Marie Roeloffzen; Maria Vendrik, not an auditor, but an "expert" *(perita)*, brought in for consultation on the Church in the Modern World; Ida Grillo, war widow, president of the Italian Catholic Action group in Tortona; Marchesa Amalia di Montezemolo, war widow, president of the Society for Spiritual Assistance to the Armed Forces of Italy.

Relaxing between working sessions are (from left) Macrina Chudiak, O.S.B.M. (not an auditor); Claudia Feddish, O.S.B.M. (U.S.A.), Ukrainian rite, superior general of the Sisters of St. Basil the Great; sideview of Sabine de Valon, R.S.C.J. (France), superior general of the Religious of the Sacred Heart and president of the Superiors General in Italy.

José and Luz-Marie Alvarez-Icaza received in audience with Pope Paul VI. This Mexican couple, parents of twelve children (later expanded to fourteen), was the only married couple invited to the Council. They were Co-Presidents of the Christian Family Movement in Latin America.

Suzanne Guillemin, D.C., superior general of the Daughters of Charity of St. Vincent de Paul, shown here in the preconciliar "cornete," which prompted Europeans to call its wearers "God's geese." Guillemin had pioneered the habit change before coming to Vatican II as an auditor. See the "new look" in previous pictures.

Mary Luke Tobin, S.L. in contemporary dress, pictured on her community's grounds at Nerinx, Kentucky, in May 1988. See Tobin in habit in earlier pictures.

Rosemary Goldie (Australia), former executive secretary of COPECIAL and only "Curial Woman" as under-secretary of the Pontifical Council of the Laity for nine years, a position she shared with Mieczyxlzw de Habicht. This picture was taken in Goldie's office in Piazza S. Calisto in January 1989, where Goldie defies modern technology by turning out major works on her manual typewriter.

Catherine McCarthy, former president of the NCCW, is now retired in San Francisco. In this picture, taken in September 1989, she displays one of her prized possessions—the original Latin copy of the Decree on the Apostolate of the Laity, which she received from the hand of Paul VI. In a symbolic gesture of the laity bringing the council to the world, the pope gave a copy of the text to three women and three men.

Marchesa Amalia di Montezemolo, war widow, invited as a symbolic gesture to "honor the women who are, with their sorrow, an eloquent condemnation of war, and a symbol of the deepest hopes of humanity for a just and Christian peace."

Marie-Louise Monnet, the first woman to enter the council as an auditor on September 25, 1964. She came from the family of Cognac Monnet brandy makers, where she received her first lessons in networking worldwide. She later demonstrated her skills as founder and first president of MIAMSI, International Movement for the Apostolate in the "Independent Milieux."

CHAPTER FIVE

THE NUN IN THE WORLD

═══ ❖ ═══

A Specialized Service Corps

When the water becomes stagnant, you break the dam. Vatican II was a recognition of the ecclesial stagnancy and irrelevance that was becoming more obvious with the advance of the modern world. John XXIII dared to break the dam when he called the council and set the agenda of *aggiornamento*. All the pent-up questions, emotions, frustrations, and aspirations came pouring out over the course of the four conciliar years. This dam-bursting swept away much of what had been revered as *religious life*. Part of the problem was that those of us within did not know we were stagnating. The old adage "Keep the Rule and the Rule will keep you" was full-coverage insurance for this life and the next. Experienced watchers realized that it was time to flush out the old water and get a live current circulating.

"We believe that the time has come for the religious life of women to be given more honor and to be made more efficacious." With these words, Paul VI began the announcement of his intention to invite a symbolic presence of women as auditors to the council. The word got out that "even nuns" would be going to Rome. The news was sensational because the so-called "good sisters," even in apostolic congregations, were operating from a monastic spirituality of asceticism and flight from the world that left them generally out of touch with realities outside convent walls. Like children, they were expected to be seen, not heard, although they were capable, qualified women, running a high percentage of the world's finest and most efficient educational, medical, and social institutions.

The paternalistic mindset prevailed among many of the conciliar bishops. Cardinal Antoniutti, prefect of the Sacred Congregation for Religious and president of the commission on *Perfectae Caritatis,* refused to allow the women religious to participate in the commission's discussion of their lives. Repeated requests were turned down, and the cardinal is supposed to have said, "Try again at Vatican III or IV."

Regretfully, almost thirty years after the women participated in the conciliar preparation of *Gaudium et Spes,* the same Roman sexist mentality prevailed and was evident in the preparatory text and guidelines for the 1994 synod on religious life. Women religious could not be full voting members of the synod — a privilege reserved to the clergy (including men religious). It was considered a big concession when twenty presidents of women's religious congregations were allowed to be present at the synod (among the two hundred or so bishops and others). Their status was that of part-time observers. This had an oddly familiar ring, reminiscent of Paul VI's cautious announcement in 1964 that female auditors could be present at certain solemn rites and congregations "during which questions will be discussed that might particularly interest the life of women."

The conciliar women were convinced thirty years ago that they were on the road to becoming full church members, in keeping with the dignity and equality accorded them by Vatican II's own teaching. They saw the way opened up for forward movement. They envisioned women as progressing beyond their silent listener role to being speakers and voters, especially in areas of their own expertise. This was also the mind of John XXIII and Paul VI. Vatican II was the courageous first step. We still await the second.

The council fathers saw the need for a built-in mechanism for ongoing *aggiornamento* in the church and a communication channel to keep the pope and curia abreast of world developments, so they called for the reintroduction of a periodic synod, and Paul VI acceded. The women religious wanted to insure they would be a part of it. They drafted the following petition to SCRIS:

> It is indispensable to have sisters represented at the synod, since they form a specialized service corps in the church, dedicated to all her [sic] interests, and deeply involved with her [sic] daily life. Together with lay women, they are increasingly conscious of their dignity as human persons (*Pacem in Terris*). They can make their full contribution to the church and human society only if they are permitted to participate in an organic way in the new structures of the church, particularly in the synod.

No one knows what became of the petition. I applaud the women's foresight and acumen as they attempted to avoid the unnecessary future hurdles of fighting for representation on boards and congregations that legislate norms and policies that affect their lives. The sisters wanted *a voice, not honor.*

More Than a Tailor's One-Night Job

It seems to me that communities of women religious took to heart the *aggiornamento* intended for religious more than men's communities did. Perhaps this is because most men's communities (apart from those of Brothers, who opt for a nonclerical way of life), being largely composed of priests, were caught up more in liturgical renewal. Because of the church involvement they already enjoyed as priests, plus the extracommunal engagements this necessitated in most cases, they had mini-breaks from community life. These included temporary substitution of regular clerical or civilian garb for that of the monastic habit — a concession never permitted to women religious, even when visiting their own families. I suspect it may also account for why many men's communities still hold on to the friar or monastic garb, while most women's communities do not. A practical point I observe is how readily monks and friars can don and doff this garb, draping an extra layer of dress over their civilian shirt and trousers, whereas for women it necessitates exchanging one outer layer for another. The sisters' one uniform habit was their communal, professional, social, business, and recreational attire. Clothed as they were in the garb of a century or more ago, they were most conspicuous in any gathering, although, ironically, their founders' aim was that they wear the regular woman's dress of the time.

A certain magical aura surrounded those who donned the religious habit. Some were even sent out to teach in classrooms the next day, despite their lack of training, as they embarked, at least in the U.S., on what was often termed the "twenty-year plan" of obtaining a degree in summer school. In the theology and spirituality of pre–Vatican II days, they had "left the world" to answer a "higher calling" than their sisters who chose to marry or remain single outside the convent. This state of mind was alive and well in the

1950s, and the uniform black/blue and white ankle-length skirts and veiled heads, served to create visually the cloister walls that "set them apart" literally, psychologically, or both.

No wonder then that the habit change caused weeping and gnashing of teeth. Much more was at stake than "a tailor's one-night job." Habit modifications and the shift toward contemporary dress symbolized a deeper and more painful reality as sisters embraced the modern world, in keeping with the new theology of *Lumen Gentium* and *Gaudium et Spes*. Belgian Léon-Josef Cardinal Suenens took a particular interest in sisters' renewal. His book *The Nun in the World* was the 1960's *vade mecum* of both the curious and those committed to genuine renewal.

No one was more attuned to these changes, the theology behind them, and the community upheaval that accompanied them than the conciliar women religious. Suzanne Guillemin's address given to the French bishops in Rome, October 26, 1964 — barely a month after she joined the council as an auditor — outlined well the problems facing all religious of the active life, not only the Daughters of Charity of St. Vincent de Paul. She saw them as intertwined with those of contemporary people within the world explosion of science, knowledge, and technology that transform profoundly the sociological and ecclesial context in which the congregations were inserted as well as the young women who came to religious communities. "Entering actively into the movement of the church and adapting ourselves to the world of today are a matter of life or death for a community," she said, "and what is even more serious, of fidelity or treason to one's vocation in the church." Strong words from this powerful Frenchwoman.

Guillemin told the bishops of the tensions the sisters felt because their active way of life seemed to militate against the contemplative spirituality they were expected to live. The dualistic philosophy prevalent among spiritual writers compartmentalized their lives through a hierarchy of faith and works. By way of contrast, Guillemin was advocating that "our manner of going to God, our mode of union with God, and the place of our contemplation, are located within our action, in the meeting of the people we encounter side by side at this moment. As St. Vincent said, 'A sister who finds the poor ten times in the day will find God there ten times a day.'" This was the emergence of a new vision that discovered the new contemporaneity of the communities' original vision by turning to their sources in the spirit of their founders. This called for a "renewal of spirit and structures."[1]

Clearly, the sisters could no longer take refuge in the security of old customs and practices, an infantile self-effacement, and a static retreat from new and pressing demands of their professions and apostolates. To enable them to cope, new and concerted efforts needed to be made in regard to formation and education, discipline and community life, and the missionary spirit. Not only was organized national effort required but also international and intercongregational collaboration to pool resources, cut costs, enrich experiences, break down old barriers, and open up new frontiers of communication, personal fulfillment, and missionary endeavor. Guillemin's talks touched on all of these areas.

Symbols change slowly and often painfully. So it was with the religious dress. Each community could tell its own story. Jerome Maria Chimy told of both flexibility and openmindedness of the sisters in particular situations and the tenacity with which others held on for dear life to the traditional dress. As superior general she visited the sisters in communist countries. Speaking of her visit to the Ukraine, she said:

> I could not wear the habit. I went as a secular, and I had no trouble with that nor had anyone at the generalate. You should have seen all the sisters around dressing me and wondering who would get to do the headpiece. Even those from the Ukraine were involved. They were very openminded. If you want to wear this, you wear it. In the Ukraine the KGB knew I was a nun, even though I wasn't in uniform, and they followed me around.[2]

Experimentation started with the 1968 chapter in Chimy's community. "As the superior general, I had to take the lead," she explained:

> When I went on visitation, I wore a modified headpiece. In Yugoslavia this came as a bit of a shock to me, though I didn't take it personally. When the vice-provincial saw me in the modified headpiece, she turned her back without greeting me and never came to see me during that visit, although I asked for her. No one said anything, and I didn't admonish anyone. After the 1970 chapter, the vice-provincial told me she hadn't the courage for that much change. She apologized and hoped I still loved her. Of

course I did. If I had admonished her, it wouldn't have worked in that community, located as it was in a village where the women wore long pleated skirts, aprons, and a kerchief. In the Ukraine the sisters were not allowed to wear any kind of religious dress or insignia, or they would be put in prison, so habit changes were not a question where survival was central. In Brazil, even before the council they had gotten rid of the lower half of the scapular because it wasn't practical for their work, where regular transportation was by horse and buggy.[3]

The manner in which the subject of habit change was introduced to the various communities was crucial. Chimy's policy was to lead but not force anyone into the desired change. As a result the sisters came round to accepting it in their own time, and with less lasting hurt feelings. Guillemin had her unique way of introducing change, as Beatrice Brown, D.C., graciously related to me.

> Whenever and wherever Suzanne met with groups, she spoke simply and eloquently, often telling an appropriate anecdote, such as the following: In 1964, the sisters had simplified their habit throughout the D.C. world, and Suzanne told a large group of sisters about her visit to the Rue du Bac infirmary. Understanding the putative sentiments of the elderly concerning the fabled "cornet," she assured them that in the infirmary there would be perfect freedom about giving up the cornet in favor of the streamlined coif. Indeed Mère Guillemin told them how General de Gaulle had exclaimed, "What? Changing the cornet of the Filles de la Charité? Well, one might as well propose changing 'le drapeau de la France [the French flag]!" Thus relaxed, the infirmary sisters were asked about the proposed change. With touching dignity, a recognized spokeswoman replied: "We feel that if our cornet is no longer the official habit, we shall not cling to it. We wish to wear whatever our sisters wear, in solidarity with Vincent's Daughters throughout the world."[4]

A little kindness, understanding, and freedom won the day.

Tobin, generally considered a prime mover among the auditors, also worked on habit changes for her community. Goldie, recalling some of the humorous conciliar scenes, related how "Mary Luke Tobin, American superior general of the Sisters of Loretto, smuggled into St. Peter's by some trick or another an attractive young nun to model an experimental costume before a cardinal, from whom she wished to obtain hierarchical approval." It was not a typical "superior's" action in those days.

Tobin told her own horror stories of dealing with Cardinal Antoniutti, prefect of SCRIS.

> I never saw eye-to-eye with him. Every time I think of his name, I can see him instructing me what to do. I could see his eyelids flutter, but he wouldn't look at me. He gave me instructions, while never looking me straight in the eye. He kept saying, "Now, now, now, you know... we don't want to have anything contrary to the church." I had to have some battles royal with him about the religious habit. All we were asking for in those days was a simple veil and suit with a skirt a bit below the knee. I think I still have a photograph I took to him of how the sister was going to look. There she was in her little dark suit and white shirt. He took his pen and pulled her sleeve down to her wrist — drawing with the pen — and her skirt all the way down to the floor. Then the veil had to be pulled out so that the hair didn't show.
>
> We were just beginning the first stages of these changes in the States at the time, and I thought we had to go to him about them. Antoniutti wanted us to remain totally immersed in black serge. What defeated that was the implementation of the council with a document that came out in 1966, decreeing that every religious community hold a special chapter initiating experimentation within two years of the council. We were to do away with everything we wanted, even if it went against Canon Law, provided that it didn't interfere with the nature and purpose of the institute. We held on to that statement for dear life.[5]

Tobin was not sorry to see the end of her exchanges with the Prefect of SCRIS:

> My last meeting with Cardinal Antoniutti took place in Rome after the council, only a short time before his death. We exchanged greetings, and he said to me seriously, "I want you to know, Sister, that what I did in regard to innovations in religious life, I did for the good of the church." I appreciated that acknowledgment and responded, "I, too, your Eminence. What I have done to encourage these new developments in religious life, I believe I have done for the good of the church." We parted in a friendly man-

ner — two persons expressing their love for the church in two
very different ways.[6]

In those days, they could meet face to face and disagree.

Guillemin's position on the dress of women religious was stated
in an address to the American Sister Servants on retreat in Paris
in 1967. The habit question came at the end in the context of
"essentials." "I hope, sisters," she said,

> that religious life will be strong enough to retain what is essen-
> tial, but the difficulty lies in determining the essential. There are
> those who believe that religious will no longer wear a religious
> habit. To those who say that St. Vincent had the first Daughters
> wear a secular habit, I would add that he immediately established
> *uniformity* in dress. The habit is a symbol of our consecration
> and at the same time a protection for each of us. A Jesuit Father
> has stated that "giving up the religious habit is not only an exte-
> rior thing. A religious who takes off her habit tends to highlight
> her *womanliness*." Once the habit is gone, consideration has to
> be given to hairdos, perfumes, cigarettes, etc. We must carefully
> distinguish between the apostolate of the laity and the apostolate
> of religious women. Sisters in lay attire who work in public hos-
> pitals or schools bring God there, but how many are conscious
> of God's presence? Sisters wearing religious habits are a public
> witness of God and of the church in today's world.[7]

One can only surmise how this Jesuit authority defined "woman-
liness." The implication was that one cannot be "womanly" and
"religious." This understanding was contrary to the recognition of
woman's dignity and uniqueness that was just emerging at Vatican II but had not yet been internalized and embraced, even by such
prophetic women as Mère Guillemin.

What Did the Sisters Want?

The original draft of the conciliar document *Apostolicam Actuositatem* was, as Canadian Bishop Alexander Carter of Sault Sainte
Marie declared, "conceived in original sin of clericalism," that is,
without any lay input. Subsequent drafts remedied this as bishops
realized that the church committees looked foolish without laity. One
would have thought that a similar process of integration would take

place in regard to including the sisters in writing and amending *Perfectae Caritatis,* since, as Bernard Häring logically remarked, they constituted the majority of the religious of the world.[8] Not even the ten women religious auditors were given a look in, and they were the superiors who were expected to implement the changes being legislated.

The sisters knocked, and other friends in court petitioned for them, but Cardinal Antoniutti refused to open the door, so they were never permitted to work in commission on the document that was to affect their lives so radically. When entrance was denied them at the front door, they went to the back door and the route of indirect influence through the pope and commissionary bishops. Constantina Baldinucci related that "the religious representatives were not asked so much for interventions or explanations about their lives because the council fathers had bigger problems to deal with and discuss." This was not good enough for Baldinucci, the religious representative of the Italian nation, so she asked Paul VI through Msgr. Magee whether the sisters could write some of their problems to present them to the council, and the pope agreed. Baldinucci gathered the desires, problems, and expectations of the representatives of the different nationalities and typed up a protocol-like text, which was read to the representatives and given to the pope to present to the council. Later, Baldinucci was gratified to hear bishops say they left the council much more aware of the problems and concerns of women religious.

Forming a United Front

In addition to the weekly meetings of lay auditors, the women religious met regularly at one or other of their motherhouses or in Palazza di Santa Marta, where about two hundred council fathers, mostly French-speaking, were staying. Most frequently they met in the provincial house of Maria Bambina in Via Saint' Ufficio (Baldinucci's community) because of its central location and proximity to St. Peter's. "There was always communication between us and the Vatican," Baldinucci explained. "Except for the present pope [John Paul II], our congregation served the popes in the Vatican." It was a big, hospitable house that had Giovanni Cardinal Colombo of Milan as a guest during the first and second conciliar sessions and Mary Luke Tobin during the fourth session. It was there that many liturgical commission meetings took place in 1965, and they had many "experimental" Masses in different languages. It could be called a "second little Vatican Council of ecumenical overture,"[9] commented Baldinucci, because many bishops, general superiors, and auditors came.

The topics most frequently discussed under the chairship of Msgr. Guano or Bishop Gerard Huyghe were formation, obedience, poverty, depersonalization, enhancing the good use of sisters' talents, renunciation of a cloister tone in active institutions, education, how to be true leaven among the masses, cooperation among communities, overcoming separatism, discernment as to where sisters should concentrate their energies and be less involved in manual work that others can do, and bonding with male religious institutions for support in implementing renewal.

Besides the specific problems of religious life, the leaders dealt also with problems of the apostolate and cooperation with the laity, e.g., the coordination of associations of female associates, collaboration with laity, overcoming prejudices, the need for a realistic study of the present position of woman, problems of promotion, the particular characteristics of women religious that must be saved, their place in the ecclesial community, the need for instituting dialogue with laity and hierarchy, the need for commissions of communication and experimentation between laity and religious for international unions of superiors general.[10]

The sisters' input demonstrated their emerging sense of themselves as ecclesial women:

> The renewal of religious life should manifest the same characteristics as that of the whole church, that is, it should be theological, ecclesial, scriptural, liturgical, ecumenical, and pastoral. Each religious institute should be encouraged to undertake experimentations while safeguarding the *founder's spirit* and *sound traditions*. Obsolete books and articles should be discarded. Recognizing that the Holy Spirit works through the whole community, not just superiors, widespread consultation and dialogue were necessary. Realizing the unity of love of God and neighbor, apostolic activity is of the very substance of that vocation, not just part of it, as they involve themselves in works for the betterment of human existence. Because of baptism, every religious

is both contemplative and apostolic. The particular apostolate of each institute must be seen within the context of the whole church, needing collaboration among hierarchy, laity, clergy, and religious, with members of each group duly represented in governing bodies that affect their lives and activity. Specifically, sisters should serve as permanent consultative or acting members of the Sacred Congregation of Religious.[11]

A clarion call went out for freedom and responsibility. Let all religious assume a greater personal responsibility in fulfilling their total commitment to the virginal, poor, and obedient Christ. Celibacy does not destroy human love but should free it from selfishness and exclusiveness. Religious obedience exacts initiative and responsibility from the subject, as well as promptitude in embracing the decisions of the superiors. Religious authority has its source in Christ who came "to serve and not to be served." Its function is to direct and build up this religious community in charity. Religious poverty is both personal and communal. It should be manifest by simplicity in buildings and furnishings, communal and effective concern for the poor, and a refined sense of justice and honesty in all its business affairs (e.g., payment of employees, profits). Community life is not founded on the principle of uniformity but on charity, encompassing a diversity of gifts. The unifying bond of the Eucharist is visibly expressed by genuine human love among the members. Enclosure should be relative to the end of the institute.

Back to Essentials

The social, scientific, and technical evolutions that were modifying the world itself affected the traditional positions of religious life and forced it to purify itself. A deepened theology of the religious life was the first requirement. It had to be stripped of sentimental, moral, or philanthropical justifications.

There was a profound unity of religious life in its theological and ecclesial root, which expressed itself in diverse forms. Vows were not practiced the same way in the cloister as on missionary roads. Problems of collaboration with the hierarchy were extremely different when it was a question of religious women. Religious life is essentially apostolic because one cannot conceive of a search for God that bypasses God's mystical body. A thorough study of a spirituality proper to the active life was called for to help eliminate the dualistic split between the duty of one's state in life and her search for God. Active and contemplative life render the same homage to God and the same message to the world, but with different primary approaches — in the world of action or in the cloister and divine office.

To safeguard and realize the specific vocation of each institute, it was important that each congregation under the impulse of the Holy Spirit work to deepen its vocation and seek to realize it in view of better service to the church. Each founder in her day answered a current need of the church; each would respond differently to needs today.

The theology of the vows ought to be rethought in their apostolic import. Vows must be assumed personally by adult religious, capable of free acts. The practice of the vow of obedience was one of the major problems existing in communities because of a shift in contemporary thought and evolution in the human sciences and the emphasis on fostering responsible obedience and initiative.

To form religious in view of a perfect response to their vocation was an urgent obligation for major superiors. First, it was necessary to form the young and then promote the integration and growth of an adult religious personality, promoting harmony between the acquisition of the secular sciences necessary for action and the development of the religious sciences. The creation of juniorates was more and more indispensable, in which young religious found a community milieu adapted to their life as students, under the direction of religious properly prepared for this purpose. Formation of local superiors and continuing formation for all was necessary because of the generation gap often experienced between young sisters and local superiors of the old school.

Congregations ought to unite in order to assure the best formation of religious, leaving behind a confining, detrimental individualism. Unions of religious, particularly conferences of major superiors, needed to take some initiatives in view of the common good, while totally respecting the proper life of each institute.

Religious-lay collaboration needed to be promoted because a mutual misunderstanding existed and contributed to the recent crisis in vocations. Evangelization required that clergy, laity, and religious be more deeply inserted into the church, with an appreciation for the particular vocation of each, by mutual respect, collaboration, contact, and friendly exchanges to help barriers fall and eliminate prejudices.

The language of "superior" and "subject," "mother general," "provincial," etc., was recognized as reflecting the Roman military model still operative in religious communities at the time. The Daughters of Charity had a different vocabulary of "Sister Servant" and "Sister Companion," although in practice the distinctions of rank operated just like in other communities. To "outsiders," these details must have seemed trivial indeed, but when Mary Luke Tobin stated that she was no longer "Mother" but plain "Sister," her titular relinquishment symbolized the equality of rank and file being inaugurated after the biblical model of service that castigated lordship over anyone and calling any human "Mother" or "Father."[12]

Sister Look-Alikes Do *Not* Always Think Alike

Despite the camaraderie that developed among the sisters and the attempt the representatives of each nation made to see and understand the problems of all, some deep divisions prevailed when it came to talking about mandating concrete changes. So-called conservatives and liberals had their representatives here as in the council at large.

Twenty-five years later, Tobin could laugh off some of the differences as she recalled the main outline of events of an afternoon tea party in an Italian garden at Sabine de Valon's motherhouse of the Madames of the Sacred Heart. This took place early in the third conciliar session and shortly after the female auditors arrived.

> Valon wanted to have us all agree that we would not go along with some of the progressive ideas that were being promoted for the decree on religious because she said she would really oppose any developments that were not exactly according to the Holy Father's wishes. I began to get hot under the collar. She said there was a group of priests in Rome who urged her to urge the sisters to oppose anything contrary to the Holy Father's will, "so let's all agree...." Well, I was so mad by this time that I said, "What priests?" She didn't tell us, and I later heard it was a group of Jesuits. Whoever they were that wanted to control her and have her control us, I knew it was not in our best interest. "I can't agree," I said, "because I see this council as the voice of the

whole church. We cannot oppose that kind of progress." I could just see them clamping us down forever. I said, "I don't think the Spirit is on our side in opposing it." Then we gabbed around for some time, and no one signed her document. So maybe that's the best contribution I made to the council. Who knows? Valon was scared as to what was going to happen in terms of renewal. She could have relaxed because there was no great progress in that document.[13]

A thorough interview conducted in 1965 by Maria José Sirera, A.C.I., was significant, both in the variety of topics discussed and in the responses given by eight of the ten women religious present at the council. He concluded that the sisters were all enthusiastic about deepening their vocations; they had a sense of a more alive and challenging church; they realized the need for evolution in their way of life to respond to a new era and contemporary young women who might want to join them; and they were sympathetic to youth and the demands they faced.[14]

In some instances the women religious talked about transcendence and the supernatural as if they were divorced from the immanent and natural and made negative references to the materialistic world and the young women wanting only purely human development. This dualistic, preconciliar language did not lend itself to the reform and renewal called for by the council. It was the basis for division and the failure to implement necessary change in religious life as well as in the church at large.

I was struck by the openness of mind to the larger human issues outside the community, no doubt somehow conditioned by circumstances, such as the presence of non-Christian world religions experienced by women like Ghanem and Khouzam. They seemed to bring this breadth of vision to the questions of their own religious life, giving them a refreshing perspective that went beyond that of the more insular-minded. I suspect that their concerns for uplifting the status of all women and seeing this as necessarily also involving men was colored at least somewhat by their experience of fundamentalist Muslims and others who explicitly supported women's inferiority. Women who had traveled widely, such as Baldinucci and Guillemin, also had widened their horizons and developed an ability to sum up situations and put things in perspective. Thomas, coming from postwar Germany, being involved in the field of nursing and in contact with laity, medical experts, and other professionals, also evidenced a healthy outlook that valued religious life but did not see it as a privileged, sacralized realm above the rest of the world.

Missing from Sirera's conversation were Guillemin, who may have been on one of her weekend visits back to Paris, and Chimy, the only woman religious who was a newcomer to the council in the final session. Chimy's evaluation of *Perfectae Caritatis* at a later date (May 23, 1993) was that

> there was nothing there; it contained no vision at all; it simply stated things as they were. We needed more than that in a council document. Some wanted to leave the religious alone. It was thrown together in a hurry. The sisters felt that they were not wanted by some bishops, and there was one council father who said he would rather have laypeople working with him than religious because the sisters were there only for the money. They were not where they were needed with the poor or even in schools but in top management jobs in hospitals. It was mostly Latin rite bishops from the U.S. and Canada who were saying these things. Our bishops were not, but then we were a minority, and we had no big institutions or hospitals.

Tobin remarked on the cold shoulder some bishops gave the sisters at the council. She had a difficult time trying to track down Archbishop Lawrence J. Shehan, head of the U.S. bishops' administrative board. She went to his hotel begging him to put in a word to get the sisters represented on the commissions that made decisions about their lives. "I brought him a statement from the American religious, asking for a deliberative or at least consultative voice. Well, you can imagine," she said, with the tone of one accustomed to dismissals from on high. "We didn't even get to first base. He said he would ask the bishops about it, but that was the last I heard of it." Perhaps as the Sister Formation movement caught on, especially in the 1960s, bishops were not pleased because communities were holding back the sisters until they had obtained their degrees and a solid theological formation. This meant that they were not sent out on mission for about six years, instead of the customary two required by Canon Law. This was frustrating for bishops who were opening up new schools and were so financially strapped that they could not operate without the sisters as "cheap labor."

Collaboration

One of the buzz words of the council was collaboration. This generally meant the new discovery of working together that took place in the commissions that wrote and rewrote the conciliar documents. It was a new experience for the bishops of the emerging world-church so strongly symbolized at the council, and this led to increased emphasis on collegiality, meaning bishop-bishop and bishops-pope relationships. This expanded further to hierarchy-laity relations and the concept and practice of subsidiarity when lay auditors arrived and were generally consulted and included in the discussions already underway. A further dynamic of male-female interaction occurred when the female auditors arrived, and this focused more sharply the issue of human dignity and equality. This also introduced the clergy-religious, religious-lay, and religious-religious factor of inter-relationships. With the Protestant and Orthodox observers present, there was a heightened sense of ecumenical sensitivity, while within Catholicism, opening up to the diversity of rites was a new window for many who hitherto were totally ignorant of them and considered anything non-Latin to be non-Catholic. Within religious communities themselves the superior-subject dynamic also had to be integrated more positively. What most people on the outside (meaning those who did not belong to religious communities) did not realize was the challenge of collaboration that faced the women religious as they were confronted with relating in a meaningful way to sisters in other congregations.

My own memory of diocesan communities in Ireland in the 1950s and 1960s was that of six groups of strangers — all Sisters of Mercy within a thirty-mile radius. We were no closer to them than to the other congregations within the same territory. There was rivalry between our schools when it came to obtaining scholarships and high school results — the gateway to students' future achievements. Approximately once a year the mother superior, assistant, and bursar from my own community visited the parent convent from which ours was founded about one hundred years earlier, and their three counterparts from that convent paid a reciprocal visit to ours annually. We never met sisters of the lower rank and file and especially none of our own age group, except those who happened to be students in the same university, training college, or hospital.

When I came to the U.S. in the early 1960s on the eve of Vatican II, I encountered other communities, Mercy and otherwise, for the first time. They too were mostly strangers to one another. Absence from the motherland and the need for companionship drew the Irish groups closer together, and the need for learning the American ways and surviving, making retreats, and attending summer school led us into closer contact with the hospitality of U.S. Mercies and other communities. At Marillac College, owned and operated by the Daughters of Charity (Guillemin's community) in St. Louis, with sister teachers contributed by other participating communities, I experienced firsthand the formation and collaboration ideals that the women religious at the council talked about, and the pipe dream was more wonderful on paper than in flesh and blood. During the three years I studied for my basic degree, I lived with the Sisters of Loretto (Tobin's community). Three other students from an out-of-state community also boarded there. At least eight or ten other communities of young sisters resided in the neighborhood, where they had a directress and a house of studies. While all were in class together, the clearest division was between the Daughters, or "cornets" (most numerous), and non-Daughters, or "veils" (the rest of us). I recall a major breakthrough in communications when the Daughters were allowed to eat their sack lunch with the rest of us at a picnic out on the lawn. Normally, the non-Daughters partook of their sack lunch with a hot beverage provided by the Daughters in a separate dining room.

Over in Rome the women religious auditors suffered the growing pains of multileveled collaboration, while the younger generation of sisters in shared formation programs was introduced to it as a way of life. Establishing a level of trust sufficient to draft joint statements that would allow for real differences was not easy. Hospitality served as a bridge builder. Baldinucci sometimes invited the international group of sisters to dinner. On November 18, 1965, toward the end of two years working together for a common cause, she invited them for a final meal together before they went their separate ways. She said, "It was a moving experience of intimate nostalgia for the auditors as the council drew to a close. The experience shared in the Vatican basilica under Michelangelo's vault was that of living in a pentecostal time and feeling its responsibility for making all the forces converge to put the council's direction to work when the group dispersed."[15]

That was the grand finale, made possible only by working together through the more difficult times. Chimy remembered that there were

clearly divisions among the religious auditors, as some were progressive, while others resisted change. Americans and Germans were
the most progressive, but it was a question of different personalities
more than nationalities. "If the pace is too fast, you can lose people.
Rome wasn't built in a day either. We wanted change but not radical
change because of the sisters in different countries. You may want
change yourself, but you might not have others to stand by you."
Thus spoke Chimy's voice of experience. She continued,

> An outstanding speaker in our group was Mary Luke Tobin.
> She was very active, a go-getter, and she was making everybody
> work. But she was quite critical, and that could sometimes be
> divisive. She wanted to have more respect for sisters, more free-
> dom, not to be ruled too much, to update prayer, dress, mission,
> etc. The main thing was that we didn't have a say in things that
> concerned us. There was too much emphasis on obedience to the
> pope. It wasn't that the sisters wanted to go against the Holy
> Father, but we wanted to be heard because we felt we had some-
> thing to say. It was a question of taking responsibility within the
> church.[16]

Attending the joint community meetings was a priority for most of
the sisters, unless they had another pressing meeting or conflict. Feddish was an exception, and she came only very seldom. According
to Chimy:

> The few times she was with us she was very much in favor
> of change, but she had trouble as general with the Ukrainian
> province. Her own province did not change as quickly as ours.
> She would be at the council, but after that she went back to the
> apartment, so she was not very much with us. She was very care-
> ful because, mind you, Slipyj wasn't for women except to work.
> Maybe he was disoriented after Siberia, but people said he was
> like that also in the Ukraine. He was not for the advancement of
> women at all, so that was why we couldn't discuss these things
> with Claudia. She herself would have been for women, but she
> was under Slipyj's thumb.[17]

Feddish and Chimy were friends, but their respective communities
were not always on friendly terms, despite their Ukrainian Byzantine
origins. "Claudia tried to break down the barrier of unfriendliness,"
she said. "When their sisters came to Rome to visit, Claudia always

brought them to visit us, and we visited them. The council did bring us together, and the Union of Superiors General was formed. In our group there was animosity, but at least there was a confession of it. At first, we tolerated one another. I remember one day we got together and joined hands in a circle, and we were so excited that we were there together and forming deeper bonds of friendship."

Baptism Makes Us All Celebrities

A major thrust of Vatican II was a retrieval of baptism as the most basic and all-encompassing sacrament that made *everyone* "priest, prophet, and king" (*sic*). The significance of this was far-reaching because it rehabilitated 99.9 percent of churchgoers as *the church,* together with the hierarchy, who had a total monopoly on it since the aborted Vatican I (1869–70) had defined papal primacy and in-fallibility and left that partial ecclesiology hanging, so that the part came to be equated with the whole.

The new inclusivity caused seismic shocks that resulted in iden-tity crises in other areas of the people of God. Foremost among these was religious life, hitherto regarded as the *state of perfection.* If there was now a universal call to holiness (*LG*, V), why religious life? And so the laity-religious tensions mounted at the council. Did the re-habilitation and exaltation of the one necessitate the displacement and denigration of the other? Some bishops, such as the Polish An-toni Baraniak, speaking for the many Polish bishops not present at the council because of communist rule, described *Perfectae Caritatis* as "a ruin" that undervalued religious at a time when "enemies of the church try to destroy religious communities, the nerve of the Christian life."[18]

The problem stared the female auditors in the face as lay and religious women met eyeball-to-eyeball as auditors in the same St. Andrew's tribune at the council. Their dress drew a real line of de-marcation. The women recognized the problem and confronted it as a lack of information and understanding, which they set about rec-tifying. The basic premise they soon established was that *they were all laity* first and foremost, not clergy, so they were not in compe-tition with one another. Miceli of the secular institutes — with one foot in each group, so to speak — spearheaded the move toward collaboration. Baldinucci related how Miceli invited all the women to a friendly meeting chaired by Emile Guano, on November 11, 1964. The proposal was made that the women divide themselves into study groups for more specific collaboration.[19] Minutes from a 1964 meeting listed those present as Baldinucci, Ghanem, Guillemin, Khouzam, Thomas, and Tobin from the religious and Bellosillo, Goldie, Miceli, Monnet, and Roeloffzen from the laywomen. The discussion centered around four areas, and one person was responsible for each. Tobin was in charge of collaboration among religious and laity. Goldie would prepare a summary of conciliar interventions specifically concerning women. Bellosillo and the WUCWO team would collect the study and the experiences concerning the conciliar themes of the promotion and education of women in view of their role in church and society. Roeloffzen was responsible for the study concerning questions and experience especially of young women.

Guillemin was the liaison person for all questions dealing specifically with religious. Furthermore, all the women auditors were asked to collaborate with the men in studying the different themes of Schema 13. Deadlines were set and adhered to.

Gertrud Ehrle was one of the architects and a strong advocate of lay-religious collaboration. Speaking of her recollections of the council twenty years later, she recalled:

> Another item which preoccupied me was intensifying the contacts with the religious congregations. Fortunately, there were quite a lot of sisters among the auditors, and I derived great pleasure from the fact that Sister Juliana from the congregation of the Poor Servants of Christ was sitting next to me. This reinforced our belief that only by laywomen and sisters working together will we be able to achieve the goals of women in the church and today's society.
>
> At a private audience during the period of the council, I had the opportunity to submit this request (i.e., closer cooperation between laywomen and sisters) to the Holy Father, Paul VI. To my great joy he accepted my proposal favorably and encouraged me to continue my efforts in this direction. Together with Carmela Rossi, former president of Catholic Action in Italy, I paid a visit to several mothers general in Rome, asking them how this goal could be accomplished. Today this cooperation is an accepted fact in many regions of the world.[20]

Your Constitution Is Yourself

"Collaboration is based on involvement with dignity and respect for all," Chimy emphasized with conviction:

> What we want as women is to be accepted on an equal basis, and having to fight for it is not very pleasant. If it weren't for Virgin Mother, we wouldn't have Christ. You and I and everyone else is born of woman, so bringing out the dignity of women is important. You don't have to read a big book of constitutions to find out what you have to be. It's what you do. And we are watched. The early Christians were known by how they loved one another, and now what do we see? See how they fight with one another and jockey for the high places. As far as I'm concerned, *your constitution is yourself.* Let people look at you, and they will read and know who you are.
>
> We lament the vocation shortage, but we need to ask ourselves some questions. Our young people today need to get better examples. I am concerned about our empty churches. We have to get *everyone* involved from the youngest to the oldest, and we have to discover solutions to our problems *together,* not thinking that we or the priests have all the answers. And we have to take this beyond our own denomination too.[21]

Aggiornamento French Style

A few examples from Guillemin's *modus operandi* will serve to demonstrate how the consultative, collaborative process began to be exercised in religious communities. Here again, I am indebted to Beatrice Brown for the anecdotes.

> Mère Guillemin had assembled the Rue du Bac sisters to distribute to them the new Book of Hours. That completed, she related another anecdote. The elderly sisters had been asked if they would feel deprived when their venerable "community catechism" gave way to the Divine Office. Someone, speaking only for herself, said, "Oh no, Ma Mère. For years I have cherished the hope that we might one day pray the Divine Office." The others, hearing this heartfelt testimony, applauded feelingly. Ma Mère beamed as she related the incident.

The great dining hall of the Maison Mère [motherhouse] had long been a place of silence, even on Sundays. One Sunday, Mère Guillemin tinkled a little bell. Silence already reigned, so the sisters wondered what was expected of them. Before long Ma Mère spoke. "I have been thinking," she said, "about our venerable custom of washing our silver at table. I think we might consult the youngest among us to discover what sage thoughts they have. Sister X [a young novice or seminary sister], what did you think when you first observed this ritual? Tell us without hesitation." A black-clad, white-fichued novice rose and told the group in a genteel voice that it reminded her of camping trips. Everyone enjoyed this fresh point of view. The mother general threw her head back and laughed aloud. Another novice voiced her opinion. "I thought it was a dangerous practice; it's really not sanitary, you know." More laughter and some applause followed, especially from the interviewer. More opinions were solicited and heard. The directress of the seminary (novice mistress in those days) must have been praying for the *coup de grâce*. It came. "I have now heard confirmed from the mouths of babes the professional opinions. From now on, we shall have conversation with our food." And so it was.

From these stories Brown gathered that Mère Guillemin knew how to prepare the sisters and other religious for change. She presented her case with grace, charm, and fortitude so that others not merely accepted but embraced the changes proposed.

Brown had her own personal experiences of Guillemin during a year's study she spent at l'Institute Catholique, while residing at the motherhouse in Paris in a suite adjoining that of Ma Mère. She found her "amazingly accessible to a loose cannon like me." When given an appointment, Brown came with a prepared speech. "A novel approach," said Guillemin smiling, "proceed, Beatrice," and she listened carefully. To Brown's impressions of the courses and professors at l'Institute, she said, "Tell them what you think." In her prepared speech, Brown had expressed concern "lest Vincent's country girls become monastic," because she had seen some signs of it. Guillemin planned visits and a tour guide to take her to several of the Daughters' houses in Paris, so that the worried Beatrice found that her fears were unfounded. Brown's summation of Mère Guillemin was that "she was a prophet. I liked her statement, spoken a day or so before she died: 'les évenements c'est Dieu' — God is in every circumstance of our lives."[22]

Hands across the World

A major instrument of collaboration officially established right at the closing of the council was the International Union of Superiors General (UISG). Several of the religious auditors were partial to this and participated actively in bringing it about. Ghanem and Guillemin originally conceived of the idea.[23] The project was submitted to Cardinal Antoniutti, Prefect of the Sacred Congregation for Religious. After much hesitation it was accepted, and the outlines of the statutes for this assembly were then developed and presented "for experimentation." Sabine de Valon and her secretary general, Françoise de Lambilly (a very gifted woman who was fluent in Latin), were also instrumental in founding UISG, "seeing it as a funnel through which the Holy See could speak to religious and religious to the Holy See. This was their creative idea. But Mother de Valon was lost when Sister de Lambilly then went to be secretary general of the UISG, for her vision and leadership had been very significant as the right hand of the superior general."[24] After the council, Guillemin was asked to become president of UISG, but she declined because she wished to devote more time to implementing conciliar renewal in her own congregation.

Guillemin expressed her conviction of the importance of UISG. "The organization of an International Union of Superiors General at the conclusion of Vatican II crowned it all. Although this Union has no hierarchical power, it constitutes a powerful factor of unity. It may well become the place where in the coming years the ideas and the future of the religious life will be elaborated."[25] She saw it as creating new opportunities for responding to responsible tasks in religious life and the involvement of women religious in ecclesiastical organizations at the Roman level.

Tobin said that UISG invited the heads of different congregations after the council, and they decided to elect a governing board. Tobin had been asked to talk on government, which she did with significant prior input from Marie Augusta Neal, S.N.D. The place was in an uproar. Some were very disturbed. That afternoon elections were held for board members, and Tobin was elected. Next morning Archbishop Paulo Philippe, O.P., chair of the Commission for Religious, led a discussion about her talk. Some said it might be all right for Americans, but it would not be appropriate for others. Philippe announced that they would hold another election. "After he had given us a kind of scolding, some mother general from Brazil came up and embraced me. She couldn't speak English," Tobin remembered, "but she was really on my side. It was funny." Two other American women were also nominated — Elizabeth Carroll, R.S.M., and someone else, as well as Tobin. "Once again, I got the most votes, although Philippe was trying to keep me out of it," she said.

> I was glad to be elected because I said what needed to be said. Most of the voters knew I would do that. I saw communication as a big problem, especially in dealing with bishops. I suggested earlier that a liaison committee of religious superiors and bishops be established as a kind of working, talking group that could discuss common problems. I saw UISG as serving this need and going even a step further to the international level.[26]

Pamela Dowdell, F.M.M., current secretary general for UISG, provided the following historical information from the archives:

> By a decree of the SCRIS, the UISG was canonically erected on 8 December, 1965. On 10 January, 1966, Cardinal Antoniutti, who was then Prefect of the SCRIS, wrote to the general secretary in these terms:
> As you already know, during the fourth session of the Ecumenical Council Vatican II, the project of an organization for the benefit of superiors general (i.e., of women religious) was studied at some length and on 8 December, 1965 that study was brought to a conclusion with the erection of the International Union of Superiors General.
> In order to assure the functioning of such an organism and particularly to guarantee the preparation of the first General Assembly of the Union, which is to be held in Rome next autumn, and after having consulted all the Very Reverend Mothers who were "Auditrices" at the Ecumenical Council, the SCRIS proceeded with the election to the positions of the Executive Committee and of the Council of the said Union, with a provisional mandate until the first General Assembly.

President: M. Maria del Rosario, superior general of the Religious of Jesus and Mary.

Secretary: M. Françoise de Lambilly, general secretary of the Society of the Sacred Heart of Jesus.

Councilor: M. Sabine de Valon, superior general of the Society of the Sacred Heart of Jesus.

Note: In May 1960, M. Sabine de Valon, an "Auditrice" at the council, had been designated president of a small group of superiors general motivated for the organization of a union. This transitional group was called "the Roman Union of Superiors General."[27]

Symbols of the Church Suffering

It was important for Paul VI to invite two war widows as auditors as a protest against the violence of war and a plea for lasting peace. While the women religious were discussing habit modifications and various changes they deemed necessary to reform and renew their lives, these could be considered bourgeois issues compared to the real issues of life and death faced by sisters behind the Iron Curtain in communist countries, where no semblance of religion was permitted. It was significant that the two Ukrainian Byzantine rite sisters, Chimy and Feddish, were present to represent those suffering sisters, because as superiors general of their congregations they had a foot in both the free and the communist worlds. In this way, a little window was kept open in the otherwise closed curtain of silence.

Chimy visited Czechoslovakia five times in secular dress because it was not very far from Rome, and she and her companions could go by car and take things to the sisters. "We had no difficulty," she said:

We told the officials we were visiting the sisters, and we declared whatever gifts we were bringing. They had an eye on us and watched us carefully. They took the homes of the sisters and the Christian Brothers. They put about 150 sisters of different orders, including seven or eight of ours, into one big institution. There they had to work for their keep, cooking, cleaning, and doing the garden under a lay administrator. The idea was to keep them there until they died. They kept them from spreading the word of God. They were not allowed to go anywhere, except with special permission for a death or something serious like that, but they could receive visitors, though not very often.

It's hard to imagine that world. The priests worked in the factories or in the post offices. Officials were afraid they would hold religious services. On Sundays they stayed home and held no services because that's when they were expected to hold them. At night they held the services without lights to avoid suspicion. The people organized themselves into an underground church in Czechoslovakia. Our sisters had nineteen vocations when I was there. They were all working girls, and they came no more than two or three at a time to learn about religious life.

One of the sisters' homes was made into a museum; another became a store. The sisters teaching in a school had a residence and it was made into a kind of hamlet for two families, and they wouldn't give it back. In the Ukraine they did return them eventually, but it was a hard fight. One nice residence had been turned into a court of justice. When freedom came, about nineteen or twenty of our sisters in religious habit came right into that house; they didn't knock or anything, and they said, "This is our house." A lawyer greeted them politely. He was astounded and said, "Yes, I know it is your house, but we have no other building yet." They say you have to be courageous. You can't show them you are afraid. You have to stand on your own feet.

All our sisters, wherever they lived, had permission to have the Blessed Sacrament kept in a little glass or container on the table. When this KGB man came in, and it was his first time in the house, he just grabbed that glass. The sister got so frightened that he was going to desecrate it that she knelt down before him, and this is what she said, "Please. You have taken everything from us. We have nothing to look forward to. The only thing we have left is this (she didn't mention what it was), who is helping us in our suffering. Please don't destroy it." She said he had compassion somehow and gave it to her, and she consumed it immediately.

But our sisters never lost faith, although it was very hard. God was with them, and somehow they were able to exist the way they did.[28]

In the hospitals the sisters often had a profound influence even on KGB who were ill. They experienced spectacular conversions, resulting in professions of faith from most unexpected individuals.

Yugoslavia was not as bad as the Ukraine. Chimy was there in 1968, and the KGB followed her around. She marvelled at the depth of spirituality among the sisters under persecution.

A Mini-Vatican II of Religious Congregations

Women religious imbibed the inductive method of the council and utilized it in preparation for their own renewal chapters. Even before there was question of their being present as conciliar auditors, women religious were following deliberations carefully and moved ahead with necessary change in their own congregations. This was true especially of the American sisters and Tobin's community in particular. In response to my question about how the council changed her, she explained to me why she was better prepared for the council than some others. "We had our general chapter in July 1964. It was monumental for us, and we made many, many changes, and at that time we reduced the number of prayer obligations, etc. We didn't go as far as we went later, but we made big changes, and so we were already involved in experimentation and renewal in 1964."

When asked whether this was as a result of what was going on in the council, she said,

> I would say it was more as a result of our getting together in our own commissions and asking ourselves why we were doing different things and why this burdensome stuff was virtuous. I think it was more common sense and themes that ran through the council — emphasis on more value type things than just reciting prayers. People going away to study brought back new ideas, and that affected our educated community. Every sister had her degree, and many went to graduate school. Six had a Ph.D. We operated two colleges. We had read the theologians — Jean Danielou, de Lubac, etc. — so we were ready for the council and were hoping that more would happen.
>
> In addition, the Leadership Conference of Women Religious was good, and we had come through the Sister Formation movement, which was a progressive step. I was first made president of LCWR in 1964, and I held that position until 1970. During those years, I set up a commission of sisters in the U.S. that I considered the best heads, minds, and hands, and I asked Marie Augusta Neal to head it up. She chaired a wonderful commission

of theologians, sociologists, artists, literary figures, and writers, who devised the "Sisters' Questionnaire," for all the sisters in the U.S. I think it was probably the single most effective instrument for moving the sisters into a new position. Marie Augusta was the one who, though not a council member, affected us most by her reflections and training. Sister formation was important. We saw the value of sisters' education — that was already in the works.[29]

In preparation for the 1964 chapter, the Loretto sisters followed the pattern used by Pope John in preparing for the Second Vatican Council. A central planning committee and subcommissions were set up to deal with four main areas: theology of religious life, community living, habit, and apostolate. The work was done in stages and aimed at the widest range of participation from the community at large. The sisters were asked to go completely through the constitutions, custom book, directory, book of common prayers, ceremonial, and any other books in common use in the institute and see what changes they would suggest. Specific recommendations ranged from emphasis on the centrality of the Eucharist to rising and retiring time, vacations, home visits, and silence during meals. The practice of silence was rethought in the context of charity and mutual support.

Modifying the habit was a major concern because of the visible image it presented of relevance to the contemporary world. Many experts were consulted, and visits were paid to dress, suit, shoe, and millinery shops before deciding on a modern habit and veil with a few color options.

The main concerns of the apostolate committee were that sisters were not known as persons; their role in the parish and civic community was too marginal; and it was their own fault if they were looked upon as "minors." A horarium essential to monastic life was seen to be an obstacle to an apostolate of charity exercised outside the convent.

At the opening of the General Chapter at the Loretto motherhouse in Nerinx, Kentucky, on July 16, 1964, Superior General Tobin wove the various threads of renewal together. She said, "The Sisters of Loretto will go on record as a result of this chapter as supporting the program of Pope Paul VI that the church should seek relevance to the modern world."

Younger sisters who entered religious communities after the main reforms and changes were in place may find reports of such renewal chapters to be very commonplace. The emphasis on sisters being adults, accepting freedom and responsibility for their actions, developing their own persons, being involved in different apostolates, taking recreational breaks with friends when needed are just good common sense — something that did not always prevail in pre–Vatican II days.

All of this is very familiar to those of us who lived through it thirty or more years ago and had to discover by trial and error what apostolic religious life was all about — a process that is never ending. The very Sisters of Loretto whose 1964 chapter launched them into the vanguard of renewal, were on the eve of the chapter (like many other communities) still publicly acknowledging trivial, childish faults, kissing the chapel or dining room floor in reparation, and at times as penance eating their breakfast kneeling in silence before going out to their daily work as college presidents, school principals, or highly competent teachers. Think of the giant step demanded of religious women coming from this environment to become auditors at a world council, to be expected to face the press and cameras and express their critical appraisal of conciliar action! Tobin was ahead of the game in the U.S. Small wonder that all the auditors I met singled her out as being friendly, outspoken, and a prime mover for change, when many of the other sisters there were still timid and retiring in accord with their training for the cloister.

Making personal decisions was out of the question in the olden days, as blind obedience to superiors and a written rule were idealized as the highest form of perfection, and consultation was generally unheard of. Many sisters were warped for life and never attained maturity.

Religious communities operated from the same dualistic philosophy that pervaded the church and equated sanctity with the grim asceticism of denial and condemnation of natural pleasure, especially in the area of sexuality. Entering the convent was "leaving the world," and one can only wonder what ever happened to the creation that God delighted in as "very good." Vatican II's attempt to read "the signs of the times" in a more favorable light also influenced the direction of renewal in religious life. Tobin cited changes in the novice's profession ceremony. "Some of the ceremonies have been funereal rather than joyful. . . . A novice might once have had to say something like this: 'I am accepting this world-despised, somber habit.' "[30] The reception and profession ceremonies in my own community included the text "Elegi abiecta esse in domo Domini" (I have chosen to be abject in the house of the Lord). Not exactly the theology of human dignity advocated by the council!

When a superior general like Tobin was behind the changes and implementing conciliar renewal, most of the community was willing to move forward. However, when the community was ready to move, and leadership was not, problems resulted. This was the case with Sabine de Valon.

I was unable to meet Valon, who is seriously ill and residing in Lyons, but Sr. Maribeth Tobin, R.S.C.J., who was assistant general from December 1964 to December 1970, had a keen memory for details of the personalities and circumstances. She provided useful information that was graciously communicated to me by Maureen Aggeler.[31]

> It was a critical time for our congregation because of the changes, and a critical time for Sabine de Valon, as our superior general, especially....
>
> The reason she was at the Vatican Council was because she was president of all superiors general in Italy; she represented them. Very intelligent, fluent in Latin and Italian, she worked with members of the commission on *Perfectae Caritatis*. She went every day to the council sessions with her secretary general, Françoise de Lambilly, a very gifted woman who was also fluent in Latin.... The Vatican Council was communicated to the whole Society by means of the Society's 1964 General Council, which brought all the vicars to Rome. Through them and through letters, Mother de Valon indicated the changes desired by the church, particularly that cloister was lifted, the religious habit would be updated, and the class of coadjutrix sisters would be abolished. The theme of her "circular letters" to the whole Society, and probably of her talks whenever she gave them, was: "The church says...and we will be faithful to the church." But there is strong ambiguity present in her letters, where a change such as the removal of cloister is announced and at once qualified. She was in conflict about the changes because they meant a departure from a long tradition and a shift away from centralized government to provinces.

Throughout the Vatican Council, Mothers de Valon and de Lambilly talked with the motherhouse community every day about the proceedings. They were very enthusiastic about it and happy to be present, aware of the privilege that was theirs. They were also intently involved, aware of the significance of this moment for the whole church, and keenly aware of its meaning for the Society of the Sacred Heart. A woman of action, Mother de Valon established a center in Rome for training "missionary volunteers" in response to the church's new thinking on missiology. For some years, a section of the motherhouse (118 Via Nomentana) was given to this project. In response to the desire of the church that congregations merge where feasible, she collaborated with the Sisters of the Sacred Heart in Egypt to test out the possibilities. By mutual agreement, they decided against it after a year's trial.

In March or April of 1965, Mother de Valon called a meeting of all the mistresses of novices to discuss implementation of Vatican II. It was at this time that she had a heart attack, and her health deteriorated from that time on.

In the fall of 1967, Mother de Valon called a special General Chapter in response to the church. For the first time there were representatives from throughout the Society, not just the vicars. For the first time there was parliamentary procedure, which allowed everyone equal voice and vote. At this session, the term of the superior general was discussed. Until then, a superior general was elected for life. Capitulants noted the ill health of Mother de Valon and talked of four-year terms and six-year terms, renewable once. During this difficult period, Paul Molinari, S.J., of SCRIS was helpful to many, including Mother de Valon, in sorting out the desire of the church, as expressed at Vatican II, and the particular circumstances. Eventually, the Cardinal at SCRIS [Antoniutti] came to the Chapter to receive Mother de Valon's resignation "in the name of the church." She left for Egypt within twenty-four hours and returned to Rome some years later, when she took up residence at the Trinità.

Irish Snapshots: The Quality of Mercy *Is* Strained

Other communities could duplicate, perhaps with less drama, at least segments of this story in regard to personalities, attitudes, fears, ambiguities, hopes, frustrations, and actual achievements. Because my own community was diocesan and independent of the five other Mercy motherhouses in the same diocese in Ireland, in keeping with Catherine McAuley's original idea of small, independent houses that maintained the family spirit, we had no central government to initiate changes. The impetus for renewal came instead from the bishop of Ardagh and Clonmacnoise, Cahal B. Daly, then an intelligent progressive thinker, who organized lecture series in theology for the sisters in the diocese, prodded the superiors into changes in the Rule and Constitutions, and began a movement that eventually backed us into a diocesan union under the direction of one of the most hated and loved men in Ireland, Redemptorist Freddy Jones. I think we were number nineteen on his list of dioceses that followed his lockstep procedure, without much change of heart or minds.

An incident still vividly etched on my memory from the late 1960s is that of a visit — my first — to a neighboring Mercy convent. It took place in summer while I was home on vacation. Our newly elected superior was attending a meeting with the bishop and the other five Mercy superiors in the diocese — it was the early stages of union talk. Sister Alphonsus Brady asked me to model for the group a modified habit we were thinking of adopting in the United States. It was a princess line black dress with a white collar and came well below my knees. I also wore a black veil with white trim, and I think my hair was showing slightly. As I waited out the Big Powers' meeting, a very hospitable sister escorted me around and brought me to meet the community assembled on the front lawn for recreation. I knew nobody. As I approached, I could hear comments like, "Here comes the mannequin." As I was then practically taken apart with eyes and hands, someone told me, "That's no habit. It's a little girl's dress."

I then faced his lordship the bishop and the six mother superiors. No one said anything. Finally Cahal B., as we fondly called him, blinked his eyes, nervously adjusted his glasses, and said, "Thank you, sister. You may leave now." Then and there I decided that never again would I ask anyone about what I should wear. I went back to the U.S. and with approval our group in the U.S. made the switch over to a black suit, white blouse, and modified veil with hair showing. Our community in Ireland allowed us to adapt to different circumstances in the States. Change in Ireland followed within a year or two. Changes to ordinary street clothes came later, and I kept my promise to myself never to ask permission for that again.

At our last diocesan chapter of the Sisters of Mercy of the Diocese of Ardagh and Clonmacnoise in 1990, I told this story to demonstrate how people's minds change. I concluded by saying, "Now as I look around me more than twenty years later, I see a lot of people in 'little girls' dresses.'" Some resented being reminded of this historical event.

For another perspective on religious life in the "olden days" (called *sean aimsear* in Gaelic), I asked one of the oldest members in my original community, Sister Imelda Hennessy, who still had a keen sense of history and enjoyed writing with a flourish. "What I recall most," she said, "was the penitential lifestyle."

> Rising at 5:30 a.m. was a daunting start to our day. There was great emphasis on community prayer and community living. Manual work was an important aspect of our charges. The heavy brush was an honored agent of our activities. Then followed the Hoover, and now all this housework is done by paid help, which in itself is good because it creates a job for grateful staff. The "white veils" (novices) of this time had some important affairs to attend to on their Spiritual Year — notably the farmyard, which meant looking after the chickens and eggs.
>
> Before the days of electricity, the oil lamps had to be attended to before the community rose each morning, and woe to you if they went out for lack of oil! Visitation of the sick and lonely was a must, especially on Sundays. All in all, it was a great time of achievement in the missionary and educational fields. A colony left for America in 1960 [Imelda was one of the four originals who went]. Buildings were erected and extended for the Primary and Secondary schools at home. From a modest beginning the Secondary School has become an important educational center, catering for hundreds of teenage girls and boys. The school itself is the biggest job creation unit in the town, judging from the number of teachers' cars parked outside. It also provides jobs for caring staff.
>
> Silence was strictly observed and Feast Days provided a welcome permission to chatter. Now life is more free and easy. Gone

are the days of "small leaves" and permissions for various purposes. Poverty now is very liberal by comparison. Although Pope John Paul has appealed to us to appear as religious, many of us have ignored his wish. All the colors of the rainbow now appear in our apparel. The veil has become an anachronism. Many people have been disedified at this lack of respect for the pope's wishes. Some have said to me, "If nuns and priests do not heed what the Holy Father says, what can be expected from us?" To which I replied, "In times of crisis, it was the laity for the most part who saved the church." And on that hopeful note, I close my recollections of the *"sean aimsear."*[32]

Sisters Seeking Insertion into the Church:
Italy and Beyond

Baldinucci never considered her position of auditor a purely personal privilege. According to the mind of the pope who invited her, she too felt the need and duty to consult others who knew the situation of women religious in Italy, so that they could help her assume the responsibility of making known their problems to the council. On January 21, 1965, she met with Angelo Dell Acqua (sub-secretary of state) to seek clarification and direction about the role of the auditors. He clarified that the position of female auditors must be understood in a "passive sense," but they should contribute study and experience to the commission for amending the schema. As to soliciting input from other Italian superiors on the problems of religious life, Dell Acqua replied, "Do it right away. We need it before Easter. Deliver the document personally to me."[33]

Baldinucci scheduled two sisters' meetings — one in Milan (February 15–16, 1965) and the other in Rome (February 19–20). In preparation for the meetings, she distributed a questionnaire that dealt with the issues of renewal, adaptation, theological education, joyful service in religious life, integrated spirituality for mature religious, ongoing formation and education in collaboration with other congregations, the creation of an atmosphere of trust, and promotion of cooperation between religious and hierarchical authorities. These topics formed the basis for the meetings that were chaired by Paul Molinari, S.J., council expert. It became clear that the sisters wanted to remain faithful to the valid traditions of their institutes while adapting prayer life and the apostolate to the needs of the times. They were willing to cooperate with the diocesan apostolate where possible, and they needed specialized clergy who were willing to participate in their formation program and spiritual direction.

Armed with this information and national support, Baldinucci was then ready for the next stage of her consultation and dialogue with the parish priests, a meeting that she called for September 28, 1965, to explain to the eighty-four parish priests, deans of colleges, and chaplains of hospitals and religious houses who came from various dioceses the anxiety the sisters experienced in trying to live their religious lives in accordance with the council, while being overworked and not understood by priests.

While Baldinucci was talking to the priests in Italy, Guillemin was talking to the bishops in Paris. The questions, findings, and responses were remarkably similar. When the bishops returned to the council, one heard many of the similar recurring refrains: the importance of formation that avoids maternalism (excessive authority) and infantilism (passive renunciation of one's personality and responsibility, confused with obedience) and promotes the responsible freedom of mature adults. Those unfamiliar with the so-called "good old days" of women religious being silent, sweet, and smiling, seeking perfection in "blind obedience," may wonder why so much is made of the meetings recorded here. It is because *they were new and revolutionary*. It was unheard of for sisters to call meetings of priests and bishops, address them, and tell them what to expect from the sisters in the future. Where did the sisters learn to be so audacious? *At the council.* They saw the inductive method of consultation and dialogue in operation in their own auditors' meetings and in the top conciliar commissions in which they participated. First and foremost, they had the example of the pope, who invited experts and auditors, women as well as men, to tell what they experienced and thought. The women were fast learners, and they shared their Roman experience, convinced that this was the mind of the church and the way forward.

A Separate Identity

In addition to the tensions and misunderstandings that existed among women religious and laywomen, there was the greatly misunderstood phenomenon of the secular institutes, represented at the council by Alda Miceli. Establishing her identity, she explained:

> It was important that these institutes were represented because they were something new in the church, to have laypeople or Christians who were not part of a recognized religious community and who had a consecration as lay Christians in the world. Very few bishops at the time of the council knew about the secular institutes because they were a novelty then. Therefore, in the preparation for the council, they were simply put in with the religious congregations. That led the members of the secular institutes to submit a request to the council commissions to distinguish between the religious communities and the secular institutes as such by making specific mention of them. They wanted the Congregation for Religious to be also for secular institutes specifically as a distinct entity, and that was done, of course, after the council. The request was made not simply by the lay members of the secular institutes but also by forty-three bishops with whom they had spoken and who signed the request that was sent to the commission.[34]

Clearly, the secular institute members did not want to be seen as "religious" in the traditional sense, but as consecrated Christians in their specifically *secular* vocation and work, as French Paul Marie Cardinal Richaud explained to the council. Part of the tension and confusion became clear in discussing vocation shortages in religious communities. Speaking to the Italian mother general, Giovanni Colombo noted:

> Secular institutes are on the rise today. They are very useful because of the witness that only they can bring, but they are not a substitute for the religious communities, which are indispensable to the church. Without such communities, the church could not do what it does. They are a visible witness of celestial values. Secular institutes cannot give this *visible witness* because they are *secular* and therefore not distinguished from the world by wearing a specific habit, which maintains the semblance of difference.[35]

On the Pulse of the Church

On December 5, 1965, three days before the council ended, Baldinucci, in the name of the female religious auditors, sent a letter to Paul VI, thanking him for the privilege of including them among the conciliar auditors. It said:

> Now we know the church. We have felt its pulse, we know its problems, which are to be solved in the light of the gospel. We feel ourselves to be in the heart of the church. We know better now how to insert ourselves into the church in a way that is both docile and capable. We do not want to disappoint your hopes. What we had the grace to hear during the council will become a program for all of us at this important, delicate turning point, under the guidance of the Holy Spirit. At the base of our renewal will be the conciliar decrees. The theological foundation and methodology of our apostolate will come from the new enthusiasm engendered by the council, and will be our sure spring for love of neighbor, love of the cross, and the hope for future glory. Your humble and devoted daughters, *auditoras*.[36]

Two days later, the pope met with all the auditors. He repeated his satisfaction and gratitude for their collaboration and contribution to the actualization of the council, including the "discreet and efficient way they operated." He encouraged them to continue to work with increased conviction and dedication to the church of Christ, while assuring them of his encouragement and warm thanks.[37] He presented each auditor with a copy of the New Testament and commissioned them to go forth and bring the gospel and the council to the whole world.

Like the rest of the church, women religious discovered that they could never *leave the world* for a sacralized realm apart, no matter how high or thick their boundary walls might be. Their place was *in the world*. Habits and customs that led them to think otherwise were a delusion. To be of service to church and world, they needed to become most authentically themselves as persons and as congregations devoted to apostolic need. The shift from *nuns* (monastics) to *sisters* (Marie Augusta Neal's distinctions) had begun, and the road had to be found by walking it.

CHAPTER SIX

Bridges Replace Walls

$$=\!\!=\!\!\Diamond\!\!=\!\!=$$

No Emancipation in a Closed Circle

"Woman cannot achieve her emancipation in a closed circle." Thus spoke Pilar Bellosillo at a meeting of WUCWO in Brussels in May 1965. She was sharing a truth learned by experience as a conciliar auditor. Vatican II set in motion the machinery for multileveled conversations, conversions, and revolutions. "Dialogue" and "collaboration" were buzz words that emerged from the council with its many concentric circles opening out onto the world. From the women's perspective I have already highlighted three interrelated areas that demanded conversation, understanding, and collaboration: lay-religious, religious-religious in different congregations, and different rites. Another major area that proved to be particularly expansive was ecumenism, and women had their own specific, progressive exposure here, in addition to what the council already offered.

John XXIII opened Roman Catholic Church windows when, disregarding curial opposition, he was led by the Spirit and invited Protestant observers to the council. John was still theologically old-fashioned enough to think that a return to the Roman fold would ultimately result from this magnanimous ecumenical gesture, but apparently the Spirit had something else in mind.

The women auditors felt some kinship with the Protestants as they looked across the sanctuary at them, guests like themselves sitting in the best seats in the house. By comparison, however, the women were latecomers, as the Protestants took up residence from day one of the council. Capturing the comical side of it all, Tobin summed up the situation: "They observed; we audited; none of us spoke."[1] At a later date, however, some observers were allowed to speak; not so the women. It is scarcely surprising that no Protestant women were

198

among the invited guests, although Cynthia Wedel, then president
of the National Council of Churches in the United States, had every
right to be there.

Opening up the Catholic Church ghetto to ecumenism was a revolutionary gesture by any standards. Previously, the one true church
was equated with Roman Catholicism. Protestants belonged to the
soul of the church, but not its body. They were not seen as part of
the Mystical Body of Christ, as Pius XII had described the Catholic
Church. Catholic-Protestant relations were previously forbidden, especially in the area of church services, funerals, etc. So-called mixed
marriages, while discouraged, were tolerated, but they were not permitted the festivity of a church celebration or candles. They took
place in the sacristy or rectory. In a predominantly Catholic country, such as Ireland, shopping in Protestant stores or even going to
a Protestant shoe repairer was discouraged and viewed somewhat as
supporting the Protestant church. Attending Protestant universities,
such as Trinity College, Dublin, was seen as endangering one's faith,
even if one was studying physiotherapy, and written permission from
the archbishop was required.

Along came Vatican II, and the "heretics and infidels" are now invited as brothers (there were no sisters invited). The old pope opened
church windows too much, some said. His successor went even a step
further. He asked pardon of the Protestant observers for the Catholic
sins of the past! Now we are invited and encouraged to meet, talk,
and pray with Protestants and Orthodox. Catholics have something
to learn from them. *Unitatis Redintegratio* promoted this, made con-
cessions, and called the whole Catholic Church to reformation. It
too made mistakes in the past and must shoulder some of the blame
for division in the body of Christ. It must now become an *ecclesia
semper reformanda* (a church always in need of reform). No wonder that *Dignitatis Humanae* had a hard time winning the necessary
support and votes to get it passed. It meant religious freedom, not
just for Catholic minorities in predominantly Protestant countries,
but also for Protestant minorities in Catholic countries. Previously,
wrong had no rights. Now there was a reversal of age-old Catholic
teaching. This appeared to be shaking the rock of papal infallibility.
The conciliar women had to contend with all this disorientation and
reorientation as well as everything else in the strange Roman experience. And the Roman clergy were further discombobulated by the
presence of women.

Apparently, not even the wives of the observers were recognized or permitted to be in view at first. According to Margaret Pawley, wife of Anglican observer Canon Bernard Pawley and the archbishop of Canterbury's first representative in Rome, "a sound test of the progress of ecumenism in those years [was]: the progress of the clergy wives."[2] They moved from being totally absent to being welcomed as participants in the conciliar celebrations. Presumably, the Roman Catholic women auditors' presence may have helped create this more inclusive climate by the final session.

Correctly, Catherine McCarthy explained, "The observers' wives really had no connection to the council. Somewhere I heard of a little reception for them and the female auditors, but nothing of depth.[3] I think they were few and far between. They were there only as 'wives of observers,' whereas we were there *in our own right* as invited auditors and staying right with the whole thing." Some of the wives remarked that the Catholic women seemed to know a lot more about their church and its goings on at the council than they did, so ecumenically, the auditors and wives were mismatched. The conciliar women missed the comparable exchange of ideas that was possible between their male counterparts and the male Protestant observers. An attempt was made to remedy this, as I will explain later.

The fact that women auditors perceived all conciliar sessions and activities of interest to them is borne out in their references to the overall themes, not just the few that mention women specifically. This is also true of the ground broken in terms of ecumenism. All those to whom I spoke noted the significance of ecumenism in their own experience and the role the Taizé community in Rome played in it under Max Thurian and Brother Roger's leadership.

A New Discovery

For Bellosillo, coming from Catholic Spain, ecumenism was both a discovery and an experience. "The discovery was blinding as I let myself be led by a double movement — forward and in depth," she explained.

> One of the deepest impressions made on me was when Paul VI asked pardon of the separated brothers (there were no sisters present at the time) for Rome's share in the blame for the separation. Presumably, up to this time it was all the fault of the

others, and Rome was the one true church to which all must return. Recognizing the sinful elements in the pilgrim church was
new, and so was the idea that the church was in need of continual reform and renewal. At Vatican II a new road to unity was
being discovered, one that can no longer be achieved by having
all the separated churches return to the Roman fold from which
they strayed in the sixteenth century and since. You can't achieve
unity by making the separated churches go back to where they
were before the split. The new day is one of communion. Rome
has neither an exclusive corner on the truth nor on the path to
salvation. A new road must be made jointly as all are converted
anew to Christ and his spirit.[4]

Bellosillo continued with enthusiasm, relating that a major factor in reaching this discovery was the person of John XXIII. The
spirit of unity was already present in his approach right from the
beginning of his pontificate and the first publicity about the council. Already in 1960, John created the Secretariat for Unity, which
was later raised to the level of a conciliar commission and headed
by Agostino Cardinal Bea. By all accounts, Bea was an extraordinary person, who shared the pope's vision of unity and knew how to
empower his working team. He capitalized fully on the Protestant
observers' presence, having them study the various conciliar texts
from the perspective of a blockage to unity and what would promote unity in every possible way. The result was an enrichment not
easily assessed, in terms of biblical sources, which helped the inter-
nal coherence of conciliar doctrine. With her knowledge of church
history, Bellosillo could appreciate the significance of this new ecumenical dialogue and how Vatican II was the first council since
Lyons and Florence that undertook the reconstruction of unity as
an established end of the council. "The shift in attitudes and understanding was remarkable, and it was experienced in action as well
as in theory. The road to unity was new. It was not a question
of having them return to Rome. No, the way was that of communion. *We all must go this new road together. Everyone must go
it,*" she said. The obvious but difficult concept to realize was that
the Reformation took place in the sixteenth century. The reformers
who left the church of Rome three hundred years ago are no longer
around, and contemporary Protestants, for the most part, never left
anything.

Ecumenism was a new discovery. I always paid great attention to what was new. I remember spending sleepless nights when I tried to put some order into all that was coming at me from the Spirit. Sometimes it was a matter of establishing a new hierarchy of values. This made me forget about things that were outdated. Getting rid of the old was painful, but getting the new was very rewarding. The surprise of discovering the marvellous clarity and coherence of the work of God was indescribable. The light, delight, equilibrium, order, and peace were without doubt the fruits of possessing the truth. One perceived the light. All this reality which we lived remained and was enriched progressively. Ecumenism was such a marvel and one of the chapters of the council that impressed me most within the general renewal. This was what I already called a discovery because afterward the experience came.[5]

This remarkable testimony gave the lie to anyone so naive as to think the council women were merely passive decorations. Bellosillo continued:

The newness of ecumenism was possible because of the overall thrust of the council in going back to the sources or origins of the church, to recuperate and renew the church with a second Pentecost. John XXIII listened to the great biblical prophets who spoke about rebuilding the house which was in ruins, and he also heard the message in the prophets of the present. John hadn't the complete view of *aggiornamento* at first, but little by little he understood that the thing he had to do was to go to the sources, to get to that church that was born at Pentecost. It wasn't a question of making only partial reforms. Nothing could really be solved by looking piecemeal at specific problems, but the whole church had to be recuperated from its very foundations, since the council had to be a second Pentecost. Ecumenism was part of the new growth in the spirit that came from an honest review of the past. The history of decline in the church was recognized as well as the growth due to the commitment of those who dared to live the gospel message anew at specific junctures throughout the ages. We needed to reevangelize ourselves and others on the model of the catechumenate process, which is now taking place in Spain and many other countries. *That's the council.*[6]

Tobin took the conciliar ecumenical experience in stride because it was not completely new to her. "Even before the council, I had become interested in the ecumenical movement, so it was thrilling for me to see the church progressing on this front." Writing in 1980, she reflected,

> Although fifteen years later there is still much foot-dragging in this area, some hopeful steps were taken at Vatican II. The pope prayed publicly in a vesper service with the Protestant observers; and in view of the long years of separation, this was a welcome event. Bilateral dialogues between Protestant churches and the Catholic Church were set up, and not only have such commissions continued but they have quietly overcome much misunderstanding and have arrived at new agreements in the course of their progress. However, official leadership in both Catholic and Protestant churches has been very slow to implement these recommendations.[7]

Switching back in time, she said,

> It is hard to remember now that, for the first time, communities of Protestant Christians were acknowledged as "churches" by Vatican II. Many of the old barriers indeed had fallen. The establishment of special relationships with Jews was inaugurated, and structures were recommended for that purpose. Attention was called to Paul's statement in Romans, "the irrevocable call of God to the Jewish people." There was insistence that all texts be purged of any anti-Semitic tones and that dialogue with Jews be continued.[8]

She cited the text from *Nostra Aetate* that deplored hatred and persecution of Jews and added, "This deploring, of course, will not suffice unless action is taken. The eradication of anti-Semitism necessary will be a continuing task, so deep-seated are its seeds in Christian history."[9]

Going back to the conciliar experience, Tobin relived the exciting, euphoric days.

> It was a delightful experience to become acquainted with the many outstanding Protestant leaders who were present at Vatican II, especially those from the United States. Methodist Albert Outler, Douglas Horton of the United Church of Christ, and

Presbyterian Robert McAfee Brown were among those I enjoyed meeting. I did not suspect at that time how profoundly some of us would share activities in coming years.[10]

Brown may be surprised to find that his poetic talent, manifested during the council, has been preserved. It demonstrated the lighter side of very serious discussions, insights, and exchanges, as well as the depth of trust engendered through the ecumenical exchange. Cleverly, it also captures the drift of the council. And so we read, "To a Kentucky Spring Chicken (with apologies to Ogden Nash)," by Robert McAfee Brown:

> One of the significant things these days about having been head of the Sisters of Loretto
> Is how symbolically appropriate it is that the word almost rhymes with *aggiornametto*.
> For it is no fluke
> That when we think of *aggiornamento* (and Lorento), we think immediately of Sister Mary Luke.
> When she and Sister Ann Richard invaded St. Peter's as almost the only women in a Council of over 2000 bishops (male), the authorities thought that they could cope with a 2000 to 2 ratio, only there was in their calculation this slight catch:
> That it turned out to be an even match.
> And if the Curia thought that Sister Mary Luke would remain obscurely docile,
> It just shows how little they understood her conception of what it means to be an apostle.
> For she has known how to relate continuity and change
> In ways that cover the possibilities of reform, renewal, adaptability, worldly apostolate, contemplation, learning, draft board visitation, the education of bishops, and other things of the widest possible range.
> And when she is pressing the church about reforming guidelines
> She's not satisfied just to receive a slight concession on the height of the sisters' hemlines.
> The women who think it is *avant-garde* to be associated with Women's Liberation
> Should take Sister Mary Luke into consideration.
> For her accomplishments show this very important truth (no matter in what order you list 'em):

That if you work hard enough, pray long enough, size up your
  opposition, rally your supporters, and plan your tactics with
  sufficient care and divine help, you can still bring about
  change within the system.
With that kind of record behind her, she will surely (one day)
  find the heavenly host most anxious to meet her,
But with eternity available for Sister Mary Luke to rearrange
  the angelic structures and the celestial appointments, one can
  only whisper, "Be on your guard, St. Peter."

The Taizé Experience of Ecumenism

In addition to the general ecumenical experience that pervaded the
council, the women had their own specific story on the road to unity.
For most, it began at the council. Besides the enrichment contributed
to council documents, the observers provided the opportunity to
live ecumenism through stimulating contacts and dialogue. Here the
Brothers of Taizé became prominent. Their small community set up
in Rome during the council invited three or four guests to lunch at
their home almost every day. Here again Bellosillo's testimony was
enlightening.

> These lunches also became part of our story because they con-
> tributed to letting us into a world of ecumenism which was far
> from us. With good reason, many considered this community a
> bridge that facilitated communication between both shores — the
> Catholic world and the Reformed. That way a deep friendship
> started to grow on the basis of prayer in common, reflection,
> and agape-shared meals.[11]

Alda Miceli elaborated on her encounter with Taizé, as she recalled how they invited the laywomen auditors and finally prevailed
on some of the sisters to come too:

> One thing that struck me forcibly on coming into the Taizé apart-
> ment was that almost a whole wall was taken up with a portrait
> of John XXIII. I kept looking at it, and finally Brother Roger
> said, "You must be wondering why we have that on our wall."
> He told me that the Catholic bishop of Taizé knew the Brothers
> were anxious to meet John XXIII, although they were "separated

brethren." John said he would be very happy to meet them, provided they didn't talk about theological questions. They came to John, and he received them as a father, but not for theological discussion. After that he invited them to the council and provided them with accommodation because otherwise they would not have been able to attend the council. So it's not surprising that they had a large portrait of John presiding over their meals. He put the roof over their heads.[12]

Wise old Pope John knew the transforming dynamic of shared meals. Conversations begun on the council floor continued in a more relaxed manner over lunch, and the walls of separation came tumbling down.

Weaving a New Fabric

Once the ecumenical conversations began seriously at the council, Catholics realized how much they could learn from Protestants, especially in the area of lay formation. "The council experience could not but include the ecumenical dimension," explained Rosemary Goldie. "From the fifties there had been contacts with the WCC on the part of COPECIAL and the ICO. It was possible, therefore, to hold a small and confidential meeting in January 1964 at Glion, Switzerland, concerning the laity." Its focus was theological and dealt in depth with "The Respective Roles of the Laity and the Specially Ordained Ministry within the People of God." With the help of the Secretariat for Christian Unity, a group from WCC met with a group called by COPECIAL. Among the participants were lay people, council fathers, and periti who were actually engaged in drafting the schema on the church, laity, the church in the modern world, and ecumenism. Bishop Johannes Willebrands, Bishop Emilio Guano, Charles Moeller, Fr. P. Hamer, and Rosemary Goldie were there, as well as Lucas Vischer, Nikos Nissiotis, the archpriest from Moscow, Vitaly Borovoi, and Madeleine Barot, who was in charge of the WCC's department for cooperation between women and men in church, family, and society. Goldie, from the inside, logically concluded, "So when in the course of the year the nomination of the auditors occurred, the idea emerged of an ecumenical reflection on the participation of women in the life of the church."

A follow-up informal meeting on "Formation of the Laity," took place without the cloud of secrecy September 7–10, 1965, at Villa Cagnola, Gazzada (Italy), headquarters of the Institute of Religious Studies of the Lombard Episcopate. Its aim was to exchange ideas and experiences as well as discover shared insights and theoretical and practical problems dealing with active participation of the laity. The consultation was jointly organized by COPECIAL and the department on the laity of the WCC. Goldie was one of the prime organizers, and she invited Tobin, among a total of forty participants from different countries and denominations. At least two other women were present, Janet Kalven and Inga-Brita Castren. Conciliar auditors Mieczyslaw de Habicht, Patrick Keegan, and Martin Work were present, as well as expert Maria Vendrik, who gave a presentation on "Methodology and Techniques."

What took place here unobtrusively was a bringing together of laity, women and men, plus women religious, as well as non-Catholics. In other words, it reflected several of the council ingredients on a very small scale, except that they were not just side by side and separate as in the aula, but were all thrown in together and actively involved in the group work of discussion, shared prayer, and socializing.

> Each day the whole group came together at the close of the morning's work, whether for the Mass concelebrated by Archbishop D'Souza with the Catholic priests present, or for a Protestant service of worship led by Rev. T. A. Adejunmobi, Baptist, general secretary of the Christian Council of Nigeria, and Rev. Dr. E. P. Nacpil, Methodist, professor at Union Theological Seminary in Manila, or again for a service of Orthodox prayers, presided over by Fr. Paul Verghese, Syrian Orthodox Church of India. Evening prayers were jointly prepared and led by Catholic and non-Catholic participants.[13]

Dr. Ian Fraser, Scottish participant, summed up the meeting:

> At Gazzada there was evidence of a growing community of thought on the life of the church in the world, and the place of the ordained within that life. From the time of the consultation in Glion, 18 months previously, the enlargement of common ground was clear. This was not because there was a movement of *us* to *where they stood*, or of *them* to *where we stood*. It

was because we were undertaking a fresh exploration together under the Holy Spirit. It is because, when the churches are serious about God's purposes, God seems to prepare new ground on which they may walk together.[14]

Inga-Brita Castren, of the Lutheran Church of Finland, an observer at the meeting for the World Young Women's Christian Association, also reported:

This Consultation brought together about 40 participants from all confessions, laity and clergy, men and women representing also all the continents. In spite of this very great variety the Consultation experienced not only an amazing degree of deep spiritual and human fellowship, but also a surprising degree of theological unity. In the discussions and working groups it would have been difficult to realise *who is who,* from which church they came, if we had not known; there were above all common concerns and problems, and to a great extent also a common biblical theology of renewal.[15]

The consultation unanimously adopted a resolution stating the priority of training the laity and recommending that it be done as far as possible by joint cooperation of Catholics, Orthodox, and Protestant churches, sharing insights, personnel, facilities, and other resources; and that this consensus should be communicated to their respective churches and organizations through the proper channels.[16]

When the women's meeting took place a month later with an overlap of some participants, previously formed contacts and bonds were renewed and deepened, so everyone was not starting all over again as strangers. It was this type of networking and interweaving, while adding on new members, that strengthened the conciliar web and sustained the work begun elsewhere. Goldie deserved much credit for this. When Tobin wrote her with her agreement to give a presentation on "The Different and Developing Roles of Nuns in the Church Today," she added a postscript pertinent both to Gazzada and Bracciano, "Our followers in the year 2000 should be grateful for your pioneer work" (July 26, 1965).

Walking toward Unity *Together*

The women auditors needed further opportunity for dialogue with ecumenical peers, so the Secretariat for Christian Unity and the World Council of Churches' Department on Cooperation between Men and Women in Church, Family, and Society jointly sponsored a meeting at Vicarello (Bracciano, Rome) from October 22 to 24, 1965 and then until October 29 in Rome, during the final session of the council. The meeting was jointly organized by Dr. Madeleine Barot, secretary of the WCC department, and Rosemary Goldie, then executive secretary of COPECIAL.

Since the beginning of the council in 1962, Catholic and Protestant women had been meeting and talking in many local communities. In the U.S. increasing cooperation took place at the national level between United Church Women and the National Council of Catholic Women, especially regarding the Anti-Poverty Program. The Grail and YWCA also initiated many ecumenical contacts.[17] What was significant and different about the Vicarello meeting was that it was the first time that these ecumenical women met to talk about their common concerns *as women* and *as Christians*. The Secretariat for Christian Unity and several Catholic offices were deluged with requests from all over the world for assistance in establishing ecumenical contacts. "A Joint Working Committee between the World Council of Churches and the Vatican had been established, but it was made up entirely of men and had an agenda so full that there was little possibility of giving attention to the concerns of women at any foreseeable time."[18] So something had to be done before the council ended. A combination of factors created the optimum moment for a meeting near Rome. The women auditors were there; both Protestant and Catholic men who were ecumenical leaders were at the council and could share their expertise with the women. Besides, it gave Protestant and Orthodox women an opportunity to sample the Vatican Council in operation.

Goldie and Barot drew up a preliminary "draft memorandum" in August 1965, working out the details of place, time, topics, participants. They decided on the main topic of conversation, "forms of life and service for women in our respective churches." The meeting should devote itself to two parallel considerations: (a) information about the present situation in various churches; and (b) reflections on woman's place in the life and ministry of the church.

They proposed that twelve to fifteen participants from both sides would be invited and a concerted effort should be made to get representation from women's religious orders of both sides, including deaconesses. The cautious tone and low-key approach signals how novel and daring the venture actually was, and the conveners did not want to kill its potential prematurely by spotlighting it before the women, the main beneficiaries, had an opportunity to profit from getting to know one another. It was wisely stipulated that "the meeting will have a strictly unofficial and informal character, with minimum publicity. It will not make any public statements without prior approval by the authorities of the R.C. Church and the WCC." So strictly were these prescriptions adhered to that most people have no idea that this first women's ecumenical meeting ever took place.

Practical points were clarified in advance. For example, "travel expenses will be the responsibility of the individual participants. Hospitality will be provided for the weekend by the Unity Secretariat." Cardinal Bea personally covered the remaining cost of the Bracciano meeting.

The meeting was to have two parts — first the women get together outside Rome. Then, having established friendly relations and become more informed of each other's churches and ministries, all move to the council in action in Rome, where special programs for the WCC visitors could be arranged by Goldie and Barot. They also envisioned holding a reception so that the visitors could meet all the "auditrices," but they did not propose that all the auditrices attend the two-day meeting in Bracciano.

The conveners proposed that the Catholic contribution could be brief presentations explaining the developing roles of nuns in the church today (Tobin), types of service for laywomen in WUCWO (Bellosillo), secular institutes, and women's role in the church in light of the council.

Due to Goldie and Barot's expert planning and organizing, the meeting took place on schedule. It brought together for the first time about thirty Protestant, Orthodox, Anglican, and Roman Catholic women from fourteen countries — Australia, Belgium, Cameroon, England, Finland, France, Germany, Greece, Holland, India, Italy, Spain, Switzerland, and the United States. Twelve were Protestant, one Orthodox, and fourteen Roman Catholic. They were sisters, deaconesses, theologians, leaders of lay organizations, and council auditors. Among them were two future presidents of the WCC —

American Dr. Cynthia Wedel and Swiss Dr. Marga Bührig. The auditors present were Goldie, Bellosillo, McCarthy, Tobin, and human rights' expert Maria Vendrik. Marie-Ange Besson, assistant secretary of COPECIAL acted as secretary and was assisted by Ann Richard, S.L., Tobin's "prudent companion" in Rome during the council. Rev. Paul Verghese, director of the Division of Ecumenical Action of the WCC, and Rev. Bernard Häring, council *peritus,* were present as observers.

First Women's International Ecumenical Meeting[19]

Barot and Goldie introduced the session with an explanation of how the meeting came about. Barot began. "Women have long been hoping for unity," she explained.

> The scandal of separated churches weighs heavily on their hearts. For a long time there has been study concerning the best use of the education and gifts of women, the problems of women today, and the Christian solution to these problems. When the women of the WCC heard that the Catholic women had been appointed as auditors at the Vatican Council, there was great enthusiasm and a desire to meet with these women auditors and other Catholic women to discuss the role of women with them.

From the Catholic side, Goldie explained:

> This meeting is part of the experience of the council. The ecumenical aspect is perhaps the newest aspect for most of us. The Secretariat for Promoting Christian Unity wanted to take advantage of ecumenical contacts for women and called upon the COPECIAL office to arrange for this meeting. In the theme of this meeting, "Roles of Women in the Church," we see a whole range of new forms of service opening up. This began to be felt in the Vatican Council in the discussion on the Church in the Modern World (not in the Constitution on the Church — a significant fact) and on the Lay Apostolate.

Barot noted that so many different kinds of groups were represented that they defied categorization, but they had tried to include various kinds of service. A whole day was spent telling the forms of service performed by women in and through various churches and organizations. Cynthia Wedel commented:

Although this was a well-informed group — people with wide personal contacts — it was amazing to see our surprise as we discovered over and over again in the course of that day how much we have in common. All of us share the concern for missions, social action in our communities, young people and better family life. All are seeking more vital forms of prayer and devotional life. All want better education and training for the laity. All have an increasing number of women studying theology. All feel a dangerous gap between the leadership of the church and the average lay person in the local congregation. All feel restive under the restrictions placed upon women by the church at a time when the secular world is rapidly removing such restrictions.[20]

Story-Telling with a Mildly Political Edge

Because I have never read any of this material in publications (I am working from the primary texts of minutes from the meeting), I believe it is important to let a wider audience in on the informative, enriching content of this landmark ecumenical women's exchange. Maria Meersman (assistant secretary, World Movement of Christian Workers) explained how the "Christian Workers" group is not a trade union or political party:

> The aim is to help one another to become better persons, better Christians, in and through their daily lives and daily work. The training is not done apart from the work. Training leads to conversion, not just in the religious sense, but all must learn to work to change the whole milieu and therefore build a better world and church — making a link between daily life and religion.

Mrs. André Chardin (Adult Catechumenate) worked in research to meet the needs of an unbelieving world and then the family apostolate. The family must be missionaries open to all — neighbors, friends, and professional contacts. Chardin observed that "the role of catechesis within the church for children is too often not adapted to children. It seems to be the role of the Christian family to question this kind of teaching. Within the family itself there must be a liturgical life worked out by the members."

Mrs. Athena Athanassiou (member of the World YWCA Executive Committee) explained how in the Greek Orthodox Church in her homeland there is no *diakonia* or organization with a special mandate because all men and women have the right to work for the church. The diaconate is carried out entirely by lay movements. She continued: "The position of women is very central in Greek Orthodoxy — they are the pillars keeping up the traditions. Many Orthodox women attend theology faculties at the Universities. Catechism is taught by women, and they conduct all the Sunday schools where Scripture is taught from first grade through all the classes." Since Greek Orthodox comprise 80 percent of the people in Greece, it is difficult to integrate the YWCA ecumenically.

Dr. Alberta Kücker (Central Committee of German Catholics) recounted that in Germany there are more than three hundred Catholic organizations nationally, consisting of teachers, nurses, professional women, and students. Its task is to inform, inspire, and promote a new understanding of the church today. They also train professional catechists, parish workers to help priests in social work, and laity to help in developing countries.

Frau Hildegard Leuze (president of Evangelische Frauenarbeit in Germany) noted that women's work in the Protestant churches in Germany began after World War I with the right to vote. After World War II women began to recognize their social responsibilities and took part in social work. Much of the welfare work done by women consists in caring for convalescent mothers both temporally and spiritually. Studies show that German professional women have better health than married women who are housewives — perhaps because professional women's rights are recognized, they have developed more interests, and therefore they lead more satisfying lives. Special schools have been opened to prepare women more adequately for their tasks as wives and mothers.

Dr. Cynthia Wedel (associate general secretary of the WCC in the United States) recalled how over a hundred years ago parish groups, mainly of housewives, came together in missionary societies to pray, collect money, etc. Now they have broadened their interests to the church's total mission, concerned especially with how women working outside the home or volunteering can be integrated more into the church. United Church Women includes all major Protestant and Orthodox groups in the U.S. They engage in social welfare work — race relations, international groups for children, community service. They promote the World Day of Prayer and engage in ecumenical dialogue with the NCCW.

Another American, Catherine McCarthy (president of NCCW and conciliar auditor) explained the NCCW as a federation of Catholic women's organizations representing about 95 percent of the dioceses in the U.S. They have seventeen program committees dealing with questions like international problems, inter-American affairs, and citizenship. They influenced recent changes in the immigration act. Catholic, Protestant, and Jewish women have worked together for many years. President Kennedy asked them to cooperate in the anti-poverty program and in improving the status of women.

Maria Vendrik (member of WUCWO's Bureau) said the National Catholic Action Center in Holland is not limited to women. It is a center of study and service concerned about the gap that exists between church leaders (clerical and lay) and the thinking and desires of the wider membership who do not feel at ease in the church.

Bellosillo outlined a basic understanding of WUCWO as a federation formed after World War I to give women a united voice in the problems of the day. Some organizations deal with evangelization, while others penetrate civilizations with Christian ideals. Most are nonpolitical, encouraging common reflection that leads to common action. An important concern is the promotion of women as women and as Christians. WUCWO has a democratic structure, formed of delegations representing all members. It aims at being at the service of each individual woman as well as each member organization.

Baroness Yvonne Bosch Van Drakestein (president of the English Grail) described secular institutes as "the latest shoot on the evergreen tree of the church," as Pius XII named them in his 1947 encyclical *Provida Mater Ecclesia*. Members of secular institutes lead a dedicated life committed fully to the apostolate. They have no religious rule or dress. They must be secular in every sense, living with and among people. An important aim is to form and provide specialists in all fields and professions who are imbued with an apostolic spirit.

Nicoletta Crosti (International Grail Movement) gave further insight into the Grail movement and its basic idea that women have a role to play in the history of salvation and the church. They are a community of love, service, and worship, mainly interested in education and formation of young people, helping them experience Christian values and striving to improve the field of catechetics.

Sister Brigitta (assistant general, C.S.M.V.), an Anglican sister, gave some historical background on the disbanding of religious orders in England during the Reformation and their revival during the Catholic Movement. Anglican sisters say the entire Divine Office daily, plus two hours of private prayer. Education is their chief work, but they also conduct homes for the mentally deficient, unmarried mothers, alcoholics, and drug addicts. They have men and women Associates and Oblates — who may be married and who observe a rule of life according to their circumstances.

Deaconess Gertrud Thoma (head deaconess, Stuttgart) enlightened the group about the two offices in the Lutheran Church — ministry of the Word and the diaconate. She explained the emphasis on the universal priesthood of the laity since Luther's time, but while all can transmit the Word of God, ordination provides order, the best way of doing things. Deaconesses are a church organization that cooperates with other ministries by nursing, by caring for the elderly, children, the mentally deficient, and prostitutes, and by teaching and working as parish helpers. There is a community of faith, life, and service among the deaconesses, and they are celibate.

Deaconess Elizabeth Souttar (head deaconess, diocese of London) demonstrated a denominational difference in the ministry of deaconess in the Church of England. There are two forms of service for women — lay worker and deaconess. Lay workers have to be recommended by the council, have two years' residence during which they study theology, do pastoral and social work, and receive a licence from the diocesan bishop, who determines their work and salary. They may take a higher degree in theology. When approved, they spend a month in spiritual preparation. They are then ordained by the laying on of hands, and they make a life promise to work for the church. They take an oath of obedience to the bishop. They are free to marry and keep money, but their work must be approved by the bishop. The ordained deaconess conducts services and preaches retreats. Ordinarily, they do not preach at Holy Communion service or administer the chalice, but permission to do so is sometimes given. A commission in the Church of England is studying the question of Holy Orders for women and the role of deaconesses.

Dr. Marga Bührig (co-director, Bolderhaus, Zurich) said that the Reformed Church in Switzerland is closely connected with the state. The Evangelical Lay Academy serves as a meeting place for people of the same professions or situations in life. Since 1963 the sacrament of orders has been open to women. The Zurich church ordained eleven women theologians, some of whom were married.

Facts here were in advance of the theory. The state universities opened their doors to women in theology. But since women could not take the church exams, the universities had to offer exams to them. Finally the church took the initiative and ordained women. However, there still remains a problem. Too often the ministry makes them enter into the old structures of the church, thereby losing something of their charismatic witness.

Mrs. Porter Brown (general secretary, Board of Missions of the Methodist Church) was the first woman to hold an executive position on the Methodist Church board. She related that it is often difficult to find qualified women for such positions. Women want to have a family as well as take their place in society. "The mother of a family will live longer without her family than with them. Our duty is to provide a place where mothers can continue their contact with the world because they need to have intelligent opinions and to shape the world by their voices." The Methodist Church requires at least one-third of the mission board to be women.

Inga-Brita Castren (consultant for Christian Education and Ecumenical Questions — World YWCA) belonged to the Lutheran Church of Finland and was an observer at the women's ecumenical meeting because of her position in World YWCA. It aims to serve the spiritual and human needs of girls and women so that they can form a worldwide fellowship. Ecumenism is a major concern in the quest for a community of prayer and joint social action.

Mary Luke Tobin spoke about changes taking place in religious communities of Roman Catholic sisters. Cynthia Wedel recalled that "one of these was presented visually when she [Mary Luke] and Sister Ann Richard appeared in their very attractive new habits, with short skirts, loose jackets and short headdresses. (They looked charming, but complained that they felt the cold very keenly!)"[21] Tobin cited Paul VI's complaint that "Sisters have been too marginal to the currents of thought in the church and in the world." Cardinal Suenens's book *The Nun in the World*, found an audience already waiting. The Sister Formation movement has played an important role in educating sisters; many sisters are highly trained in theology and in other fields and are therefore capable of entering into very serious study and discussion of religious life. Sisters are entering such new positions as government poverty programs and inner-city projects. They are more concerned about the pastoral needs of the church and working more closely with laypeople.

Blame Interpretation, Not the Bible

Bührig added a scholarly biblical and theological perspective to the overall experiential reports and testimonies of the other women. "There is no fixed biblical doctrine on the place of women in the church and in society," she said. Questions arose from specific situations, such as the Corinthian experience and women being quiet in church.

A dynamic understanding of the Bible is needed because the word is always addressed to someone in a situation. What is central to revelation is Jesus Christ, and we need to confront our own situation with his message and in dialogue with the knowledge and thinking of our time. Women's liberation is a late fruit of the gospel preaching, and secular society is asking the church why it opposes women's emancipation.

In Genesis, humans were created in God's image as man and woman, not neutral, so God is not male. In pagan religions the gods were male and female, a fact that is important for Christian anthropology. There is a complementarity that is not identity, but equality. Man and woman are created in the image of the Triune God, a community of fellowship and dialogue. Together man and woman receive the command to increase and multiply and dominate the earth. This has become separated in Christian thought; woman is thought of only as mother (as if she could do it alone), and man is thought of as reigning over creation. Both man and woman are taken together in the name Adam.

In the New Testament both man and woman are in the Body of Christ, and baptism is for both as full members of the People of God. Galatians 3:28 goes the furthest in the New Testament, stating that there is neither male nor female but that all are made one in Christ by reason of baptism.

Not to be married was considered a great misfortune in the Old Testament. But since both men and women are full members of the Body of Christ, both can choose marriage or celibacy for the Reign of God. The teaching in Galatians 3 lifted woman's status; before she had no choice. This whole question needs rethinking today, even in the secular world where celibates are needed for important positions. Two lines are indicated in the New Testament: one freeing woman for total service within the church; the other, restricting her.

In 1 Corinthians 11, woman is not told to stop prophesying in public, although she has to keep her head covered, since an uncovered head was a sign of prostitution. Paul mentions many women as co-workers. While this in itself does not prove anything, it suggests that in certain circumstances women were free to serve fully in charismatic ministries that had not order as we know it today.

In 1 Timothy 2:15, reflecting a more hierarchical structure, women were told not to speak in public. Here woman is sent home to be a mother — returned to her former place in society. Why? Perhaps women were too ecstatic and charismatic to fit into the more institutionalized church. The consequences of all this for today are that we must take seriously the questions asked by a changing world, paying attention to the findings of sociology, psychology, and anthropology concerning the equality of men and women. The question of equality needs to be looked at in the context of church renewal and the whole body of Christ concept where all contribute to the common good, even if it means forgoing some rights.

New Incarnations of Theological Principles

Discussion followed with responses from Bernard Häring and Paul Verghese. Häring saw Paul's restrictions in Corinthians as influenced by his own Hebraic background, wherein women were not invited to the synagogue. Nevertheless, Paul goes on to speak of the liberty of all God's children; this freedom is not to be used selfishly but for the common good. In Corinth when the Christian community wanted to be accepted socially, women unveiled or speaking in the assembly would have been at odds with their social oppression at the time. Häring emphasized the fundamental freedom and equality of women with men in Genesis. He noted how God is sometimes presented in Scripture as father and at other times as various images of woman. He recalled Jesus' companionship with women and how Mary Magdalene was entrusted with bringing the resurrection message to the apostles.

Häring concluded that theological principles must be incarnated in new ways. Woman's place in the church today is changing. A great privilege of woman is to serve — to be a deaconess. While priest-hood of women may not be practical now, other steps need to be taken first to make sure women are not mere auditors but active members of the commissions if they are ever to bring the message of the risen Christ to hard-headed theologians and bishops. The role of theological teacher is an important one for women.

From an Orthodox position Paul Verghese stated that the Bible is not a direct norm for sociological cultural standards today, but we can develop three theological categories that are biblically based: freedom, community, and loving, compassionate, suffering service.

Other points were made concerning the mutuality of love in mar-riage, and male dominance over females was seen as an aberration stemming from an unwillingness to become totally dependent on God. Note was made of some high positions held by outstanding women in the first three centuries, when widows were fully ordained ministers to care for the poor and virgins were deaconesses.

Bührig got the last word with an exhortative comment that women should seek together for a new meaning of service because of the limitations it has traditionally meant for them.

Many Things in Common

The substantive discussions indicated the caliber of women who were at the council and the level of conversation they were interested in and capable of carrying on — a far cry from the light pleasantries of afternoon tea talk with observers' wives. Because the women's ecu-menical meeting included a wider range of women than the officially invited auditors, the purpose was to broaden the circle of dialogue, not only to Protestant and Orthodox women but also to involve a broader spectrum of Catholic women in the council doings and thus to spread its influence and momentum. The result was dynamic. Wedel recounted:

> The first outcome of our discussion, therefore was a deep feel-ing of oneness. Like the early Christians, we began to feel that "we had all things in common." Any suspicion of one another with which we may have come to the meeting evaporated in the understanding and mutual affection which quickly grew. A sec-ond result was a speedy process of learning from one another. As we identified our common problems, we all found new ideas and

learned of new materials which others had developed or tried. Reports were constantly being interrupted with, "Where can we get that?" or "Can we come and see how you do it?"[22]

From Bührig's presentation Wedel concluded:

"The present subordination of women in the church can be traced not to the biblical record, but to later interpretations of that record. She left us feeling that recent biblical scholarship may help to change some of the traditions which have gone un-questioned for many centuries. She pleaded, however, for real renewal and change in the church, rather than merely working for a higher status for women in the church as it now is.[23]

Many feminist scholars today agree that Peter's barque needs to be overhauled from stem to stern. To use a post-Christian Mary Dalyism: "A woman's asking for equality in the church would be comparable to a black person's demanding equality in the Ku Klux Klan."[24]

Agenda for the Future

Besides the camaraderie and euphoria of this sisterly exchange across denominational lines, the participants proposed practical suggestions for future cooperation through study, service, and prayer concerning several questions about woman's self-perception as a person, wife, mother, worker; the world's perception of her; the church's view of her; and the Bible's view.

Second came the question about how woman can contribute most fully to the life and work of church and society, within religious life, secular institutes, and other organizations as single or married ac-tive Christians, tending to human needs and creating a climate where ecumenism is realizable.

These questions entailed the reassessment of the single woman's role and the value of celibacy; the married woman balancing work or voluntary service outside the home with family commitments; op-portunities for a woman with grown children; woman's potential for service within the church in policy-making and administration at every level; woman's contribution to the development of theology.

The Vicarello women drafted a statement requesting the Secre-tariat for Unity and the World Council of Churches, cosponsors of the meeting, to consider appropriate means for achieving ongoing follow-up. They suggested setting up a committee of six women who could easily attend meetings in Europe to promote ecumenical collaboration on joint projects responding to urgent needs, highlighting the Woman's World Day of Prayer and Church Unity Octave, as well as general secular involvement.[25]

A Roman Welcome for Protestant Women

After the meeting at Vicarello four days were passed in Rome. Briefings, attendance at the Public Session of the council on October 28th, and a series of lectures and receptions afforded further opportunities for mutual knowledge and understanding. During the week, the group was received by Cardinal Bea and Bishop Willebrands at the headquarters of the Secretariat for Promoting Christian Unity.[26]

Wedel rounded out the story.

Father Thomas Stransky of the Secretariat staff and the Rev. Lukas Vischer of the World Council of Churches briefed the women on current activities of the council. Father McManus of Catholic University gave a helpful explanation of liturgical change and renewal. The group were guests of the Ladies of Bethany at a most interesting ecumenical center called Foyer Unitas, and of the Taizé Community at an apartment which they maintained in Rome during the sessions of the council.

The climax of the week was attendance on October 28 at a great public session of the council at which Pope Paul promulgated five decrees. This was done in the setting of a mass concelebrated by the pope and a group of cardinals from all parts of the world. The glory of St. Peter's, the color and music, the hush of an enormous congregation, the solemnity of the mass and the simple decisiveness of the pope's statements combined to create a feeling of having been in the midst of a great moment in the history of the church and of the world.[27]

The five decrees promulgated were *Christus Dominus, Perfectae Caritatis, Optatum Totius, Gravissimum Educationis,* and *Nostra Aetate.* Another enthusiastic description came from Deaconess Elizabeth Souttar, "delighting in the multicolored pomp and ceremony of the celebration, a little bit preconciliar perhaps," added Goldie. Souttar wrote:

> I wish I could convey the impression of brilliant color and movement — the glittering chandeliers, more than 2000 bishops in white miters, Cardinals in scarlet, Swiss guards with halberds, officials in black velvet with white ruffs and gold chains, the diplomatic corps in evening dress and orders, the Knights of Malta, and at last the pope himself, walking slowly in to the singing of the choir. . . . The pope came in passing close to us and giving us his blessing. I believe that no one of us will ever forget the feeling of love and of unity which we experienced at that moment of communion when together we knelt, Roman Catholics, Anglicans, and Protestants, in an authentic friendship of sharing, although unfortunately not yet full sharing, within and outside the aula.[28]

Once the women auditors and now the Protestant women observers appeared in St. Peter's, it became easier for others to be admitted also for a limited time. Douglas Horton told how Bishop Ernest Primeau of New Hampshire and Cardinal Ottaviani (of all people!) had asked Mildred Horton if she had ever attended a conciliar business session. She had not. Primeau sent his *peritus* and their friend Msgr. Paradis to the office of the secretary general and got Mildred an application blank, and she obtained an entrance pass for November 14–19. Horton commented on it as "the earliest date in history (as far as I know) for admission of any Protestant woman to the council."[29] Paradis "had to face a veritable inquisition for such a precedent! . . . It was a red-letter day for Mildred," as Mary Luke Tobin took her to the auditors' tribune and introduced her to its other occupants. Horton commented, "Let no one say that *aggiornamento* has not hit this council."[30]

Wedel further testified. "Those of us who were Protestants came home from the week in Rome with new appreciation for the Roman Catholic Church, a vivid sense of the Holy Spirit at work among us and a determination to find ever more constructive ways in which women may contribute to the renewal and unity of Christ's Body, the church."[31] According to Bellosillo, Barot and Bührig remained on in Rome for the remainder of the session and were able to gain further insight into the conciliar workings from the inside.

Women Met and Talked

Of major significance were the bonds of friendship formed during this first formal international gathering of women that crossed denominational lines. For Bellosillo, the most important thing was not the topics discussed but the encounter itself, the fact that women from different denominations actually got together and talked. The effects of that first encounter were far-reaching. Age-old barriers were broken down, and a new age of progressive development emerged for women to do things together. "We discovered the extraordinary potential of this female collaboration. We held follow-up meetings, and in 1968 a mixed working group — an official organism between the Vatican and WCC, known as WELG, Women's Ecumenical Linkage Group — was appointed." It consisted of Bellosillo from the Roman Catholic Church and Bührig from WCC. It was a brand new experience.

Women of other denominations told the Catholics about their experience of married clergy and extensive lay involvement in the church's mission at home and abroad. It was new for Catholics to meet not just permanent deacons but women in such a category. At that time, laity were in the early stages of answering responses in church that previously were rushed through by altar boys. There were no lectors or distributors of communion, other than the clergy. Here were women in other churches talking about *ordination*. During the council St. Joan's Alliance raised such questions within the Roman church, and it was now public knowledge that Gertrud Heinzelmann had challenged Rome's discriminatory theology and practices against women and called for major changes, even before the council opened. These were considered fringe positions. The Vicarello contacts brought the issues closer to the center. Seeds were sown; leaven was planted; and new fires were lit.

The bonds created among the women have persisted throughout the years. In 1985 or 1986, the European Women's Forum invited the "mothers" of the Forum — Madeleine Barot, Pilar Bellosillo, Inga-Brita Castren, and Marga Bührig. Barot remarked, "They will soon have to start calling us the grandmothers of the Forum, since we are all getting on in years." The torch ignited at Vicarello needs to be handed on to a new generation of women who will continue to talk, share tears and laughter, dare to climb new walls, tear down barriers, build new bridges, and join new hands to help save the world

from destruction and the church from fossilization. I find this goal
well illustrated in a 1976 poster that reads: "We will meet all of us
women of every land; we will meet in the center; make a circle. We
will weave a world web to entangle the powers that bury our children."[32] Let the word go forth from Vicarello and Vatican II: *women
are on the move together.*

CHAPTER SEVEN

Bring the Council to the World

═══ ❖ ═══

The Church Is Proud to Have
Glorified and Liberated Woman

"A Council which proclaimed a few great truths without setting up the means to oversee their implementation after the council would be like a short spring not leading to a summer or to any harvest."[1] Thus spoke Léon-Josef Suenens, one of the main architects of Vatican II, in the conciliar plan he submitted to John XXIII in 1962. Giovanni Battista Montini (later Paul VI) contributed further to its overall structure, so as to highlight the millennial significance of this council of the church about the church and to ensure its lasting impact.

Part of the plan was that while the council was still in session, post-conciliar commissions would be announced to "de-congest the council," creating a sense of the seriousness of its intent to carry through on the *aggiornamento* just begun. The commissions could be attached to the various curial congregations, and "this would create a sort of breath of life blowing between the Centre and the periphery," giving diocesan bishops input and scope for pastoral implementation.[2] Suenens suggested that the great commission of Matthew 28:19–20: "Go...Make disciples...Baptize...," should constitute the backbone of the council's work, serving as a standard by which to examine the church's conscience as it looked inward to its own structures and outward in its mission to the world. Just as the council began with a message to all of humanity, it should end with a final solemn message to the world. Suenens suggested that it could be addressed first to the Orthodox, then the Protestants, next to all who believe in God, and finally to atheists, reassuring all of the pilgrim church's trusting belief in Christ's promise to be with us to the end of time.[3]

Montini specified various groups that constituted the mystery of the church and about which doctrine needed to be expressed: "bishops, priests, religious, laity, various forms of ecclesial life, different ages of life, young people, women, etc." In the context of church-world relations — ecumenism, civil society, learning, art, science, work, economy, other religions, the church's enemies — he suggested that specific messages be addressed, "messages in which the church's own principles would ring out strongly, and which with a certain prophetic spirit, would sound an appeal, in each sector of humanity to which they were addressed, to welcome in a new and sympathetic way the light and salvation of which the Catholic Church is the only source."[4]

By the council's end, Montini was Pope Paul VI, and he had the opportunity to implement his own earlier suggestion about closing messages. The connection is clear in that messages were addressed to "Rulers," "Men of Thought and Science," "Artists," "Women," "The Poor, Sick, and Suffering," "Workers," and "Youth." Three or four people representative of each category were brought forth to receive their specific message. The conciliar women would have preferred to have been included in each category, rather than be isolated and paraded as an additional, separate group. **Mary Luke Tobin** captured the scene.

> On the last day of the council, a great outdoor Mass was celebrated in front of St. Peter's. At its conclusion, part of the program involved the presentation of certificates of honor to distinguished persons in various categories. Four philosophers, for example, were so honored; they walked across the platform and received from the hands of the pope some special insignia of recognition. Then four literati, four musicians, and so on, were singled out for praise. Finally, four women [there were really only three] were walked across the stage. And the announcer proclaimed that "women should be honored for their contribution to the church."
>
> I turned to my nearest neighbor in the bleachers, Father Godfrey Diekmann, and said, "But women are not a *category* in the church. They should not be honored as women more than men should be honored as men. Men *and* women are the church, aren't they?" Father Godfrey looked at me and said, "You're right, Sister; you women need to help us see this."[5]

I agree with Tobin. The recurring theme of the conciliar women was that they were *laity* in the Roman Catholic Church, and everything that pertained to laity pertained equally to women and men. On the other hand, I can also see a point in which it was necessary to highlight visibly women's presence in the church in a new way that publicly stated the shift to which the council committed itself. Women were not treated equally as laity. Vatican II declared this wrong, and things would be different in the future. That was the purpose of women's record-making symbolic presence. It was one of the major conciliar shifts initiated and needing to be given a symbolic boost at the council's end, to ensure that lasting effects had to follow. It could not be a return to exclusive, sexist business as usual in the church or anywhere else. And so in the spirit of Matthew 28, women were commissioned to go forth and make a difference, telling what they had heard and seen and doing what they needed to do to change the face of the earth for the sake of God's reign.

León Cardinal Duval of Algiers, assisted by Julius Cardinal Doepfner of Munich and Raul Cardinal Silva of Santiago, read the following message, which was received by **Laura Segni**, wife of the former Italian president, **Luz-Marie Alvarez-Icaza**, and **Marie-Louise Monnet**:

> And now it is to you that we address ourselves, women of all states — girls, wives, mothers, and widows, to you also, consecrated virgins and women living alone — you constitute half of the immense human family. As you know, the church is proud to have glorified and liberated woman, and in the course of the centuries...to have brought into relief her basic equality with man. But the hour is coming, in fact has come, when the vocation of woman is being achieved in its fullness, the hour in which woman acquires in the world an influence, an effect, and a power never hitherto achieved. That is why, at this moment when the human race is undergoing so deep a transformation, women impregnated with the spirit of the gospel can do much to aid mankind [*sic*] in not falling.
>
> You women have always had as your lot the protection of the home, the love of beginnings, and an understanding of cradles. You are present in the mystery of a life beginning. You offer consolation in the departure of death. Our technology runs the risk of becoming inhuman. Reconcile men with life and above all, we

beseech you, watch carefully over the future of our race. Hold back the hand of man who, in a moment of folly, might attempt to destroy human civilization.

Wives, mothers of families, the first educators of the human race in the intimacy of the family circle, pass on to your sons and daughters the traditions of your fathers [sic] at the same time that you prepare them for an unsearchable future. Always remember that by her children a mother belongs to that future which perhaps she will not see.

And you, women living alone, realize what you can accomplish through your dedicated vocation....Especially you, consecrated virgins, in a world where egoism and the search for pleasure would become law, be the guardians of purity, unselfishness, and piety....

Lastly, women in trial, who stand upright at the foot of the cross like Mary, you who so often in history have given to men the strength to battle unto the very end and to give witness to the point of martyrdom, aid them now still once more to retain courage in their great undertakings....

Women, you who know how to make truth sweet, tender, and accessible, make it your task to bring the spirit of the council into institutions, schools, homes, and daily lives. Women of the entire universe, whether Christian or nonbelieving, you to whom life is entrusted at this grave moment in history, it is for you to save the peace of the world.[6]

A formidable agenda indeed! But the women took it to heart and were determined to make a difference. Paul VI asked the women to bring the world to the council. Now it was time to *bring the council to the world*. The message was a mixture of the idealism and romanticism the conciliar women tried to overcome, and the prophetic edge that emerged in the overall conciliar experience. Liberation they wanted, not glorification. The path ahead was not clear-cut, but the general direction was indicated. Women knew they would have to make the road by walking it, even without previous visible footprints.

Eileen Egan, the only woman quoted in the U.S. bishops' Peace Pastoral, evaluated the message to women as "forward-looking." She commented, "It was ironic that in his address to the women at the close of the council, Pope Paul VI told them it was up to them to save the peace of the world. Yet the discussion on peace, and the whole theology of the just war which has brought the world to the brink of war, is a male matter."[7] Egan and others of the peace movement hoped the council would ban nuclear weaponry, just as the Second Lateran Council banned the crossbow in 1139.[8]

Small and Inadequate but Strong in the Spirit

The timid, self-conscious women, feeling awkwardly out of place in an overwhelming episcopal gathering, and shrinking from the spotlight of cameras and reporters' interviews in the fall of 1964, resembled the disoriented, fearful apostles, hiding in the upper room after Jesus' death. However, like the twelve after the tongues of Pentecost, the women emerged on December 8, 1965, changed, strong, and convinced of their identity as church with a mission in the world. They experienced the new Pentecost of Vatican II, and they were given the tongues to tell others about it. Personally, they were changed. Their eyes were opened. They felt an obligation to spread the good news. Members of religious communities knew their specific privilege was intended for others not represented at the council, and they were forthcoming in sharing their treasures. The international networks geared up for post-conciliar implementation with a measure of euphoria and trepidation.

Ida Grillo was asked to speak to many Catholic Action groups and to discuss her experience. Being an auditor was a boost to her, and she saw it as timely that women were finally given recognition in the church. "My education was very traditional," she said. "The position of women during my earlier life was very different from what it is now, and the question of women's ordination never came up. I have always seen men as priests, so it's difficult to imagine a woman in that role." Her grandson, Pietro, said his father says it is right for women to become priests, so the discussion is taking place in this household, and a new generation will be more open to new developments.

Amalia di Montezemolo, war widow and a "woman of the home," was

> later often asked to share her experience as an "Uditrice" with interested groups of persons from all walks of life. She accepted such invitations willingly, preferring only to speak with small

groups rather than to large audiences. She spoke of the great emotion she felt in finding herself caught up in such a grandiose and exceptional event as an Ecumenical Council. She spoke of the deep impression and emotion of experiencing the living Body of Christ in that assembly, the strong presence of the Holy Spirit as the One who inspired that gathering of more than two thousand bishops from all over the world together with the pope. Among the places which asked her to share her experience was Venice, where the then patriarch, Archbishop Albino Luciani, later Pope John Paul I, asked her to speak to a large number of the committed laity of that local church. I remember her saying that because of her lack of any special theological preparation or particular ecclesial experience, she felt "small and inadequate" before their expectations.[9]

Books, Not Orders

With the burden of office, **Pilar Bellosillo** realized what was at stake:

> Once the council was over, it was difficult to know where to begin to implement it. That was the challenge all institutions faced, and little by little different ways emerged. Sometimes reforms were made too hastily, with unfortunate consequences. The WUCWO reflected deeply, and the Third World Congress of the Laity in 1967 was a foundational congress of renewal.[10]

Afterward, Bellosillo and Vendrik surveyed Catholic women throughout the world as to their actual situation. The survey had three parts — freedom of women (1) in the family, (2) in society, and (3) in the church. "The answers were passionate and surprising because they showed the maturing process of women. The years from the 40s to the 60s were very important (*muy importante!*) in terms of woman's maturation, becoming an adult, learning to think for herself, and judging what her life was all about." Bellosillo still remembered an answer that came from a woman in India. She said: "The priests think we women are stupid, so they give us orders. *We don't want to be given orders but books to inform ourselves.*" This marked WUCWO's president indelibly. "Three human groups reached their adult age at that time," said Bellosillo, "(1) people of color, (2) the proletariat, and (3) the world of women, which also cuts across the other two groups."

John XXIII recognized the awakening of feminist consciousness as a sign of the times, which was important for Christian believers and all of humanity. Signs are important because it is through them that God speaks to us. The church as a living community inhabited by the Spirit needs to pay attention to what's happening throughout the world. "God has not become dumb but continues to speak in our age," so through WUCWO Bellosillo experienced the communal dimension of discerning God's word and implementing conciliar teaching in conversation with life.

Given Pius XII's impetus, WUCWO worked for the promotion of women. Pius spoke to the women in Rome for the great world congresses. Bellosillo recalled that after World War II, "he told us we must be brave and accept the challenge of history which obliges us to go out of our homes into society, but to do that we have to form our own personality. Accept the challenge, go out, but be prepared."

The survey indicated that women were ripe for this. After the council, the main objective for WUCWO was the formation of women.

> We set two priorities — (1) education and (2) participation of women in society and in the church. The teaching of *Gaudium et Spes* is demanding in terms of human dignity with its consequent freedom and responsibility, so that people will be judged according to their conscience. Women must be educated for this responsibility. Education for them must be a process of liberation from everything that oppresses woman from within — ignorance, passivity, fear, and from the outside — society.[11]

A team under the direction of Marie Salas studied the new orientation toward education, especially Paulo Friere's approach to liberating education, and devised very simple but impressive methods. They had two objectives — (1) to work directly with women and (2) to work indirectly to change societal oppressive structures. Convinced of the truth she experienced over and over, Bellosillo stated, "Liberation begins *when a woman can define herself.*"

The conscientization process was used effectively in Latin America, Africa, Asia, and Europe, especially Spain.

It is a short process that doesn't stretch out into long courses —
that comes later — but since what a woman is made of is very
healthy, her consciousness is awakened, and I was astonished to
see how soon they became real leaders of their group. It was
a historical moment in Africa because they were just emerging
from colonialism, which was another sign of the times. Decol-
onization of the church was also afoot, from being basically
missionary with foreign priests from Europe to becoming an
African church with African priests. I could easily see what
great qualities human beings have. I worked a lot with African
women. The African Christian militants were marvellous, and
in a few years they readily assumed even political responsibilities. The Governor of Dar es Salaam said it made no difference
whether they were woman or man; as long as they were the best
one for the job, he would give it to them. African women represented WUCWO at UN meetings and took the floor to express
their views. In this stage, education for women implied the as-
pect of participation just as much in society as in the church.
At a Pan-African conference in Rome, the women committed
themselves to all aspects of development in their own countries,
including evangelization in the church.[12]

Once it had launched the educational program for liberation,
WUCWO opted to work for the promotion of women in the church,
picking up on the resolution adopted by the Third World Council of
the Laity. A special WUCWO commission studied Canon Law and
petitioned for a revision of the code that would eliminate discriminatory canons that denied women equal rights in the church. The 1983
revised code reflected some of their recommendations.

When the Congregation for the Doctrine of the Faith published
the declaration *Inter Insigniores* against the ordination of women in
1977, it did so without prior consultation of WUCWO, although the
congregation claimed to have consulted women. That was one of the
many wars Bellosillo encountered with Rome.

Private Initiative

"The council was very open. Soon afterward many things were
closed as progress halted or slowed down. This direction of openness
and closing was obvious to me in regard to three particular themes:

(1) women in the church, (2) ecumenism, and (3) private initiative in the church," said Bellosillo. Here she demonstrated how lay initiative and responsibility advocated in the council and its documents was threatened and curtailed soon after the council.

On January 6, 1967, Paul VI created two new organisms that had been called for at the council: (1) the Pontifical Council of the Laity, requested in *Apostolicam Actuositatem*, and (2) the Council for Justice and Peace, requested in *Gaudium et Spes*. They recognized areas where laity were already working, but because of that there was conflict between the Council of the Laity and the already existing International Catholic Organizations (ICO), created in 1953 as an umbrella for diverse lay groups, including WUCWO.[13]

Goldie, executive secretary of COPECIAL, and Mieczyslaw de Habicht, general secretary of the ICO, were named as the undersecretaries of the Council of the Laity, while the first secretary was a Belgian cardinal. That marked the end of the COPECIAL, and the ICO was threatened with a similar fate, with more drastic consequences.

The new Council of the Laity was composed almost totally of those responsible for the Catholic Internationals, and because they were laity they wanted to be an original organism within the curia, different from the other curial offices. When Paul VI reformed the curia, the Council of the Laity appeared to be equal to the others, "which is exactly what *we did not want*," explained Bellosillo. Since the Council of the Laity could fulfil the role of the ICO or at least reduce its activities, the ICO seemed to have no further reason for existing. However, the laity saw the organisms as essentially different. For them, the Council of the Laity, at the level of central government, was an organism of *official* character, and the ICO as an expression of free lay initiative was *private* in character. The laity wanted the conference and its autonomy respected and with it the identity and character of *private initiative* or *subsidiarity*. "We were convinced that this was the spirit of Vatican II. We feared excessive centralization and intervention of the official church, which was contrary to the spirit of the council," stated Bellosillo, then president of the ICO and a consultant for the Council of the Laity (as was Karol Wojtyla).

A tripartite structure was set up, consisting of the secretary of state, the president of the ICO, and the secretary and undersecretaries of the Council of the Laity. The life of the ICO was saved by a historic meeting in Fribourg in 1969, but only after a tough battle with dramatic episodes. Bellosillo relived the scene. "They say women are not tough, but at that moment they needed to be. At such critical moments, men don't dare do what women have to do in standing up for their rights."

If the ICO as an integrating organ of lay organizations was supplanted by a hierarchical copula, what would happen to lay autonomy and the distinctive lay competencies in the temporal sphere that the council recognized? The problem lay with the office of secretary of state, which was always jealous of lay freedom and autonomy, despite its value in linking the ICO to other organisms. "Those who made up the Council of the Laity were not the problem," said Bellosillo, *they were our own laity.*" As ICO president, Bellosillo defended the values at stake. "The grace of office and work of the Spirit gave me great strength and enabled me to confront church dignitaries. This confrontation took place in Fribourg. I said: 'I have great respect for those representatives of the Vatican, but I have the same respect for all the lay representatives of the world."

Finally, an equitable solution was found in a suggestion put forward by Jean Jacques Mastelin, secretary of the ICO conference, in a luncheon meeting. He suggested using the UN model in relation to non-governmental organizations. Let the ICO have the status of consultation in relation to the Council of the Laity, which would respect its nature as a non-governmental unofficial organization. Happily, this was accepted by the parties involved. "The most important outcome of all this was that it saved the life of the ICO and with it a measure of lay autonomy. Today such battles may seem distant, but what makes them significant is how soon there appeared in church government the *fear of liberty and autonomy* which the council recognized and conceded to the laity." The laity had to defend real values and nourish a healthy autonomy in the church, especially when the hierarchy tried to clamp down. Without living through the growing pains of the conciliar process, Bellosillo would have lacked that perspective and yardstick for measuring subsequent developments.

The Question of Freedom

The Declaration on Religious Freedom was surrounded by great emotion and dramatic moments among the bishops, who lived in very diverse situations of freedom and lack of it. If one can consider *Pacem in Terris* the Magna Carta of human rights in the magisterium of John XXIII, the Catholic Magna Carta for the universal church can be seen in the complete set of normative documents promulgated by Paul VI with the council, especially *Gaudium et Spes* and *Dignitatis Humanae*. Bellosillo took stock and counted three main areas of progress.

1. Religious Liberty

The principles of religious liberty have been recognized for years in the constitutions of states, but it has taken the church a long time to come up with a declaration that recognizes religious liberty as a human right, not just for Catholics, but for all people across the board. That's why *Dignitatis Humanae* was such a breakthrough. The right to religious freedom is prior to all judiciary recognition because it is a fundamental human right. In *Dignitatis Humanae* the validity of this right was confronted with the Bible and found to be consistent with it.

2. Autonomy of the Temporal Sphere

The council affirmed autonomy of the temporal reality in *Gaudium et Spes* so as to avoid the clericalism of intervening in scientific questions in the name of religion and morality without being informed of the realities at stake. Bellosillo worked on several commissions for *Gaudium et Spes,* specifically that on marriage and family, where the Galileo fiasco resurfaced, so she could speak confidently as an insider, voicing the predominant understanding.

A new attitude concerning moral matters appeared here. The church is the custodian of revelation, but it does not have elaborated answers to all problems, even moral ones. Sometimes experts need to be called in, according to the nature of the problem, e.g., medical experts. Also the contingent options of Christians, even those gospel-inspired, cannot pretend to express church doctrine in an obligatory manner, since other options are possible. A balanced approach demands more than prooftexting from a single gospel reference.[14]

3. Freedom in the Church

Dignitatis Humanae did not explicitly address the question of freedom within the church's own structures. However, the overall principles apply to the church's stance in the world. Bellosillo saw this as especially challenging to Spanish ears, due to the national situation of the Spanish church during Franco's dictatorship. "The Spanish bishops were affected by the declaration, not that they opposed it, but it was a whole new discovery for them."

The document pointed to two fundamental criteria for regulating relationships between the church and the political realm: (a) mutual independence, and (b) healthy collaboration. These criteria were energetically affirmed by the council in terms of the necessary freedom of the church in carrying out its mission (*GS* 13 and *DH*). "It has happened and could happen again that this freedom has been interfered with, even by the Catholic Church, in 'proselytizing by force' or bad law." In Spain church and state were so linked that the church could enforce its religious freedom by law. Hence the significance of the topic.

The document on religious liberty also had far-reaching consequences for eastern European countries. It was new for Bellosillo to hear about this as she had not worked with people from Russia, Poland, or other Russian satellite countries. From some of the women at a feminist forum in Finland, she learned how the Roman Catholic Church's attitude even toward Marxism had changed from condemning it forty years earlier to passing no such condemnation at Vatican II. "The situation of the church in communist countries is such that despite the tension with Marxism, they understand each other and have worked out a compromise, implying a certain conformity to Marxism." Bellosillo saw this as *muy importante* because it bears witness to the kind of compromise implied in mutual respect and coexistence.

> Religious women from Eastern Europe spoke well of the political situation and had no comments about persecution. Christians support Marxist governments in some ways. In Spain the church always supported those in power, such as Franco. In eastern countries, the church supports the leaders, so there's always some compromise.[15]

Ready for the Spirit

Bellosillo recognized the difficulty of implementing church teaching, especially when it stretched people, as did Vatican II. "It's one thing to write down questions and guidelines, but living its own teaching is something else. The council laid the foundations for the church to be in dialogue with the modern world. That means *the church must not do all the talking.* It must also *listen* to its conversation partner." Early post-conciliar developments evidenced a reneging on the decentralization modeled at the council. Bellosillo and other women experienced the retreat at the 1971 synod. They wanted more said about women, but their suggestions were rejected. Listening to the "experts of life" was new and rewarding at the council, but it no longer prevailed in 1971 as the hierarchical magisterium dominated again. Canadian George B. Cardinal Flahiff's speech delighted them because he said, "Let's not be unjust to the women who are waiting since the council for doors to open," but he was ignored too. The women wanted to follow the inductive method used in writing *Gaudium et Spes,* but that too had become passé by 1971. Five of the women present refused to sign the final report. An Argentinean woman opposed them, claiming, "We have to try to keep the men happy." The women wrote their own "minority report," which they finally published unedited.[16]

During the council and since, Bellosillo recognized the importance of laying solid foundations on which new values and reconstructions can be added. "The church can never be a closed system with all the answers prepackaged microwave style. It must always leave room for the Spirit to *slap one in the face* anew. The importance of the grassroots must be realized, and little by little [*poco a poco*] we must reweave together the communitarian material of the church through reevangelization and catechizing." She was emphatic about making minority views known today, especially those that were unquestionably the views that shaped Vatican II and its directions for the church of the future. My project on the council mothers fits into this vision.

There have been many steps in Bellosillo's journey and that of the other women who travel with her. There have been rich, comforting experiences and experiences that made them suffer a lot. Her motto is: "Dare to risk yourself. If you have to wait until everything is 100 percent clear before you act, you won't do anything." In 1989 she was working with Marie Salas on a book dealing with women in the church since Pius XII. This veteran council mother has boundless energy and enthusiasm, protesting, "I feel younger and younger with the Spirit, despite my grey hairs."

The Only Curial Woman

Rosemary Goldie confessed, "I have the dubious honor of having been the only curial woman for ten years — 1966–1976," and she proceeded to tell how that came about. "Before the council, there was not even one lay man, much less woman, in the curia, not even a typist. Two women from the Grail worked for Cardinal Willebrands, but their rank was 'typist by the hour.'" When COPECIAL became redundant with the establishment of the new Pontifical Council of the Laity, Goldie and de Habicht became the co-undersecretaries. Since the new council was part of the curia, that meant that Goldie was the first curial woman, just as de Habicht was the first curial layman. Two women from the Grail were then appointed to the staff. De Habicht was retired early, and a priest took over as secretary. Goldie wondered whether she would be kicked upstairs or out. She had been teaching one course on the laity in the pastoral division at the Lateran University. "Without any consultation, either with me or with the university, I was let go from the laity council and appointed full-time at the Lateran," she said.[17]

What was the Council *of* the Laity then became the Council *for* the Laity, with *no layperson,* woman or man, at any level of responsibility in the curia. Goldie hoped for forward movement, that a layperson would become secretary, but "the movement went backward, becoming *more curial* and *less lay.*" Goldie's upset was not her personal loss of an elevated position but disappointment. A layperson should be in charge of a lay council. She wrote Paul VI a note expressing her dissatisfaction, and she also talked to him for ten minutes at the end of a general audience. With a sense of frustration, she added,

> How can we get them to realize that they need the contribution of women so that they [men] can exercise authority as they should? It is not the juridical rules on the books but *how they are implemented* that makes them so oppressive. Things could change immensely if even what already exists were used with an open mind. The main problem is mentality and approach.[18]

Having said that, Goldie was reserved in her comments about the present direction of the Roman Catholic Church, and remembering the surprise element of Vatican II, she refused to speculate for the future. The 1987 synod on the laity was disappointing, but "we can't always dwell on the negative things of the present. Look at all that has changed. We need to be encouraged by that, and the pope and bishops need to be encouraged too." Goldie enumerated other changes for the better:

> The papacy has changed since John XXIII was carried into the Vatican in his *seda gestatoria* and treated like an oriental monarch with the "frappants" on either side, the Swiss guards, etc. Paul VI simplified all that, and there has never been another tiara since Paul's symbolic gesture of giving it to the poor of the world. Now a sisters' choir directed by a very competent sister musician often sings in the presence of the pope. This was unthinkable before the council. Women with uncovered heads now read in St. Peter's in the presence of the pope. There is still an obvious omission of women's presence at the paraliturgical service on Good Friday. In the past, only cardinals and bishops came up to venerate the cross. Then youth groups of girls and boys were added. Given the presence of women on Calvary, it seems an obvious place where women should figure prominently in the Good Friday service at least.[19]

In 1995, four women were permitted to help carry the cross on Good Friday. This gesture prompted cynical remarks that the pope finally gave public symbolic recognition to what his reign has meant for women.

Goldie does not favor women's ordination to the presbyterate and especially not to the episcopacy. She believes that diversity in ministry is better maintained by keeping an all-male priesthood and episcopacy — something I do not understand. She sees no theological reasons, only cultural ones, against their admission to diaconate. In fact, she believes this must come. Women need to be given *de jure* recognition in the church with a deliberative say in decision-making. Liturgical representation of women is needed, and the function of lector is not sufficient. She concedes that ordination to the priesthood may come, but not in her lifetime and ideally only after careful study. "I am definitely in favor of open discussion," she wrote.

> After the pope's "definitive" statement, with its unfortunate peremptory tone, even Ratzinger seemed to suggest that discussion was needed. It is the only way to go more deeply into the reasons, whether for or against; to give the "intelligibility" that

was always hoped for by Archbishop Bartoletti, president of our Study Commission on Women. And, if the Catholic/Anglican dialogue is to be continued — which it must be — this question also *must* be discussed.[20]

Goldie respected Bernard Häring as a conciliar *peritus*, and she was glad he spoke out again in 1989 on the problems of birth control that have never been adequately addressed. When the twentieth anniversary of *Humanae Vitae* was celebrated with a special congress in the fall of 1988, Goldie had difficulty translating the major address into English because it was so conservative. It reminded her of some of the dreadful positions set forth by Polish Erbert Bednorz and Italian Carlo Caffara at Vatican II. Based on Thomism and the defective biology of Aristotle that it incorporated, it viewed woman simply as an aid to man in marriage, there to fulfil his needs — sexual and otherwise — beyond which man was better without woman.

Goldie hopes to retire to her native Australia, where she can once again enjoy the sea, but she is still too busy writing a major work on the laity. She was an official Vatican delegate at the WCC's 1990 conference in Seoul, South Korea, on befriending the universe. She was also a Roman Catholic delegate at the last WCC meeting in Canberra in 1992. Women who find her opposition to the ordination of women hard to understand conclude that "Rosemary has been too long in Rome." Who knows what further metamorphosis is in store when she breathes the fresh Australian sea breezes once more?

No Paper Council

Alda Miceli saw the council as particularly timely in showing

how the church is deeply united in solidarity with the life of humankind and their story. It gave indications of how people should have a stronger, more active, responsible and constructive presence, not only with a view to eternal salvation, but out of concern for the whole social reality where women and men are working. The council committed us all to human cooperation in the fields of science, technology, and work generally. This was an inspiration which makes all our social commitment a service which we offer sincerely in truth and freedom for the elevation and liberation of humankind, with religious respect for the sacred dimension of their life and destiny.[21]

Like many of the other octogenarian council mothers, Miceli continues to live her commitment to her secular institute and its principles, which the council validated.

Gertrud Ehrle is dead, but the work to which she dedicated her life continues to shine forth in a new way under the leadership of younger women. It is still *Licht über dem Abgrund,* light over the abyss of life's challenges, especially for women who continue to struggle for their full rights in German society and church. Bishop Augustinus Frotz of Cologne recalled two of his conciliar interventions that were accepted so that specific mention was made of *women* with men in *Gaudium et Spes* and *Apostolicam Actuositatem.* He saw both as the fruit of his exchanges with Ehrle in Rome, and he acknowledged that it was her persistence that really got them accepted. Because of that, he felt obliged to be present at Gertrud Ehrle's funeral in Ravensburg to make sure that she was given the credit she deserved for her accomplishment. Frotz considered his experience as spiritual director to the German Women's League as enriching for him personally and in his pastoral ministry as bishop.[22] The lay-religious collaboration so dear to Ehrle's heart and demonstrated in her solidarity with **Juliana Thomas** must also continue in their successors because Thomas too has gone to her eternal reward.

The three youngest conciliar auditors, **Anne-Marie Roeloffzen**, **Gladys Parentelli**, and **Margarita Moyano**, are now in their sixties and involved in the ongoing implementation of the last council and preparing for the next in various ways. Roeloffzen gave me information on Rie Vendrik but not much on herself. Some day, I hope to discover **Hedwig Skoda**, dead or alive, just so the record may be complete.

When asked about where the church today stands in relation to the spirit of Vatican II, **Catherine McCarthy** replied,

> I think it's doing a wonderful job. We still have some of those old codgers — some of them Irish too — who stick to the old rules and regulations, but on the whole we're moving in the right direction. Women have more time today than they used to have, and there are more important things to do than playing bridge — which I don't like. I think it's the humanity of meeting people and discussing things that are important. There's a lot of that go-

ing on, including a good two-way swap between Protestants and
Catholics. We see that within our dialogue with the Lutherans
here in San Francisco.[23]

Margaret Mealey chimed in, "I think the adversity that we see just
motivates us even more."

On her return from the council, McCarthy found a receptive audience in the NCCW. She attributed a lot of that to Mealey, secretary
at the time.

> One invitation after another came in from dioceses, asking me to
> address groups, and this was a way of inspiring and educating
> the women throughout the country on what Vatican II promul-
> gated. The council [NCCW] suffered a little too as a result of
> Vatican II because frequently a parish thought they didn't need
> the women's organizations anymore, and they established parish
> councils instead. After a few years of that, they found they lacked
> the working group they needed. Gradually, the women's groups
> were reinstalled. It was a wrench for a while. Unless the women
> were strong enough to hold together, they were just merged into
> the parish council.[24]

With due appreciation for the organization that she served and
that offered her the unique opportunity to be a conciliar auditor,
McCarthy continued.

> I think the NCCW has always been avant-garde in their resolu-
> tions and thinking, and it's because of continual education and
> the programs we have. Like the Blessed Mother, we are there
> when we are needed. We have the resources, the departments,
> and the thinkers for the church at our fingertips, plus a regional
> and national network for anything we want to accomplish.

With obvious enthusiasm, both McCarthy and Mealey summed up
the council,

> We contend that *it was no paper council* but the roots of a real
> live awakening for everyone. People were interested in hearing
> about it. The most important message for women especially, but
> also for the laity in general was *involvement*. That takes care
> of everything. Be involved. Be part of everything with whatever
> faculties you have. Push on and up into the future.[25]

Like a Great Bird Opening Her Wings

As Vatican II was opening in 1962, **Marie-Louise Monnet** had no idea that she would in two years be called to participate officially as an auditor, but she already felt the need for all people to open their hearts in response to the council that could not fail to give more prominence to the laity by recognizing their worldly apostolate. Her own dream for further international extension of the apostolate in the independent social milieux was shaping up. While some of her co-workers were engaged on the Latin American front, she became an "itinerant" in Madagascar, responding to an invitation to attend centenary celebrations for the implantation of the Catholic faith on that island. Bringing Catholic Action to this young and vibrant church, with laity and clergy working together for the good of the whole church and each being missionary to the other: this was Monnet's dream being realized.

Returning to Rome, Monnet was anxious to report to John XXIII on what she had heard and seen. "After listening attentively to my report," she said, "the pope stood up, extended his arms, and said, 'I see your movement opening its wings, like a great bird, over the world.'"[26] John's prediction came true in the post-conciliar years, especially between 1966 and 1972, with the extension of the apostolate throughout Africa, Latin America, India, Canada, the United States, and Europe. Monnet was a team player, convinced of the need for "collective evangelization." She always aimed at linking MIAMSI to other meetings and congresses in process, such as bishops' synods and significant national and international celebratory occasions. She gave birth to a movement that was bigger than herself, and she made sure the teamwork was in place before she handed on the torch. She knew when the fledgling was ready to fly on its own, and she resigned from the presidency in 1972. Paul VI received her in private audience and asked her to stay on in Rome to help continue such necessary church work.[27]

Some of the main goals of MIAMSI can be seen in the requests the movement made of the Latin American bishops in 1972. They asked

that the specific place of the laity in the church be affirmed, safeguarding the link between life and faith; that they apply themselves to vitalizing their preoccupation with evangelizing people in the independent milieux whom the church too often judges as "incurable"; that they struggle against the passivity of Latin American women faced with male domination, which tends to marginalize them in the world and in the church.[28]

It would be incorrect to say that Monnet's vision was the result of her experience as a conciliar auditor. Rather, her nomination as an auditor was the church's official recognition of the work she had already done. Her lay apostolic work of evangelization was part of the grassroots fermentation that made the council possible, and it is no accident that some of the most helpful bishops in her early work, e.g., Achilles Liénart and Achille Glorieux, also surfaced as leaders at Vatican II. In turn, the council validated that work, giving it a necessary boost to open its wings and fly farther afield. Monnet's method for world apostolate was conceived at home in the family Cognac business. Her vocation was clarified at Lourdes in 1931. It led her to work with youth, then adults, the rich and middle class in particular, nationally, and finally internationally. Each movement had its own originality; its roots were in the church, and its work was always done in collaboration with the hierarchy. She concluded:

> while each person has her own vocation, the organizations have also a vocation that needs to be respected...I ardently emphasize it once again because I have too often seen confusion when that is forgotten. Let us remain faithful to our vocation, safeguard our originality, reflect its essential characteristics. They center around two poles: evangelization of a social milieu and the direction of the church. With this little baggage of simple convictions these movements were started and they must follow their course to the ends of the earth.[29]

When Monnet wrote her farewell letter to MIAMSI and her other friends in 1986, she was back in her native France, in poor health, and about to move into a home for the aged run by the Little Sisters of the Poor, where she could have proper medical and physical care, "but especially the spiritual and ecclesial ambience that is always at the heart of my life." She saw this move as a new step in the same evangelization process of her life — "the aged too are called to live their own mission fully in their milieu."[30] Passionately and with love, Monnet pursued her vocation to the end of her life in 1989. One can never underestimate the power either of the Spirit or of the Cognac spirits in the world!

Back to the Time of the Inquisition

"When we came back from the council," said **Luz-Marie Alvarez-Icaza,**

> we did not endear ourselves so much to the CFM as to the masses, making contact with the wider populace on social questions and Christian living as it applied to them. As part of that work, we published a magazine, *CENCOS*. One recent issue dealt with the Latin American Bishops Conference that took place in Santa Domingo in 1992. My husband went there as a newspaper reporter, and he was very critical of how Rome manipulated the meeting.

José Alvarez-Icaza, but not Luz-Marie, was a member of the post-conciliar commission on marriage and the family.[31] "It was a chauvinistic act," she said.

> My husband was elected to be a layperson involved as a consultant for the implementation. Twice a year, he and other laity — men and women — got together to discuss their experience in living out the council teaching. They sent their opinions to the pope, but sometimes the authorities didn't like it when lay opinions differed from those of the bishops. For example, during the tortures of many religious, laity, and non-Christians in Brazil, under the pretext of purging the nation of communism, it was a woman, Frances Alves, who was among the consultants in Rome. She denounced the military action and torture. Out of Alves's commission came the idea that they should make a public protest against the Brazilian government, and that it should be made to ask pardon and stop persecuting. But when Alves and the commission got home to their own countries, the laity found that different reports had been given there. Chile in particular made a protest to the Vatican. Then the Vatican prohibited the Christian protesters from publishing anything because the Brazilian government said it would consider any protest an unfriendly action from Rome. A future council must look at the mixing of the political and spiritual in the church. There should be some way to eliminate political interference from prophetic church action against evil.[32]

When asked for any further evidence of such meddling, Luz-Marie responded,

> Yes, for example, in Santo Domingo, on the pretext of enforcing the Vatican II documents, they are actually destroying the spirit of the work of John XXIII. There are detours in different parts of the world in implementing the documents. But like a child who has an accident and breaks dishes when she's beginning to walk, I believe these mistakes could be corrected, while preserving the *spirit of the council,* without changing things *fundamentally.* Now there is an authoritarian way of treating these matters that contradicts totally the spirit of the council. In Santa Domingo, the CELAM meeting was obviously controlled by the Vatican and the Roman curia. The spirit of the council was much wider and open. Now to go back to the strict marching along with everything controlled seems a contradiction to what the council wanted. Some restrictions might be necessary so as not to go out too much on a limb, but the limits are not always clearly marked. Now theologians are asked to swear to a tremendous commitment under oath. I feel that's going back to the time of the Inquisition.[33]

José supported his wife's position, adding,

> Until women are able to participate fully in the life of the church today, the church won't be able to solve either its own internal problems or those of the world. Women are separating themselves from the church because they feel underestimated and undervalued. They constitute the greater half of the world. We need equality, not domination.[34]

"And nothing is being done to help the single parents and unwed mothers," added Luz-Marie.

The youngest of the Icaza children, Emilio, got married recently in a beautiful setting out in the country. It was a very informal ceremony, with all kinds of symbols manifesting love and friendship. The priest who witnessed the marriage said only a few words and asked the couple to talk to each other about what they were representing. "Please tell us what you are thinking about," he said and sat down on the grass. All their non-Catholic friends were saying, "This is the kind of Mass we like. Where can we find this on a regular basis?" "Unfortunately," said José, "I don't know. I'm convinced that priesthood is in the depths."

Generally speaking, the Latin American women, who were younger than the other auditors, with the exception of Roeloffzen, had higher hopes and consequently deeper disappointment with the actual accomplishments of the council. They found their meager participation frustrating. While **Margarita Moyano** held that the council was *the* ecclesial event of this century and that it was a real *event,* not just documents, she refrained from replying to my letter for about six years because, as she said, "I do not like to recall an unpleasant experience, such as my participation as an auditor at the council was."[35] The main problem was that the council was not implemented. By comparison to her role at Vatican II, Moyano was a fully active participant as an expert on youth ministry in the Medellín Latin American Bishops Conference in 1968. It was a "revolutionary step of God," she said.[36] It embraced the notion of a servant church, open to dialogue, and the church of the poor that John XXIII had hoped for.

Moyano, now aged sixty-eight, is retired but still working in her parish in sacramental preparation of adults for baptism and confirmation. She has a steadfast hope that is more than optimism. "This hope is a confidence in the action of the Holy Spirit, which burst forth at Vatican Council II, flowed freely at Medellín, was the principal impetus at Puebla, and which is showing itself today in Argentina via very concrete signs... organizations of women,... basic ecclesial communities," etc.[37] Poor people are making their own voices heard, instead of having someone else speaking for them. That gives her hope that her dream for a new evangelization could really take root.

The People of God on the Move

Auditors like **Gladys Parentelli,** who were present only for the final session of the council, were at a disadvantage. For one thing, the others had bonded before they got there and were more likely to associate with those they knew. Moreover, reporters, who swarmed around the first conciliar mothers, thought they had exhausted all the possibilities for news items from the women at the third session and were less likely to look to the newcomers at the fourth session for extensive interviews, although each woman brought her own unique wealth of experience to the council and responded in her own way. Parentelli explained her great expectations and disappointment.

> Fundamentally, I hoped that Vatican II would orientate itself toward an opening to the world, that the church would open itself to the "signs of the times," that it would go along with the life of the more active and progressive Christians, that it would give a greater participation to the laity in all structures of the church, that woman would be considered a member with full rights in the church, that the hierarchy would be less authoritarian, that the church would have an organizational charter that was more democratic and less hierarchical. To the contrary, the current Roman curia is the most authoritarian, dogmatic, inhuman, and hard-hearted that the church has had in this century.[38]

She recognized the breakthrough Paul VI made in terms of starting something that would engage women more actively in the church, but "that was stymied, made inoperable, or betrayed by the Roman curia, and especially by Pope John Paul II."
From the perspective of the group she represented, she concluded:

> There was a clear letdown in the Catholic Rural Youth Organizations in the face of the results of Vatican II. They had hoped for more progressive decisions, especially in respect to the laity. Apart from this, for example, the pastor in my town in Uruguay hoped that Vatican II would decide that priests could marry. In general, people saw the decisions as far removed from anything that concerned their daily lives directly.[39]

She followed the basic lines of development on the Latin American continent — where liberation theology was born as the logical outcome of implementing Vatican II and its good news for the poor and oppressed, rooted in the gospel message of justice, especially through her participation on the Justice and Peace Commission. Her contemporary Credo gives insight into her present perspective as she continues to work for the cause of women, something that began with MIJARC and its concern for young people, farmers, and rural Catholics. She prays:

> I believe in God, our loving Mother, creator of heaven and earth, of all that is visible, which amazes me each day, and for all that is invisible, for example, music which gladdens my hours.

I believe in Jesus Christ, who became a person because a poor carpenter and a young Palestinian woman said yes; who was crucified, died, was buried, and is now seated at the left hand of his Mother, and who resurrects each day in the hearts of many just ones.

I believe in those who are persecuted, jailed, tortured, murdered, and disappeared, without our knowing where they are buried, and who cannot sit near to their mothers or brothers, [fathers or sisters] any longer.

I believe in all women creators of the world, the majority anonymous, because they participate in the divine. I believe in Sister Juana Inés de la Cruz, persecuted by the Inquisition; I believe in Clare of Assisi, who loved birds that suck nectar from aloe flowers; I believe in Teresa of Avila, founder of spirituality and women's communities; I believe in Joan of Arc, burned at the stake for having freed her people from the imperialistic invader.

I believe in the sanctity of the poor; I believe in base communities; I believe in the people of God on the move, people who pray and struggle for their liberation.

I believe in Oscar Arnulfo Romero, in Léonidas Proaño, in Albino Luciani, in John XXIII; I believe in the four women missionaries murdered on December 2, 1980, in El Salvador by a band of fascists, and because I believe in those who have given up their lives as a token of solidarity and complete love, I believe in all those who love, and I believe in myself because I am loved.

The Giant Leap from Nuns to Sisters

Sisters involved in renewal after the council insisted that the habit was only the external, and they were concerned with a much deeper kind of *aggiornamento*. Nevertheless, one should not underestimate the significance of the habit change. Such a visible symbol, equated with the sisters' very identity, became the lightning rod that often drew a barrage of verbal abuse on the pioneers of change. The tragedy of a whole congregation of IHM sisters wiped from canonical status in California under Cardinal McIntyre and denied the backing even of the Conference of Major Superiors of Women (now LCWR) by just one vote must surely now be counted among the martyrs' blood that led to widespread renewal. Cardinal Antoniutti "had told all U.S. communities of sisters that the IHM sisters had legislated changes that were 'deviations from the essence of religious life.'"[40] Anita Caspary, the community leader at the time, petitioned Paul VI to consider the group "a new form of religious life," but she got no response. In December 1969, "more than 300 sisters voted to become a noncanonical community." This "gave us the freedom to be self-determining and to make moral choices on the basis of conscience without leaning on the authority of others...the same struggle for feminist values that continues for women in all walks of life today, especially for women in the church," said Caspary. This pioneering group of women was finally recognized for their courage in a recent 1995 reconciliation service initiated by the LCWR.

While some laity welcomed the changes as breaking down unnecessary barriers between them and the sisters, others resented this *symbolic leveling.* Underlying the opposition was, I suspect, a basic insecurity, that the church and salvation were not rock based as they thought but rested on shifting sand. When you change, that forces me to change too in how I relate to you. Once the changing starts, where does it finish? Is everything up for grabs? Those of us who went through the habit change were concerned with the challenge of dressing appropriately and presenting a respectable hairdo on a modest budget, realizing slowly that styles had changed since we entered the convent as teenagers. We did not realize how much our modest changes impacted those around us. Soon the serviceable and affordable polyester pantsuit replaced the habit for many and became the sister's trademark of identification.

All religious communities had to visit the question of habit as part of the self-examination and renewal the council advocated. The preoccupation with inches and yards intensified for a time before the habit — which was contemporary when the orders were founded and had served to distinguish each specific order before the council — gave way to various generic styles that left the orders indistinguishable. This symbolized the move of the conciliar women to bring down the artificial barriers among congregations as well as between women religious and laywomen. Today, Elisabeth Schüssler Fiorenza challenges the language of division that distinguishes between *nun*-women (religious) and *lay*-women; she recognizes that all Roman Catholic women are lay, and all laywomen can be religious.

Jerome Maria Chimy was involved in the process of bringing renewal to her community with the distribution of a questionnaire for input and suggestions from the community at large, an exhortation to read the conciliar documents, especially *Perfectae Caritatis*, a reminder of the necessity of returning to the sources and the spirit of their founder, and an assurance that this was the spirit of the council. "Confidence and zeal should characterize this period which we are beginning — namely, the new spring of our Christian and religious life."[41] This inaugurated not only the personal renewal of this Catholic community of the Ukrainian rite, but it also led to the expansion of the sisters' work both in health care and education, even to the level of working with the bishops in the Canadian Catholic Conference. Claudia Feddish called and officiated at the special chapter for renewal in her community in 1969, and she completed her term of leadership in the community in 1971. Six years later, while getting off a bus in Rome, she was run over by a bus, which fractured both her feet, and she died from complications at the Gemelli Clinic on January 1, 1978.

Constantina Baldinucci, while leading the renewal process in Italy, also embarked on a tour of international travel, bringing the council message and encouragement to the Sisters of Maria Bambina on all continents. Her community continues to respond to the poor and needy, including AIDS victims. Cristina Estrada died in 1985, leaving her institute very little information on the council workings but her own greatest legacy of a saintly life, and the sisters expect she will some day be canonized. Marie de la Croix Khouzam still finds in the council documents a richness that is clearly marked with the light and the gifts of the Holy Spirit. Sabine de Valon remains seriously ill in Lyons. While the chapter on her last years as community leader is carefully researched and documented, it was not available to me. Valon's community went on to make the conciliar teaching its own, despite the initial trauma of its leader's hesitation and eventual resignation, which benefitted all concerned and made the path forward possible.

Marie-Henriette Ghanem continues to translate books and prepare programs for radio broadcasts of the Voice of Charity, part of the Lebanese radio network devoted to special religious and cultural programs. Ghanem saw the 1994 synod on religious life as an opportunity for serious self-examination and charting the course of a genuine renewal. Her personal reflection was that in the church this life will always have a place. New forms responding better to the needs of the times will arise. The old will have to adapt if they are to survive. I have great confidence in our own congregation. Since its origin, it has worked for the glory of God in different domains, teaching, catechesis, traveling missions, pastoral, care of the sick, etc. It continues in this way to modify its mode of action, especially in emphasizing a human formation that is profoundly spiritual, nourished by Scripture and the Eucharist. Hasn't every apostolic fruit its source in God?[42]

Outward from Rue du Bac

It was after Vatican II that most religious communities went about renewal and change in a systematic way. A look at **Suzanne Guillemin's** approach in 1967 demonstrated how she brought her conciliar experience to bear on the community by addressing its leaders. She noted the severe crisis religious life was undergoing as part of the wider church crisis, which is not uncommon following a council. The crisis was manifested in many ways, especially in the mass exodus of sisters from communities and priests from the active ministry, most frequently to embrace the married state. Guillemin focused on three main points that were central at the council and that had direct bearing on religious communities: the human being, the world, and the church. The shifting sands were obvious as she juxtaposed past and present thinking.

Now: The human being was generally promoted with emphasis on human rights, development of personality, personal involvement, and exaltation of human values. The world or society was recognized as impacting human development so it became a new focus for study, including society's evolution, increased social welfare, and organized governmental assistance. The church needed rethinking in itself and its mission because the state had taken over the education of its citizens, or individuals have assumed the responsibility of doing so. With the promotion of the lay apostolate and a pastoral organization of all that vibrates in the church, the older position and organization of the church required consideration anew.

Previously: The essence of religious obedience lay in the renunciation of the human being's rights and values. Religious communities and other charitable organizations attempted to help their fellow humans over against the world or society whose goods were renounced by the vow of poverty. Christian education was the church's responsibility, and religious communities were the instruments. The work of the apostolate was the prime responsibility of clergy and women religious.

What we see here is the bigger picture, as Guillemin presented it, and within which she addressed particular community questions. In modern parlance we might call it crisis management. She picked up on practical points and suggested guidelines that the local superiors could flesh out in their own circumstances, commencing with a central question.

> In regard to obedience, this may prove helpful to you in handling a young sister who complains to you that her Sister Servant does not understand her and that she cannot understand her Sister Servant. Tell her that her reaction is a perfectly *normal* one. Her Sister Servant received an entirely different understanding of the practice of obedience twenty or thirty years ago. The young sister's generation cannot see obedience practiced in exactly the same manner. Stress the point that each one must carry the weight of the *crisis of its century.* The young sister will have a better understanding of obedience and will have regained her peace and tranquillity so that she will then be ready to discuss her real problem, for which she may be responsible.
>
> Dialogues with young sisters must be increased. Do not dictate answers or solutions. Discuss some possibilities and give time to think about what was said. Young people do not want ready-made solutions. They want to come up with their own. *Bear with ambiguity.*[43]

This wise woman continued to share insights into her own manner of approaching people.

> I like to think of four virtues in particular that I consider the great ones needed today: lucidity, serenity, dialogue, and firmness.
>
> Lucidity is necessary for really *seeing* problems in their context. Serenity helps straighten things out in time of crisis.... Always try to find some point or aspect in which the other person is right. You will only then be ready to dialogue. Dialogue

entails knowing how to *listen* to our sisters. We must *hear* their opinions...not only through the ears but through the spirit, if we are to reach any kind of common ground of thought. Try to understand others;...change *your thinking* if others are right. Firmness comes last. If you place it first, all will be lost. Be *firm on essentials* or all religious life will decay.[44]

Poverty came under much discussion. In keeping with the conciliar directive that religious congregations should be faithful to the charism of their founder, the Daughters of Charity questioned whether they were sufficiently involved in the service of the sick poor. Quoting founder Vincent, Guillemin reminded the sisters of the new poor, "any others who through shame dare not make known their wants." She gave examples of new forms of poverty under experimentation in various countries. In France, five sisters would live in an apartment like the working class in their area; three were to serve the parish, visit, and teach catechism, while the other two would work as salaried nurses in a welfare hospital and pay all expenses from the two salaries received. "They will represent God in that hospital *provided* they are permitted to wear the Holy Habit," she said. "We are anxious to see if sisters can manage to infiltrate public institutions." A similar project was undertaken in Ecuador, where the sisters chose to live in a house in the poorest part of town, and the poor people rallied to help them. This type of small group living and budgeting was new in the 1960s and emerged as an attempt to respond to apostolic needs.

While searching for effective apostolic forms of religious life, Guillemin also emphasized the importance of community life and time for retreat and solitude. "Silence and recollection should never be recommended to the sisters as a means of mortification. By doing this, they become our aim, whereas union with God is our real aim. Silence and recollection may be mortification that serves as a means of becoming united with God."

While Guillemin gave concrete, practical guidelines to her community, she could also focus at length on the wider context when addressing many different audiences, whether they were bishops, a special gathering of religious congregations, international gatherings, groups of nurses and social workers, missionaries, etc. Certain recurring themes emerged. A healthy change of spirit was called for as sisters returned to the gospel message and paid attention to the working of the Holy Spirit in the interrelated areas of church, world, and institute. Static security based on the past was to give way to dynamic innovation. Spiritual isolationism must be laid aside as the Spirit was sought in everyday work — a shift from viewing the world as a place of perdition, necessitating separation of evangelization from humanization.[45]

Throughout her talks, Guillemin made connections to the new vision that emerged at the council, and she was totally committed to the new insight of religious as being the church so that their whole life was part of the whole missionary church. Vatican II spoke of the servant model of church, and sisters must be part of this with a converted mentality, steeped in authentic charity. "True, we have always been at the service of the church, but I venture to say that we have been servants in a superior position; but now we have to serve in a spirit of fraternity [*sic*]. This is the change of spirit we need." She interjected an example from real life. "Recently, a layman said, 'Why is it that the sisters always want to do something *for* us, but never *with us?*' In the future we shall have to regard everyone as our brother and sister, and urged on by the Holy Ghost, cooperate *with* them."[46]

Having picked up the historical sense of development acknowledged in the church at the council, Guillemin saw it at work also in religious communities, as in any living organism, so that true fidelity did not mean immobility, but dynamic response to changing situations. She listed several false convictions to be avoided, especially when clothed in the claims of fidelity to tradition:

1. Unity of spirit in a congregation can be maintained only by total uniformity.

2. The Holy Ghost manifests itself only to superiors. They possess the monopoly of the right inspirations.

3. The well-being of the Institute must be considered apart from that of the church.[47]

By way of contrast to these narrow forms of pseudo-fidelity, genuine renewal demanded putting on the mind of the council, inserting oneself into the local church, collaborating with laity and clergy and whatever network of public or private organisms that structure one's work in the service of humankind — in short, realizing that communities can no longer operate in a "closed circuit."[48]

Guillemin also recognized the changing role of women as a sign of the times and drew inferences for women religious.

> Connected with the societal emancipation of woman, the position of women religious is in a state of complete transformation. Formerly the task of a woman was confined to domestic duties and she was subject to paternal or marital authority; today she is culturally equal to man, can follow a profession and has equal civil rights. In the same way, for women religious also, the time has come to accept personal responsibilities and obligations. Her task will often extend beyond the narrow circle of her community and will have to be performed in cooperation with lay people.[49]

In response to social evolution, sisters will no longer be practicing charity toward the poor — from a position of superiority — but will be in their service, enabling them to procure their lawful rights. In this way they will avoid the accusation of siding with the rich. So Guillemin concluded, "This seems to be the most modern and best adapted form of poverty for our Congregations" — relinquishing power and prestige. Designations of superior and inferior will no longer be appropriate within communities, as the superior will be leader and director in dialogue and consultation with sisters, as a uniting link among them.[50]

Recognizing the new challenge of the lay apostolate and questions of self-identity it posed to the sisters, Guillemin did not see it as a threat. There was room for everybody, a unity in diversity. "A local church is imperfect unless it presents itself in its three different states: the priesthood, the laity, and the religious state. Each of them is necessary, and if in complete harmony with each other, they form the most beautiful harmony imaginable."[51] Side by side with the laity, the sisters perform the same tasks and care for the world "as a sign of God, as an appeal to sanctity, as a witness of Christian hope, as a living proclamation that God is enough for those who love Him" [sic]. One could critique this notion and its implications that laity are not also such signs. Guillemin seemed to be referring to the visibility of the religious habit and the specific questioning attention it attracted.

While recognizing the crisis in which religious life found itself in the late 1960s and the new challenges to be faced if it is to continue to be viable, Guillemin remained optimistic. She saw the Holy Spirit at work in the upheaval, leading congregations to greater authenticity and usefulness in the church. It would challenge them to produce constitutions that safeguard liberty, flexibility, and adaptability to specific needs and places. It would purify them of nonessentials and in a strange, providential way renew the church.

Several of the auditors mentioned the important task committed to Guillemin in the post-conciliar implementation. She was asked to be a consultant for SCRIS and the new Peace and Justice Council. She declined in order to give more time to her own community. Unfortunately, her premature death in 1968 deprived both the Daughters of Charity community and the wider church of her wisdom and input.

A New Kind of Madness

"It is difficult for the management of the company to understand how the vocation of the good sisters leads them to involvements such as these."[52] The company in question was Blue Diamond Coal Company. Apparently, it had a record of abuses in regard to pollution, environment, and health, safety, and labor regulations, which concerned groups in Appalachia tried to have rectified. The Sisters of Loretto (Tobin's community) purchased shares in the company's stock in order to have a say in bringing about the necessary changes. When the company refused to list the sisters as a shareholder, the community brought a lawsuit against it in 1979. The "good sisters" were not supposed to be involved in such political action. In 1974, the Loretto community developed an investment committee with the responsibility to "deliberately use our investment power as a tool for realizing social justice both through the correction of social injustice and the promotion of projects of positive social value. Where and when to invest will be determined by the potential of realizing these objectives as well as by the economic wisdom of the investment."[53]

How did **Mary Luke Tobin**, the conciliar auditor who was engaged in little wars about habits and hemlines with Antoniutti, head of SCRIS, make the giant leap to entanglement in the major social justice issues involving a coal company? Her own explanation is very logical and rooted in the return to biblical sources emphasized at the council. "Meditation on the liberative actions of Jesus, who manifested in his life that he valued persons and their well-being above every other consideration, convinced me of the necessity to involve myself with the struggles of oppressed peoples."[54] Ironically, her justice edge was also sharpened by contact with contemplative monk Thomas Merton, whose community at Gethsemani adjoins Tobin's in Nerinx, Kentucky. Merton was forbidden to write about inflammatory peace issues. He was appalled by the revelations of the Nazi death camps exposed in the long trial of Eichmann and especially by the fact that a psychiatrist pronounced Eichmann *sane*. Merton wrote, "And now it begins to dawn on us that it is precisely the *sane* ones who are most dangerous."[55] By way of contrast, he advocated the kind of "wise madness" religious communities stand for in advocating moral values.

This kind of madness was catching. It led Tobin's community to take the necessary risks involved in relinquishing control of their schools, where this seemed best, and in allowing the sisters to become adults, capable of making conscience decisions that led them into the challenging issues of peace and justice. Here Tobin found a number of threads from the council crisscrossing as she became involved in ecumenical work with Church Women United and peace missions that led her as far afield as Saigon on a fact-finding mission and to Europe, with Robert McAfee Brown, Rabbi Beerman, Harvey Cox, and others, seeking international support against the Vietnam war. Some of the theoretical conciliar discussions about lay-religious and ecumenical collaboration took on flesh, blood, and bones as she engaged in a peaceful protest of the Vietnam war by joining a group that continued to pray and sing in the Capitol rotunda in Washington, D.C., and she ended up sharing the indignity of a night in jail with two other people in cramped space, under a glaring light.[56]

By degrees and through her political involvements with people, Tobin became more convinced of the essential but overlooked connection between individual piety and social responsibility. "Never, I reflected, could faith be restricted to the narrow circle of personal piety alone."[57] She found herself becoming more deeply involved in the interrelated oppressions of the poor, especially in Third World countries, justice for women, and the arms race and nuclear threat. At the council, several of the auditors were touched by Paul VI's bringing the message of *Gaudium et Spes* to the United Nations even before it had been formalized into a document. Many times since, Tobin brought the message across the globe and to picket lines, finding her home, like Mother Jones, "wherever there is a fight against wrong." She reflected,

> I believe it is crucial for Christians to recover a sense of the values of Jesus — that all persons are equal. Compounding the difficulty of working for feminist goals is the unfortunate reality that many women are not even aware of their subordination. I am convinced that only when women reach a greater consensus about the inequities they undergo, can the movement grow strong enough to change a sexist church and society.[58]

One door closes, and another, followed by another, is continually opening as Tobin continues to read the signs of the times in the light of the gospel and with the support of her community. She brings Vatican II to the world and constantly pushes out its frontiers. Her peace missions and justice protests, whereby she continues to put her life on the line for Christian convictions, are carrying out the conciliar mission to "hold back the hand of man" and "save the peace of the world" (Conciliar message "To Women"). She can also be found at the Women's Ordination Conference and Women-Church meetings, where the struggle goes on, indicating that indeed "the hour is coming for woman's vocation to reach its fullness" in a diversity of ways not yet imagined" ("To Women"). Eliminating all discrimination is just the basement construction for a sturdy and reliable house.

A Word from the Loyal Opposition

Joseph Dunn cited Lutheran observer at Vatican II George Lindbeck for his diagnosis of why more significant changes have not come in the church since the council. It is because "the Roman Catholic Church still has not learned to deal with a loyal opposition — it has not learned how to make a distinction between a loyal opposition and a disloyal one." Dunn made Lindbeck's concluding words his own: "And no church can, it seems to me, really have the kind of renewal that was projected by the Second Vatican Council, unless it learns to live with those who, out of love for the church, for God, for Jesus Christ, criticize the church."[59]

Many women who stay with the Roman Catholic Church today, including some conciliar auditors, find themselves in the position of loyal opposition. This is true of Bellosillo, to name one. Her promi-

nent position in WUCWO and as expert at the 1971 Synod on
Justice in the World convinced her and four other women of the need
to speak out, no longer through male proxies, because the pontifical study commission on Women in Church and Society (1973–76)
failed to tell the truth. This was not an isolated incident but a cul-
minating point in a series of postconciliar events that continued to
erode the ground gained by women. The chief aim of WUCWO was
"to improve the position of women through education and participation both in the human community and in the church."[60] Following
the council, WUCWO's working group "Women in the Church"
(later changed to "Women and Church") carried out a second worldwide study, from 1966 to 1969, on the "liberty of women in society
and in the church." The Third World Congress of the Lay Apostolate in 1967 put forth a resolution based on the equality of all
persons through baptism, St. Paul's condemnation of all discrimination (Gal. 3:28), the conviction of the interrelatedness of woman's
socio-cultural position and her ecclesial place, and the evolving social
position of woman toward full equality of rights in most countries
in the world. It concluded: "The Third World Congress of the Lay
Apostolate expressed the wish that the church grant women their
full rights and responsibilities as Christians and that a serious doctrinal study be undertaken into the place of women in the sacramental
order and in the church."[61]

The "Women in the Church" group began their consultation on
Canon Law in 1969. In essence their memorandum "requested that
discriminatory measures with regard to women should be reformed
and that there should no longer be a contradiction between *the affirmation of the gospel principle of equality of the sexes* and *the
justification of inequality* in practice and in discipline."[62] The memorandum was presented to the Commission for the Revision of Canon
Law by the Juridical Commission of the Council of the Laity. "What
created the greatest problem for the Council of Laity was the request for equal rights, including in the church, 'because this would
open the gates to a demand for access to the priesthood.' "[63] And it
did, with ensuing discussions that exposed the ambiguity of church
tradition, which like everything else, is culturally conditioned.

The 1971 synod was to deal with the ministerial priesthood and
justice in the world — two issues that inevitably came together in
the question of women's position in church and world. For the first
time, women, two religious and two lay women, were invited to take

part in the work of the synod on the issue of justice. The lay women were Barbara Ward and Pilar Bellosillo.[64] Ward was not permitted to deliver her prepared address at the council, for the sole reason that she was a woman. Her personality and expert input impressed the synodal bishops, leading one to ask, "Can we deprive the church of this valuable feminine potential? We do not have the right." Canadian Cardinal Flahiff was outspoken in bringing women into the discussion both of diversified ministries and of social justice:

> Many people have mentioned the growing diversification of ministries in connection with the ministries properly belonging to lay people. But no one has raised the question of *the ministry of women*. This is my question, are all these new ministries to be reserved to men? ... We should be failing in our duty toward rather more than half of the church if we do not even speak of the subject.... Given the progressive recognition of women's equal rights both *de jure* and *de facto,* given the injustice of all discrimination with regard to women, should we or should we not raise the question of their possible role in new ministries?[65]

Flahiff presented the recommendation from the Canadian bishops, stating that representatives of the Canadian Catholic Conference asked their delegates to recommend to the pope that a mixed commission be set up to study in depth the question of women in church ministries. They said, "Despite a centuries-old tradition against the ministry of women, we believe that the signs of the times (of which the fact that women are already successfully carrying out apostolic and pastoral tasks is not the least) are pressing us to study the present situation and the possibilities for the future. If we do not begin this study already now we are in danger of being overtaken by events."[66] The synod sent the request to the pope.

Nothing happened until March 1973, when Paul VI created the commission, which was doomed to failure from the beginning because it was not sufficiently representative of the world church. It was too in-grown, since seven of the ten men worked in Rome as theologians or were members of the dicasteries, and several disciplines were not represented. Three were laymen and one of them never appeared. There were fifteen women, including Bellosillo. Study of priesthood for women was outlawed. The women from Vatican II expected the inductive method used for *Gaudium et Spes* to be followed. It was not.

Women sought outside expert advice, which was initially denied. Five of the women on the commission sent a letter of resignation to the pope. They saw the futility of the commission, since it evaded its real task at every turn. A reply came three months later, promising that things would change. The women agreed to continue. Nothing changed. When it came to writing the final report, the five women were joined by a sixth in writing their minority report — a usual procedure followed during the council. It was not included in the dossier sent to the pope. The minority women did not publicize their frustrations or report until 1987, when they felt that in the name of justice and for the good of the church and women at large they could not keep silent any longer. Their thesis was that "the pope entrusted *all* the [commission] members with a very specific responsibility, and *all* are answerable to the men and women of our time for presenting a complete, objective and true vision of the work carried out."[67] Only the majority side was presented. Lacking was the healthy pluralism that could have been the catalyst for moving forward. The commission was worse than nothing. It gave the semblance of responding to the synod's recommendation, while masking the stagnation regarding women in the church.

The pope indicated the direction to be taken: "to collect, verify, interpret, revise, and develop the ideas expressed concerning the role of women in modern society.... This already expresses all the work of observation, research, and reflection with which you are entrusted with the aid of theologians and experts."[68] The minority's gravest reservation was that "the most central questions were not dealt with in depth,... the differences between men and women,... God's plan and the signs of the times... the socio-cultural context,... the 'document' on ministries."[69] There were problems from the very first meeting, where the question of ministries for women was raised; *all* the women members of the commission refused to accept such a proposal. The final statement, which was neither discussed nor approved in commission, still contained the masculine and feminine stereotypes the women clearly opposed earlier. The same battle was waged again, although the conciliar women got more results in eliminating some outmoded stereotypes from *Apostolicam Actuositatem*. Karl Rahner responded to a commission consultant with a fundamental critique of the majority report and the unfounded, ahistorical conclusions drawn from Scripture and church tradition.

The minority report concluded with a statement of the members' goodwill and how they were

> anxious to contribute to the awakening within the church of a healthy, critical conscience essential for the stimulation of the renewal to which the church is constantly called in order to live the gospel and to witness to it.... For them, in reality, the problem of women must be situated in a wider context: there is a need to establish a new scale of values, to draft a new type of relationship between men and women which should gradually replace the present model based on concepts of superiority and inferiority, and which is linked to debatable roles and stereotypes, fixed for centuries or even millennia. It must be demonstrated that the struggle for the Christian liberation of women is part of the struggle against all injustice and against all oppression bearing down on humanity. It amounts even to conceiving a new society and a new church in which men and women will be in real and authentic cooperation for the advancement and the salvation of the world.[70]

The women struggled to preserve the vision of Vatican II in its opening to inclusivity. The quest for truth continued in the unequal synodal tug-of-war. Subsequent synods dealt with significant topics, but each was a missed opportunity to carry forward the conciliar message. The world was left uninterested and untouched. The post–Vatican II generation of women — young, old, and in-between — looked to Rome for bread and were given stones. They looked for fish and were given scorpions. They looked for wine and were given vinegar. They even offered to bake and share the bread, to make and pour new wine, but they were rejected, so many discovered Women-Church and the Women's Ordination Conference together. The bread continues to rise, and the wine is fermenting in preparation for the dawning of a new day when women from all classes, races, orientations, and religions will host and enjoy a creative, inclusive banquet for all people, with sensitivity to the rest of God's creation.

CHAPTER EIGHT

THE DOOR IS OPENED TOO WIDE
TO BE CLOSED

When John Charles McQuaid, archbishop of Dublin, returned from the council in 1965, he assured the people of his diocese that nothing would happen to disturb the ecclesial tranquillity in Ireland. "The church is as solid and as lasting as Nelson's Pillar," he said.[1] For those unfamiliar with the city of Dublin in the 1960s, Nelson's Pillar (known simply as "the Pillar"), erected in memory of the nineteenth-century British admiral, was the tallest monument in the city. It was the center-of-the-city landmark, the hub from which all bus lines originated. In 1967 the statue succumbed to a few sticks of dynamite. "All along O'Connell Street the stones and rubble flew. Up went Nelson and the Pillar too" — as a popular Irish song had it. Since then, Catholic Emancipation leader Daniel O'Connell has replaced Nelson in a less imposing statue.

So much for McQuaid's prediction about the stability of the Irish church! He was both right and wrong. Vatican II caught on in Ireland, maybe not with a bang like the fall of Nelson, but like elsewhere in the world, the face of the church has changed for-ever in that "island of saints and scholars." Many people are way ahead of the clergy in their commonsense approach to life, espe-cially since they have discovered their God-given rights to think and speak for themselves. This is true especially among Irish women. The Third International Interdisciplinary Conference on Women held in Dublin in 1987 gave a necessary boost to the development of Irish feminism. One of the conference panelist speakers is now Pres-ident Mary Robinson. With the fall of their beloved Bishop Éamonn Casey of Galway[2] and the more recent explosion of information on pedophilia, "mná na hÉireann" (the women of Ireland) are speak-ing more forthrightly in defense of their children and their right to the faith of their mothers and fathers, which many perceive to be bankrupt through the irrelevance of official church teaching and practice. There were no Irish women auditors at Vatican II, but the current fermentation in the Irish church could be the litmus test for the rest of the Western world.

In keeping with the conciliar spirit, the women of Vatican II were convinced that they had turned the corner in terms of being accepted as equal human beings and full church members. There was no going back.

A Chinese proverb states that "when a big tree falls, you hear a great crash, but when a whole forest is growing, you hear nothing." So it is that as we approach the third millennium, a new grassroots church of people is growing from beneath, and this is especially true in the phenomenal growth of basic ecclesial communities in countries of Latin America.[3] Church leaders as a group apparently are not ready. Meanwhile, the dysfunctional institutional model self-destructs with its misplaced emphasis on inconsequential details of dress code, idolatrous worship of letter-of-the-law papal teachings, and gross neglect of the core of all gospel values — Christian charity. We hear about the crisis of priest shortage, parish closings, and so-called Eucharist-less Sundays. There is no priest shortage for those who have eyes to see. There is only short-sightedness in those who will not read the signs of the times. The papal response continues to be, *no, no, no, no. No* to women's ordination; *no* to married priests; *no* to birth control; and *no* even to the language that recognizes women's existence. Women ask for the nourishing bread and wine of having their presence, their gifts, their adulthood, and their ministry acknowledged and validated, and their God named to reflect the image of their female humanity. Instead, they are given the stones, scorpions, and vinegar of a *men's* catechism and a return to the sexist language Lectionary only briefly abandoned, if at all, in some churches.

Meanwhile, the world at large is groaning under the weight of injustice, poverty for the majority, localized wars, domestic violence, and ecological destruction. There are few credible, prophetic voices to be heard from the churches — custodians and preachers of the Good News. A communications gap permeates most sectors of society along the lines of "haves" and "have-nots," generation and sex/gender inequities within families, and a multitude of deep-seated ethnic issues and historical injustices and grudges. In the Roman

Catholic Church the most obvious lines of division follow the male-female fault line that cuts through and across most other lines, creating the climate for a volcanic eruption of gigantic proportions. The warning rumbles are already audible to those with ears to hear all over the world. Women on the outside of Roman decision-making bodies that attempt to control their lives observe how the ground gained at Vatican II is blatantly being eroded. The Aurelian Wall has gotten higher and denser, even as the Berlin Wall came down. The veil of secrecy has once again surrounded Roman policy-making, even as the Iron Curtain has been drawn back. With the demise of the old communist enemy, women and homosexual/lesbian persons have become the butt of the new "Christian" backlash. A popular song captures the defensive mood: "There's a wall between you and me, A wall so high that it reaches the sky. There's a wall between you and me."

Patty Crowley, U.S. survivor of the Papal Commission on Birth Control, finished her work on the commission believing that the pope would follow its recommendations. He didn't, and Crowley has lived with that bitter disappointment since then, as she has listened to women's questions, such as the Catholic mother who asked, "Is contraceptive sex irresponsible when I have already borne ten little responsibilities?"[4] Nevertheless, she goes about her varied ministries claiming, "It's my church; no one's going to kick me out."[5]

Where Have All the Flowers Gone?

The conciliar women were clear about what they did *not* want. They wanted simply to be accepted as equal human beings with equal voice and recognition in the church and a fair share in decision-making. They did not want to be romanticized as flowers, which are pretty to look at but easily wilt (unless they are of the silk or plastic variety), or pedestalized in unrealistic ways that lay on them the burden of being paragons of superior virtue and strength and thus responsible for more than their share of saving the human race from perdition. The concluding conciliar message, "To Women," contained much of this florid language, while honestly attempting to recognize women's perennial contribution to society, mainly through the family.

The message also cut along a prophetic edge. It stated: "As you know, the church is proud to have glorified and liberated woman, and in the course of the centuries, in diversity of characters, to have brought into relief her basic equality with man."[6] Glorification was part of the romanticism the conciliar women rejected. Liberation they wanted. The Spirit put words in the church fathers' mouths, with meaning beyond their most daring expectations. They said: "But the hour is coming, in fact has come, when the vocation of woman is being achieved in its fullness, the hour in which woman acquires in the world an influence, an effect, and a power never hitherto achieved."[7] Women are discerning that Spirit at work within themselves and in their world. They are claiming their power as a united body that cuts across religious and social barriers, and they are joining hands across the world through international gatherings and technological communications.

Women can be presidents, prime ministers, and chief justices in various societies in the world. In most Protestant dominations, women can be ordained to priesthood and even episcopacy, although they continue to be treated as second-class ministers in many instances. Meanwhile, in the Roman Catholic Church, it is a major concession that girls can now legitimately be altar servers, a practice some local churches introduced more than twenty years ago.

Young women and men today, to the extent that they have any interest in a church that appears to be totally out of touch and out of step with their interests, concerns, and hopes, are increasingly asking, Why be a Catholic? Some find it embarrassing to be associated with an institution that not only fails to make progress, but even withdraws from moderately progressive positions taken earlier and fails to implement its own conciliar imperative to eliminate *all discrimination*. Even inclusive language has taken a backward step. As one woman reminded me, "By the time they get as far as including Sarah with Abraham, we will have gone on to including Hagar as well." The rehabilitation of Sophia has already taken root in mainline theological circles,[8] while Rome is still fixated in the literalism of the he-God-Father as sole designation for the deity. Increasing numbers of women recognize that they are not in the image of *that* manmade God, so they are doing their own ecumenical, biblically based reimagining.

Even in "holy Ireland," parents of the Vatican II generation are claiming, with legitimate concern, that the next generation, their children, will be lost to the church unless something changes radically to convert the hierarchy to a pastoral connection with teenagers and youth in general. This is particularly true of young and middle-aged women — the parents and their daughters. Time is running out. In recent years a new organization has been formed on the strength of more than twenty-two thousand signatures from people throughout Ireland. It is called BASIC — Brothers and Sisters in Christ. Their mission statement commits them to promoting women's vocations to the priesthood. A founding member, Soline Vatinelle, has experienced a vocation to priesthood for twenty years, and she is not an isolated case.

The high tide of Vatican II is history. John XXIII launched the big ship that has been tossing and turning in various depths of choppy water ever since. The one place it cannot sail is in dry dock — where present Vatican hierarchs seem to be steering it, while talking about preparedness for the third millennium. John Paul II wants to apologize for the church's sins of the past — inquisitions, etc. He is several hundred years too late to benefit the dead victims. His 1995 letter addressed to "women of the world" apologizes for the harm done to women by the Catholic Church. Action in the present is what women want to evidence papal sincerity and repentance. "It's a nice try, your Holiness, but you need to do more for the sisters,"[9] wrote Nell McCafferty, one of the few women who have read it. McCafferty noted how the bishops were keeping "your letter *to us* all to themselves," by never mentioning it in the public forum of Sunday Mass. Women are reserving absolution until they see evidence of the papal "purpose of amendment."

From Guests to Hosts

Women's position (or lack of it) in the church is ironic, considering the involvement of most women with the preparation and serving of food and drink in one form or another. Mothers conceive and nurture children within their own bodies, and in creatorlike fashion bring forth and nourish new life. As cooks, providers for families, fending for themselves and/or their children, they produce the bread of life, whether as wage-earners outside the home or unpaid homemakers, or provide a welcoming table for friends and the hungry. Goodness knows they have been initiated many times over with the preparation and serving of church breakfasts, potluck suppers, ordination dinners, and bake sales. Given the number of women involved in service-oriented jobs or volunteer work of teaching, caring for the sick, secretarial service, and general maintenance, as well as increasingly in leadership positions of politics, justice, science, and technology, there seems to be a particular "fittingness" or "connaturality" between women and the servant model of ministry frequently advocated today in theory. Yet it is there that their exclusion is most visible and persistent in the Roman Catholic Church. It is high time to sacramentalize the obvious and to "ordain women or stop baptizing them," as popular slogans declare. Not that every woman either feels called or wants to be an ordained priest. The issue is freedom of choice and following one's baptismal call wherever it leads. As it stands, it needs to be openly expressed that there is a two-track baptismal system in a church that has seven sacraments for men and only six for women.

There is a time to be a *guest* and a time to be a *host*. The women of Vatican II felt privileged to be the pope's invited guests. But something didn't quite add up, when they were supposed to *be* the church. It is time to stop talking about women *in* the church. Women want to be truly and fully a part of God's household and at home in their church as church, fully engaged as *co-senders of the invitations, co-preparers of the feasts, co-hosts and co-presiders* with men at the celebrations. Instead, they often find themselves unwelcome guests when they raise challenging questions.

The Most Unmanageable Revolutionaries

Small-minded, weak administrators in positions beyond their potential are like little boys in big men's shoes. They are frequently threatened by strong women. They sometimes perceive a courageous woman to have "the strength of ten men," when really she has just the strength of one woman.[10] Women religious, at least in the U.S., are one group that took the renewal called for by Vatican II to heart, as they strove to learn and implement the "mind of the church." Not surprisingly, they have also collided with Vatican officials in the process. Most leading women theologians no longer work in Catholic institutions because of a climate hostile to feminism and other creative thinking. Specious reasoning, devoid of justice, is conjured up behind closed clerical doors, and schemes are devised to remove women from positions where they are most effective. Laity are scandalized and outraged at the blatant defiance of justice and charity, and they feel powerless in the face of this latest inquisition that patronizingly says, "The people are not ready" for women or married priests. All evidence is to the contrary, and it becomes more obvious who is not ready.

Conciliar auditor Tobin proclaimed that the council was a door opened wide — too wide to be closed.[11] Renewal has no end. If it is to continue to be life-giving, it must go on and on. That makes it threatening to those who prefer predictability.

The publication of *Inter Insigniores* (Declaration against the Ordination of Women) in 1977 was surprising only in that it was the first time an official church document addressed the question, indicating how the discussion of women's ordination had come out into the open and spread since members of St. Joan's Alliance first raised it before the council, especially through the scholarly work of Gertrud Heinzelmann ("Wir schweigen nicht länger"). Had the 1973 papal commission on women, requested by the 1971 synod, done its work properly, it would have given the pope more concrete data on anthropology, ecclesiology, and culture that could have enabled him and the Congregation for the Doctrine of the Faith to write a more relevant and credible text. Paul VI was known to ignore the findings of his own commissions, and he also ignored the modest report of the Pontifical Biblical Commission that said the Bible alone could not decide the question of women's ordination. Priestly ordination for women or men was not a biblical question, since it was a later historical development, and priesthood, as we know it, is the most notably lacking ministry in the New Testament.

WUCWO responded to *Inter Insigniores,* saying it "regrets that, despite the affirmation that a large number of women were consulted in the preparatory stage to the writing and publication of the declaration, the WUCWO was not consulted...[although it] represents 127 organizations which are present in 60 countries of the six continents (some 36 million women)."[12] A WUCWO delegation met with the CDF representatives in June 1977, but by then it was too late to make any impact on the already published document. The Congregation said that WUCWO should continue its in-depth reflection on the issues of women in the church, in dialogue with the CDF. Study is necessary, but at some point it can become a mode of evasion.

Women Are *Not* the Problem

The ordination question, first raised in Europe, spread to the United States, Canada, and eventually to the other continents, especially in the context of liberation theologies. When women began serious theological studies and had the language skills and methodological tools to embark on their own primary research, the face of biblical, historical, and theological scholarship changed forever. One thinks of the groundbreaking biblical work of Elisabeth Schüssler Fiorenza and the new feminist theology pioneered by Rosemary Radford Ruether, joined and followed by a host of others in the Catholic, Protestant, and Jewish traditions, plus experts in other disciplines. More and more Catholic women, especially from women's religious communities, obtained master's and doctoral degrees in theology in the late 1960s and 1970s, enthusiastically motivated to make their contribution to the revitalization of the new church discovered at Vatican II. A goodly number were hired on seminary and university faculties when Vatican II was still in vogue and it was safe and acceptable to hire women.

During the 1970s and 1980s several Women's Ordination Conference meetings were held, with overlap from the wider perspective of Women-Church in the 1980s. More recently the ecumenical dimension has also been important. The 1995 WOC meeting in Washington celebrated twenty years of its struggle for a renewed priestly ministry and two thousand years of women's struggle for equality. Questions were raised as to whether women should want ordination if it means ordination into subordination. Women were commissioned to claim our gifts and priestly ministry in whatever form it takes. Many women are not waiting for "permission" anymore. They are moving forward.

As Ruth Wallace uncovered in her carefully researched book *They Call Her Pastor,* increasing numbers of women are involved in a variety of ministries, including priestly and sacramental actions, that are not officially designated as such. Gladys Parentelli documented well the ecclesial reality in Latin America, where women constitute approximately 80 percent of church ministers, despite their lack of recognition through ordination.[13] It takes at least twenty years to obtain official acknowledgment for established church practices, as we saw recently in the papal concession to altar girls. Priesthood is the last bastion of male prerogative, and it is proving more difficult than storming the Bastille, but the Holy Spirit has her own ways and time.

Well-meaning bishops drafted a pastoral on women after extensive consultation with them. Women requested that they write, not about women as if they were the problem, but about *the sin of sexism in church and society.* Women asked that the real problems of divorce and remarriage, spouse abuse, birth control, abortion, and ordination be addressed; otherwise, the pastoral should not be written. It went through several drafts, each draining more and more of its lifeblood, until, with Roman interference, it became another Roman club to beat women. Finally, the tired, fearful bishops shelved their decade's work, and women breathed a sigh of relief. Maybe the bishops learned from the process.

Women are not the problem. Their very presence, their scholarship, their unconventional gatherings, and their various feminist, womanist, mujerista, and Asian-American perspectives send shock waves into various sectors of the church, although the women are simply claiming their own voice and dignity as human beings, exercising their baptismal call as free and equal members of the church, and assuming responsibility for their own lives, the life of the church, and the planet that sustains them. As the conciliar women still emphasize, "We laid the foundational principles." The council at large, including women, was commissioned to implement and develop those principles. Women today are saying, "Church of Rome, please continue the *aggiornamento* of Vatican II by *implementing your own teaching in our regard.* We want to be present in larger and more truly representative numbers at Vatican III, and we want our full voice on the conciliar floor and our full voting power on all commissions and documents."

•

Women of the church everywhere, claim your power. As successors to Mary Magdalene — not the sinful woman, but the apostle to the apostles — fulfil the command of Jesus to *go and tell Peter and the other disciples what you see and hear.* Jesus is risen and continues to rise in women and all who are put down by church and society and dare to break silence about it.

POSTSCRIPT

AN AUTOBIOGRAPHICAL NOTE

═══ ❖ ═══

My editor and concerned friends urged me to conclude with an autobiographical note that they saw as particularly relevant and indeed poignant, given the topic and thrust of my book. I taught systematic theology at St. Meinrad School of Theology, Indiana, for fourteen years, and I was tenured in 1992. Nevertheless, I was fired from my teaching position in May 1995, with less than two weeks' notice, no due process, and the insulting offer of half a year's already meager salary. All of this was in clear violation of the terms of my contract, the procedures spelled out in the *Faculty Handbook,* and the school's endorsement of the American Association of University Professors' Statement on Academic Freedom.

The charge brought against me was "public dissent" from magisterial teaching in regard to women's ordination. In May 1994, Pope John Paul II published an open letter, saying that the question of women's ordination was definitively closed. In October 1994, the Women's Ordination Conference responded in kind with an open letter to the pope and U.S. bishops, which I and about two thousand other people signed, respectfully requesting that the discussion be continued. The letter was published in the *National Catholic Reporter* (November 4, 1994). In accordance with my rights as a citizen and private person (guaranteed by my contract), I did not indicate my professional affiliation with St. Meinrad School of Theology, nor did I use the initials of the Congregation of the Sisters of Mercy of Ireland and South Africa.

On April 26, 1995, I received a letter from Archabbot Timothy Sweeney, O.S.B., stating that he was asking president-rector Eugene Hensell, O.S.B., to terminate my contract at the end of the semester, allegedly because asking that the discussion continue on women's ordination made me "seriously deficient in my duty," in his interpretation of Canon 253 (although it does not mention "dissent").

On May 9, my last teaching day, I received a letter from Hensell (who signed my tenured contract in 1992) informing me of my termination.

All of this was in stark contrast to my evaluations over the years. Daniel Buechlein, then president-rector, hired me in 1981, knowing my views on women's ordination. During my interview I told him I had no personal sense of vocation to priesthood. He said that because of his position he was not actively working for women's ordination. In reply to my question as to how structures changed if there was no help from within, he said, "By hiring people like you." When reappointing me for a seven year term in 1983, Buechlein wrote, "I was pleased by the positive report which was presented by the Personnel Committee and I concur with the specific commendations.... In a very short time, you have become a valuable member of our faculty and have won the genuine respect of our students." In 1984, he wrote, "I'm delighted to grant your sabbatical request for... 1985.... May I take this opportunity to congratulate you for your marvelous contribution to our life and work here. We value your presence as well as your various and substantial contributions as a colleague. Thank you!"

In 1988, the middle of my first seven-year contract, President-Rector Hensell responded to my faculty evaluation.

> Your teaching ability is clearly appreciated by our students and your presence on the faculty over these past years has been an asset to the school. During these years of transition in the church, I realize that it is not easy being a woman theology teacher in a seminary.... I encourage you to feel "at home" on our faculty. You have manifested your ability as a faculty member and therefore you are encouraged to enjoy this very important work with a sense of confidence and a spirit of relaxation.... It is an important time for women in our church. Solid scholarly contributions to the area of theology by women are very important. We will support your efforts to the best of our ability. I want to thank you for your work and presence at St. Meinrad. I look forward to working with you in the years to come.

In approving my 1993 sabbatical to research the women of Vatican II, Hensell stated, "I think it has a great deal of significance for the church.... I wish you well in this project. Its completion will be a credit to you and a benefit to our school" (March 2, 1992). Two months later he granted me Continuing Appointment (tenure) and added:

> Your faculty review was very positive and clear recognition was given to the gifts you bring to the School especially in the area of your teaching. As you are well aware, these are very challenging times for schools of theology. Our students will continue to need solid grounding in systematic theology in order that they be able to provide the kind of ministry and leadership the church needs and deserves. Your proven ability as a teacher will be a very important asset for our school, our students, and the church in the years ahead. Congratulations on achieving this important step in your teaching career.

Four days later, Academic Dean Tom Walters wrote:

> I want to take this opportunity to formally say "Congratulations" on your Continuing Appointment to the School of Theology. While Gene's comments echo mine, I want to add that you are also to be commended on your research regarding the women of Vatican II. Because of your intellectual curiosity and desire to push the boundaries of theological research, we are a better school.

With that consistent type of commendation for my work over the years, I was not prepared for the accusation of being "seriously deficient in my duty" in 1995. The first rumor I heard about my possible firing was on March 6, the morning after the arrival of the NCCB Visitation Team, which consisted of Archbishop Elden Curtiss of Omaha, Bishop Seán O'Malley of Fall River, Rector Pat Brennan of Mt. Angel Seminary in Oregon, and Rector Pat Guidon of Oblate College, San Antonio. Curtiss, the team's chair, made it known publicly to students that he was there to carry out Archbishop Daniel Buechlein's wishes with regard to feminism, including firing me, and homosexuality. Allegedly, according to Curtiss, because I signed the open letter to the pope, I forfeited my right to teach in a seminary, and action had to be taken against me. Academic Dean Walters called me into his office to tell me this shortly before Hensell presented the oral report to the faculty on March 8.

Two weeks prior to the visitation, Bishop Edward Slattery of Tulsa and his vocation director, Tim Davison, visited the seminary and showed administrators a copy of the *National Catholic Reporter* letter with my name highlighted. I was never officially informed of this.

A week prior to Slattery's visit, Archbishop Buechlein addressed the faculty at the invitation of President-Rector Hensell. When asked what the visitation team might be looking for, Buechlein said, among other things, "They will be looking at individuals and why they are here." No one questioned his cryptic remark, but some faculty later made the connection between this statement, Elden Curtiss's recommendation that I be fired, Timothy Sweeney's initiative against me, and Eugene Hensell's actualization of my termination. Hensell told me Buechlein had been trying to get rid of me for nine years because I was a feminist theologian, although in Hensell's own estimation, I was a moderate one.

St. Meinrad administrators totally ignored letters from the Leadership Team in my congregation, at the central, provincial, local, and individual level, as well as from members of my family, leaders in other religious congregations, and individuals and groups at academic institutions who tried to initiate discussion before I was terminated.

The administrators' precipitous unilateral action against me evidenced, at best, their ignorance of the nuanced understanding of "dissent," which clearly distinguishes honest differences from those that are hostile and obstinate, as set forth in the CDF's 1990 "Instruction on the Ecclesial Vocation of the Theologian."[1] They ignored the exhortation to bishops to initiate dialogue with theologians in order to create a climate of trust and offset major difficulties, "to seek their solution in trustful dialogue," and to follow the proper procedures (40, 42). This magisterial document states that prior to removing a theologian's teaching mandate, the magisterium is required to carry out "a thorough investigation conducted according to established procedures which afford the interested party the opportunity to clear up possible misunderstandings of his [her] thought" (37).

The procedural steps are further specified in the 1975 theses set forth by the International Theological Commission,[2] which is clearly the parent document of the CDF's 1990 Instruction. For example, it states: "When one party 'unilaterally' takes over the whole field of the dialogue, he [sic] violates the rules of discussion. It is especially damaging to dialogue between the magisterium and theologians when the stage of discussion and debate is broken off prematurely, and measures of coercion, threat and sanction are employed all too soon" (Thesis 11). Furthermore,

> Before instituting any formal process about a question of doctrine, the competent authority should exhaust all the ordinary possibilities of reaching agreement through dialogue in order to clarify a questionable opinion (for example by discussing the matter in person or by correspondence in which questions are asked and replies given). If no genuine agreement can be reached by such dialogical methods, the magisterium should employ a broad and flexible range of measures, beginning with various kinds of warnings, "verbal sanctions," etc. In the most serious kind of case, when all the methods of dialogue have been used to no avail, the magisterium, after consulting theologians of various schools, has no choice but to act in defence of the endangered truth and the faith of the believing people. (Thesis 12).

Even Canon Law provides a process before action.

St. Meinrad authorities' extreme action against me was diametrically opposed to the CDF's dialogical method and the spirit of trust it requires as the hallmark of those engaged in the collaborative pursuit of truth in the service of the church. While invoking magisterial teaching in defense of their action, they failed to honor even the doctrinal principle of "hierarchy of truths" set forth at Vatican II (*UR* 11). Even more basic from a Christian perspective was their neglect of the threefold biblical process for settling differences, as set forth in Matthew 18:15. Presumably, a seminary committed to the education of future priests would be a place that could be expected to operate from a model of practical justice and charity.

On May 10, Dr. Bridget Clare McKeever, S.S.L., tenured professor in Pastoral Care and Counseling, submitted a letter of resignation to Eugene Hensell. He never acknowledged it. McKeever wrote:

> The events of the past two months have raised serious questions regarding how and where I should devote the remaining years of my active ministry. The model of church which the NCCB Visitation Committee exemplified and which, to my acute disappointment, St. Meinrad School of Theology also displayed in its response, is one with which I cannot identify and which I cannot support. The circumventing of the faculty constitution and the terminating of Dr. Carmel McEnroy's tenured contract without

due process is, in my opinion, a breach of faith not only with Dr. McEnroy, but also with the entire faculty. Regardless of how these actions are rationalized, they are unjustified and unjust.

McKeever quoted from her community's Mission Statement, stating, "Through all our ministries...we resolve to become agents of change in struggling to transform unjust structures and to promote reconciliation." She added, "I have believed in the good will and in the good faith of St. Meinrad as long as I could. However, it is no longer possible for me to do so."

In the cover letter she sent to her colleagues with a copy of her letter of resignation, she wrote:

> I believe I could have lived with the behavior and the report of the NCCB Visitation Committee, it being a hostile force outside St. Meinrad. However, when Carmel's professional life and ministry was so obviously used by St. Meinrad as a bargaining chip between ecclesiastical power brokers, I realized that my ethical boundaries were being stretched beyond their limits. I had no option but to resign.

The Catholic Theological Society of America at its 1995 meeting in New York overwhelmingly endorsed a statement and two resolutions in my favor. It viewed my dismissal "with dismay." Furthermore, it stated:

> The absence of any process to deal with the charges against a tenured faculty member raises serious concern that after more than a decade of joint efforts by American bishops and scholars to formulate processes to insure fair treatment for Catholic scholars accused of doctrinal error, due process, even that guaranteed by contract, is often jettisoned. Dr. McEnroy's is a case in point.

The society questioned the charge of dissent and asked that I be reinstated, since "in the view of the society the demands of justice have not been met." It testified that "nothing has changed in the professional role of Dr. Carmel McEnroy. She is a Catholic theologian in good standing."[3] I was gratified by the CTSA's support, and I trust the judgment of this informed group of female and male *periti*.

The outpouring of support I have received and continue to receive from men and women, many of whom I don't know, indicates the outrage of the people of God with the hierarchical abuse of power, symbolized by my unjust dismissal. They demand that the Spirit not be silenced in the people's church. In my own situation I find parallels to Jesus' disciples and friends. Some betrayed him; some fled in fear; others came to him by night; still others remained faithful to the end; and complete strangers befriended him.

In its Pastoral Constitution on the Church in the Modern World, the church assembled in Vatican Council II recognized that while it had a message for the world, it could also learn from the secular world. It is time to implement the conciliar Declaration on Religious Freedom within the church's own structures. Since I have been denied my rights by St. Meinrad School of Theology under the guise of "church law," I have no option but to turn to the civil courts for justice. My lawyer, Ronald Sheffer, filed a sex discrimination complaint with the Equal Employment Opportunity Commission, and he has received a permit to file the lawsuit in federal court. This will be done early in 1996.

In light of the contemporary backlash against theologians and women in particular within the wider retrenchment from Vatican II, it is more urgent than ever that the story of the conciliar women be told. May it empower many bent-over women with courage to stand up tall and claim their baptismal rights and dignity as human beings made in the image of God. May it validate the experience of courageous men, especially bishops and priests, who experience the cost of discipleship when they break ranks with their peers in the cause of justice and charity. May it challenge fearful women and men to dare to make a difference by declaring once and for all that the Auschwitz principle of blindly following orders is no substitute for responsible Christian action and human decency. I take the liberty to paraphrase Pastor Niemoeller's painfully true reflection on how fear paralyzes, while the enemy divides and conquers: They came for the homosexuals, and I didn't speak up because I wasn't a homosexual.... They came for the women, and I didn't speak up because I wasn't a woman.... Then they came for me, and there was no one left to speak up.

NOTES

===◆===

Introduction

1. Alberic Stacpole, *Vatican II Revisited by Those Who Were There* (Minneapolis: Winston Press, 1986).

2. Ibid., 14.

3. In a letter (August 8, 1988), Tom Stransky, conciliar *peritus* and ecumenist, wrote to me: "During the first session of Vat. II, after the daily Eucharist when all visitors, special guests, etc., were asked to leave, the only woman who had the right to remain was Blanche Shaeffer (I am unsure of the spelling), General Secretary of the World Friends' Committee. With over 2,500 cardinals, bishops, periti, ushers, lining up at the two makeshift 'facilities,' Blanche had the right to her own toilet."

4. Karl Rahner, "The Abiding Significance of the Second Vatican Council," *Theological Investigations,* trans. E. Quinn (New York: Crossroad, 1981), 20:90–102.

5. Mary Daly, *Webster's First New Intergalactic Wickedary of the English Language* (Boston: Beacon Press, 1987), 222.

6. *The Council Daybook* consisted of three volumes, the first covering conciliar Sessions I and II, the second Session III, and the third Session IV. With editorial commentary, the volumes provide documentation on excerpts from important speeches and give general news items, such as partial lists of the auditors as they became available.

7. The *Lay Apostolate* was the official bulletin of COPECIAL and was published three times a year. Its focus was directives of the Holy See, activities of the Permanent Committee for International Congresses of the Lay Apostolate, and development of lay apostolate movements both internationally, regionally, and nationally. It was the most reliable source for lists of auditors because the lists were derived from the auditors themselves, especially Rosemary Goldie.

8. First interview with Rosemary Goldie, Rome, July 1988.

Chapter 1: Women Must Come Closer to the Altar

1. Maria Clara Bianchi, *Il Postconcilio e la Suora* (Milan: S. Guiliano, 1967), 34.

2. Douglas Horton, *Vatican Diary* (Philadelphia: United Church Press, 1964–67). He has one volume for each of the four conciliar sessions, subsequently referred to as I, II, III, and IV.

282 NOTES TO PAGES 13–23

3. Ibid., I:34.

4. Ibid., I:63.

5. Conversation with Eva Jung-Inglessis, Piazza Navonna, Rome, January 18, 1990. One of her articles was "Women at the Council: Spectators or Collaborators?" *Catholic World* 200 (October 1964–March 1965): 277–84.

6. Häring, letter of December 11, 1994.

7. Horton, *Vatican Diary*, II:126.

8. Ibid., II:58.

9. Ibid.

10. During the third conciliar session, Horton related how the pope granted forty dispensations or permissions to bishops, some pertaining to fasting laws for priests celebrating multiple Masses. Most were of a trivial nature, such as granting the bishop the right to allow "pious women" to wash altar cloths, whereas what bishops really wanted was an acknowledgment of their office, making many permissions unnecessary.

11. Irish *Catholic Times*, November 28, 1993.

12. "Nine Lay Leaders Suggest More Ideas for Vatican Council," *Sign* 41 (October 1961): 14–15.

13. "The Problem of the Parish," *Ave Maria* 100 (September 26, 1964): 15.

14. "New Opportunities, New Insights — A New Identity?" *Ave Maria* 100 (September 19, 1964): 6–7.

15. "Male and Female: Changing Relationships," *Ave Maria* 100 (October 10, 1964): 22.

16. Ibid., 20.

17. Ibid., 21.

18. "Her Concern: The New Catholic Woman," *Ave Maria* 100 (November 21, 1964): 12.

19. "The New Catholic Woman: Her Children," *Ave Maria* 100 (October 31, 1964): 19.

20. "The Woman and the Council: Will Her Voice Be Heard?" *Ave Maria* 100 (October 3, 1964): 26.

21. "Male and Female," 18. Other articles in the series were the following: "The Catholic Woman as a Minority" (October 17, 1964): 22–26; "Her Marriage" (October 24, 1964): 12–14, 30; "Her Vocation" (November 7, 1964): 12–14, 22–23; "Her Work" (November 14, 1964): 12–15, 30.

22. Here I acknowledge the input of some married women who were critical of some of the women's input in the *Ave Maria* interviews, commenting that they know few mothers who are "soft-brained" or "parasitic" due to constant diets of ironing and dishwashing. While admitting that no one likes the drudgery of housework, there are creative and constructive ways to make daily chores more tolerable and integrated with the rest of life.

23. Thomas Aquinas *Summa* IIIa Supplement, 39, 1 and 3.

24. Adolph Schalk, "The Church and Women," *U.S. Catholic* 31 (1965): 26.

25. Ibid.

26. Ibid.

27. Ibid.

28. Ibid.

29. Ibid.

30. Rosemary Goldie, "The Laity in the Ecumenical Movement," *Gregorianum* 68, nos. 1–2 (1987): 309.

31. Ibid., 332.

32. Ibid., 311.

33. Yves Congar, *Lay People in the Church* (Westminster, Md.: Newman Press, 1967).

34. "Catholic Action," *The Oxford Dictionary of the Christian Church*, ed. Cross and Livingston (Oxford University Press, 1974), 254–55.

35. Goldie, "Lay Participation in the Work of Vatican II," *Miscellanea Lateranense "Lateranum"* (1974–75): 506.

36. Goldie, "Lay Participation," 504, n. 2, citing *Actes* of the Congress, Rome, 1952, 44–45.

37. Ibid., 504.

38. Ibid., 503.

39. Ibid., 504–5.

40. Ibid., 508.

41. Ibid., 506.

42. Goldie, "Una donna nella Concilio," *The Review of Religious Sciences* (Pontifical Regional Seminary, Pius XI, Maufetta), 376. Free translation by Goldie, "A Woman at the Council: Memories of an Auditor."

43. Interview with Catherine McCarthy, Mercy Center, Burlingame, Calif. (September 21, 1989).

44. Goldie, "Women in the Church," *The Month* (February 1964): 83.

45. St. Andrew's tribune was an area beside the statue of St. Andrew to the left of the main altar in St. Peter's. It was set up for the auditors. The Protestant observers were opposite them on the other side.

46. Goldie, "Lay Participation," 510–11.

47. Ibid., 512–13.

48. Douglas J. Roche, "The Return of the Laity," *Sign* 44 (November 1964): 22.

49. Ibid., 23.

50. Ibid.

51. Ibid., 22.

52. Ibid., 23.

53. Ibid., 71.

54. Interview with Pilar Bellosillo, Madrid (January 27–28, 1989), trans. Julio Moro. Carmen Bellosillo's hospitality with coffee breaks kept us going.

55. Léon-Josef Suenens, *Memories and Hopes* (Dublin: Veritas, 1992), 140.

56. Ibid., 140–41.

57. Suenens, letter of June 3, 1988.

58. "Nine Lay Leaders," *Sign* 41 (October 1961): 14.

59. *America* 107 (November 3, 1962): 972–73.

60. Ibid., 973.

61. Horton, *Vatican Diary*, III:26.

62. Ibid., III:114.

63. "Equality for Women in the Church," *U.S. Catholic* 30 (September 1964): 62.
64. Horton, *Vatican Diary*, II:190.
65. Ibid., II:196.
66. Goldie, "Women in the Church," 84.
67. Ibid.
68. Bernard Häring, letter of April 11, 1988.
69. Schalk, "The Church and Women," 21.
70. English translation reproduced in *Die geheiligte Discriminierungen* (Bonstetten: Interfeminas Verlag, 1986), 124.
71. Schalk, "The Church and Women," 25.
72. Ibid., 21.
73. Ibid.
74. Ibid., 22.
75. Ibid., 21.
76. Ibid.
77. Interview with Betsie Hollants in Cuernavaca (August 6, 1989).
78. Xavier Rynne, *Vatican Council II: An Authoritative One-volume Version of the Four Historic Books* (New York: Farrar & Giroux, 1968), 198.
79. Horton, *Vatican Diary*, III:165.

Chapter 2: The Missing Half of Humanity Surfaces

1. Douglas Horton, *Vatican Diary* (Philadelphia/Boston: United Church Press, 1964–67), III:16.
2. Ibid., II:21.
3. Douglas J. Roche, "The Return of the Laity," *Sign* 44 (November 1964): 24.
4. Horton, *Vatican Diary*, III:32–33.
5. Marie-Louise Monnet, *Avec amour et passion* (Chambray-lès-Tours, France: C.L.D., 1989), 233.
6. Horton, *Vatican Diary*, III:46.
7. Suzanne Cita-Malard, *Les femmes dans L'Église à la lumière de Vatican II* (Maison Mame, 1968), 23.
8. Denise Peeters, letter April 9, 1989, follow-up to conversation in Brussels, January 30, 1989.
9. Gladys Parentelli, *Mujer Iglesia Liberación* (Caracas, 1990), 44.
10. Interview with Lucienne Salle, Rome, January 12, 1990.
11. Monnet, *Avec amour et passion*, 11.
12. Ibid., 15.
13. Ibid., 69.
14. Ibid., 162.
15. Ibid., 93.
16. Ibid., 26.
17. Ibid., 27–28.
18. Horton, *Vatican Diary*, III:69.
19. Ibid., III:126.

20. *The Tablet* (October 12, 1985): 1065.

21. Rosemary Goldie, "A Woman at the Council: Memories of an Auditor." Goldie gave me a spontaneous free translation of an Italian article she had just completed for the *Review of Religious Sciences,* January 1989.

22. Interview with Alda Miceli, translated by Rosemary Goldie, January 12, 1989).

23. Alice Curtayne, "From the United States," *Irish Times,* October 27, 1965.

24. Interview with Mary Luke Tobin at Nerinx, Kentucky, April 29, 1988.

25. "Dominican Tertiary — First Lay Woman from United States at Vatican Council," *The Torch* (December 1964): 1.

26. I met Catherine McCarthy and Margaret Mealey at Burlingame Mercy Center, September 21, 1989.

27. Rosemary Goldie, "The Emerging Lay Woman: Vatican II and 'The Other Half of Mankind,'" *World Outlook* (May 1966): 227.

28. "Présentation," in *Mère Suzanne Guillemin conférences et témoignages* (Paris: Editions Fleurus, 1968).

29. Ibid., 142.

30. Ibid., 151–52.

31. I experienced great hospitality at the Grillo residence, January 23–25, 1989, while Marialuisa Ruffini translated, and cousin Pietro, Grillo's grandson, took over in her absence. The whole interview was very much a family project. Grillo's daughter, Maria Attilia Grillo Ruffini, informed me that her mother died on December 10, 1994 (letter of September 22, 1995).

32. Published in *Roma Clandestina,* (1946): 25–27, a book given by Amalia to Ida Grillo at the council, October 23, 1964.

33. I am greatly indebted to Archbishop Andrea di Montezemolo, apostolic nuncio in Uruguay in 1989, for the information on his mother. He also put me in touch with his two sisters in Rome. Furthermore, when he was appointed apostolic delegate in Jerusalem and Palestine in 1990, he asked Msgr. Paul Gallagher to continue the search for Gladys Parentelli, who had been living in Uruguay. I gratefully acknowledge Msgr. Gallagher's work in locating her and sending me her address.

34. Suor Maria Clara Bianchi, *Il Postconcilio e la Suora* (Milan: Scuola Tipografica San Benedetto Voboldone, 1967), 86. I met with Constantina Baldinucci at her motherhouse in Milan, where Sister Maria Clara recounted some of the conciliar memories and Sister Gemma acted as translator, January 24, 1989.

35. Ibid., 23.

36. Maureen Aggeler's letter is based on information obtained from Sr. Maribeth Tobin, who was assistant general from December 1964 to December 1970. She has vivid memories of those years, which were so critical for the congregation and its superior general. Denise Peeters knew Sabine de Valon and the Sacred Heart Sisters, so she was able to inform me as to Valon's whereabouts, and she put me in touch with Aggeler. I also acknowledge letters received from Françoise de Lambilly, Geneviève de Thélin, and archivists Ann McManus and Mary C. Wheeler. All were contacts in the detective project that yielded little fruit until I heard from Aggeler.

37. The Dernbach sisters enthusiastically included me in their Three Kings celebrations. The U.S. Sister Germaine aided me with translation.

38. Juliana Thomas, "Die Frau beim Konzil," *Kranken Dienst* 4 (April 1966).

39. Juliana Thomas, Letter from Rome, October 4, 1964.

40. Alice Curtayne, "The Silent Women at Vatican II," *Irish Times,* October 27, 1965.

41. Interview with Srs. Concepción Ruz and Elena Bava at the motherhouse of the Handmaids of the Sacred Heart, Rome, January 18, 1990.

42. Miguel Martinez and Victor de la Fuente, *Love for Ever: Saint Raphaela Mary, Foundress of the Handmaids of the Sacred Heart of Jesus* (Paris: Rameau, 1987).

43. Ibid., 27.

44. Daniel M. Madden, "Women at the Council," *Catholic Digest* (April 1965): 17.

45. Community archives. Thanks to Sr. M. Christopher Malcovsky, letter of June 20, 1989.

46. Ibid.

47. Interview with Jerome Maria Chimy at Mundare, Alberta, May 23, 1993.

48. Community Archives about Claudia Feddish.

49. Interview with Chimy. Unless otherwise indicated subsequent quotations are from this interview.

50. Chronicle excerpts from Vatican II by Sr. M. Christopher, General Councilor, 17.

51. Vegreville Chamber of Commerce brochure.

52. Marie de la Croix Khouzam, letter of April 2, 1993.

53. Ibid.

54. Marie-Henriette Ghanem, letter of April 30, 1993.

55. Dr. Augustinus Frotz, letter of July 24, 1989.

56. Interview with Helga Sourek at her home in Cologne, January 5, 1990.

57. Ibid. All subsequent quotations on Ehrle unless otherwise stated are from this interview.

58. Anne-Marie Roeloffzen, letter of September 14, 1989.

59. Horton, *Vatican Diary,* IV:82.

60. Margarita Moyano Llerena, letter of January 29, 1995.

61. Gladys Parentelli, letter of January 18, 1991. This and subsequent works by Parentelli have been translated by Rev. Cajetan White, O.S.B.

62. Interview with Luz-Marie and José Alvarez-Icaza at their home in Mexico City, April 28, 1993, and May 2, 1993. Subsequent quotations from the couple unless otherwise indicated are from this interview. Thanks to Mechtilde Swearingen, O.S.B, who made arrangements, provided transportation, and served as translator.

63. Robert McClory, *Turning Point* (New York: Crossroad, 1995).

64. Gertrud Heinzelmann, letter of June 14, 1989.

65. Cita-Malard, *Les Femmes dans L'Église,* 97.

66. Goldie, letter of January 9, 1995.

Chapter 3: Flowers Have at Last Bloomed in Our Land

1. Donal Lamont's own recollection of this is recorded as "*Ad Gentes,* a Missionary Bishop Remembers," in Alberic Stacpole, ed., *Vatican II Revisited by Those Who Were There* (Minneapolis: Winston Press, 1986), 270–82. The speech was given during the third conciliar session (1964), when there was an attempt to expedite the remaining business and hasten the end of the council. The missionary document was reduced to thirteen propositions, and Paul VI had made an unusual appearance in the aula to speak in their favor. Missionary bishops opposed the propositional approach as a denigration of their work, but they hesitated to speak against the pope. Lamont called the propositions "thirteen dry bones" that were no substitute for the nourishing bread required on the missions. He drew on the prophet Ezekiel's analogy of the dry bones coming to life (Ezek. 37). Likewise, Lamont called on the Spirit to breathe on the dead propositions, to give them flesh and blood and make them live.

2. Interview February 20, 1989, with Bishop Donal Lamont at Terenure College, Dublin, where he is in retirement with his Carmelite community. I am indebted to my sister, Rita Fitzgerald, for arranging the interview and to her husband, Padraig, for transporting me there.

3. Rosemary Goldie, "The Emerging Lay Woman: Vatican II and 'The Other Half of Mankind,'" *World Outlook* (May 1966): 228.

4. Léon-Josef Suenens, letter of March 6, 1988.

5. Gregory Baum, letter of February 26, 1988.

6. Tom Stransky, letter of August 8, 1988.

7. Interview with Tobin, April 29, 1988.

8. Gladys Parentelli, *Mujer Iglesia Liberación* (Caracas, 1990), 45.

9. Suor Maria Clara Bianchi, *Il Postconcilio e la Suora* (Milan: Scuola Tipografica San Benedetto Voboldone, 1967), 34–36.

10. Interview, January 1989.

11. Telephone conversation with Eva Fleischner, February 25, 1993.

12. Daniel M. Madden, "Women at the Council," *Catholic Digest* (April 1965): 18.

13. Partially in Mary Luke Tobin, "The Council and Sisters' Renewal," *Catholic World* 201 (April–September 1965): 41.

14. Parentelli, *Mujer,* 47.

15. Conversation with Eva Jung-Inglessis in Piazza Navonna, Rome, January 11, 1990.

16. Juliana Thomas, letter to her community, October 4, 1964.

17. Parentelli, *Mujer,* 47.

18. Interview, May 2, 1993.

19. Bonnie Brennan, letter of June 7, 1989.

20. Conversation with Seán Mac Réamoinn at the Warwick Hotel, Dublin, Ash Wednesday, 1989. Thanks to my sister, Rita Fitzgerald, for arranging this meeting.

21. "Schwester Juliana in Röm." No newspaper title or date included.

22. Juliana Thomas, letter to her community, September 24, 1965.

23. Juliana Thomas, letter to her community, October 22, 1965.

24. Goldie, "A Woman at the Council."

25. Interview, September 21, 1989.

26. Goldie, "A Woman at the Council."

27. Parentelli, *Mujer,* 47–48.

28. Goldie, "A Woman at the Council."

29. Ruth Wallace, *They Call Her Pastor: A New Role for Catholic Women* (Albany, N.Y.: State University of New York Press, 1992), 3.

30. Interview, September 21, 1989.

31. Horton, *Vatican Diary,* III:130–31.

32. Interview September 21, 1989, when McCarthy read from her conciliar journal.

33. Interview, January 27–28, 1989.

34. Alda Miceli, letter of February 22, 1990, trans. Rosemary Goldie.

35. Monnet, *Avec amour,* 204.

36. Ibid., 210.

37. Suzanne Guillemin's text. Obtained from Sr. Henrietta Guyot, D.C., Archivist for the Daughters of Charity of St. Vincent de Paul, Marillac Provincial House, St. Louis, Mo. I am also grateful to Sr. Ann Mary Dougherty, D.C., rue du Bac, Paris, for sending me a gift copy of *Mère Suzanne Guillemin conférences et témoignages,* donated by a former mother general, and to Sr. Kieran Kneaves for other retreat material.

38. Khouzam, letter of April 2, 1993.

39. Moyano, "A veinte años de Medellín," *Criterio* (September 22, 1988): 528.

40. Ghanem, letter of April 30, 1993.

41. Interview, May 23, 1993.

42. Goldie, "A Woman at the Council."

43. Moyano, "A veinte años de Medellín," 528.

44. Ibid.

45. Interview, September 21, 1989.

46. Monnet, *Avec amour,* 211.

47. Goldie, "A Woman at the Council."

48. Conversation with Lucienne Salle at the Pontifical Council for Peace and Justice, Rome, January 12, 1990. The following quotation is also from this interview.

Chapter 4: Experts in Life

1. Ralph Wiltgen, S.V.D., interview with Rosemary Goldie, November 19, 1964.

2. Roberto Tucci, S.J., is one of the few commentators who lists the women who worked on Schema XIII. See *Vatican II: L'Église dans le monde de ce temps* (Paris: Les Éditions du Cerf, 1967), especially the notes on 88, 91, 92, 99, 107, 109.

3. Eileen Egan, "To Recognize the Disguise of Jesus in the Enemy," *National Catholic Reporter* 25, no. 20 (March 11, 1988): 14–15. Some similar ideas are expressed in her letter of April 12, 1988, to me.

4. Joseph Dunn, *No Lions in the Hierarchy* (Dublin: Columban Press, 1994), 297.

5. Ibid., 299.

6. Ibid., 298–99.

7. Bernard Häring, letter of April 11, 1988.

8. Häring, "La mia partecipazione al concilio Vaticano II," *Cristianesimo nella storia* 15 (1994): 161–81, esp. 178–81, where he speaks specifically about Wojtyla's input on Schema XIII.

9. Interview, January 27–28, 1989.

10. Monnet, photocopied text from Library of the Pontifical Biblical Commission for the Laity, October 5, 1964.

11. Monnet, text from January 19, 1965.

12. N. C., "Mgr. Ancel et Mlle Monnet parlent aux évêques africains du schéma l'Église dans le monde," *La Croix* (October 11–12, 1964): 5.

13. Goldie, "A Woman at the Council." The specific reference is to "L'impegno della donna nella Chiesa: scritto del 1964 di Papa Giovanni Paolo I," *Avvenire* (August 29, 1978), 4ff.

14. Interview, January 27–28, 1989.

15. Goldie, "A Woman at the Council." When the birth control commission completed its work and turned in their almost unanimous Majority Report to Pope Paul VI, Patty Crowley voiced their expectation. "I don't think there was a doubt in any of our minds that the pope would follow the commission report." Philippine demographer Mercedes Concepción concluded, "I was sure we had made history," meaning that change was imminent after the testimonies that came from married couples all over the world. That was also the mind of Canadian medical doctor Laurent Potvin, who said, "I felt sure the problem was settled once and for all... and I was very optimistic." His wife, Colette, cautioned, "Don't be so excited. Don't you see Cardinal Ottaviani sitting up there?" (Robert McClory, *Turning Point* [New York: Crossroad, 1995], 128). Subsequent history has demonstrated how right she was, as Ottaviani and his theologian friends immediately set about undoing the commission's work by convincing the pope of their own traditional arguments. The papal encyclical *Humanae Vitae* followed in 1968. McClory's book tells the whole story.

16. Gladys Parentelli, *Mujer Iglesia Liberación* (Caracas, 1990), 50–51.

17. Ibid., 51.

18. Interview, April 28, 1993.

19. Dunn, *No Lions*, 302.

20. Goldie, "Lay Participation in the Work of Vatican II," *Miscellanea Lateranense "Lateranum" (1974–1975)* 522, n. 44.

21. Walter Abbott, S.J., ed., *The Documents of Vatican II* (New York: Herder and Herder and Association Press, 1966), 234. Austin Flannery, ed., *Vatican II, the Conciliar and Post Conciliar Documents* (Northport, N.Y.: Costello Publishing Co., 1975) 935, footnotes Pio Paschini's two-volume study, *Vita e opere Galileo Galilei*, but he makes no reference to the contemporary conciliar discussion on Galileo at the council.

22. Giuliana Bragantini, *Le donne nel Concilio Vaticano II* (Rome: Pontificia Università Lateranense, 1984), 97–98; cf. *Gaudium et Spes* 25. This was a

doctoral thesis directed by R. Goldie. I commissioned Attilia Gogel to do a free translation for my personal use. Bragantini's focus and scope are quite different from mine in that the author did not interview any of the conciliar women, except Goldie, and she uses all Italian texts, with one exception. Her first two chapters deal with lay involvement leading up to the council. Chapter 3 presents the various bishops' interventions concerning women. Chapter 4 focuses on some of the women auditors, while the fifth chapter deals with women's involvement in the church's mission in the light of Vatican II. The author pays particular attention to Italian women, especially women religious.

23. Goldie, "Lay Participation," 523.

24. Parentelli, *Mujer*, 53–54.

25. Here I am working from archival photocopied texts, comparable to those Bragantini used as the basis for chapter 3 of her book. Excerpts from episcopal interventions were often reproduced in the *Council Daybook*.

26. Bragantini, *Le donne*, 60.

27. Photocopied archival text.

28. Photocopied text from Archives of Pontifical Council for the Laity Library. See also Bragantini, *Le donne*, chapter 3.

29. Goldie, "Lay Participation," 524, n. 50.

30. Dr. Augustinus Frotz, letter of July 24, 1989 includes specific information on Ehrle and the Frauenbund as well as Frotz's own awakening of consciousness to the need to name women as such, instead of simply presuming they were included under "men."

31. *America*, October 30, 1965.

32. Bragantini, *Le donne*, 66.

33. Curtayne, "The Silent Women."

34. Interview, September 21, 1989.

35. Interview, May 3, 1993.

36. Curtayne, "The Silent Women."

37. Goldie, "Lay Participation," 525.

Chapter 5: The Nun in the World

1. Suzanne Guillemin, "Renewal of Spirit and Structures," a presentation given at a special colloquium organized by Pro Mundi Vita and held in Louvain, September 10, 1966. The French version is published as "La vie religieuse feminine et l'apostolat universel: Renovation de l'esprit et des structures," *Mère Suzanne Guillemin conférences et témoignages* (Paris: Editions Fleurus, 1968), 51–69. I cannot pass up the opportunity to mention my two-mile hike out a country road from the train station in Louvain in search of Pro Mundi Vita, which had relocated in an old Norbertine monastery.

2. Interview, May 23, 1993.

3. Ibid.

4. Sr. Beatrice Brown, letter of May 17, 1989.

5. Interview, April 29, 1988.

6. Mary Luke Tobin, *Hope Is an Open Door* (Nashville: Abingdon Press, 1981), 34.

7. Guillemin, archival material.

8. Häring, letter of April 11, 1988.

9. Suor Maria Clara Bianchi, *Il Postconcilio e la Suora* (Milan: Scuola Tipografica San Benedetto Voboldone, 1967), 38.

10. Ibid., 40-41.

11. Obtained from archival texts at the Library of the Pontifical Council for the Laity.

12. Archival texts, most apparently coming from Tobin.

13. Interview, April 29, 1988.

14. M. J. Sirera, "Unas 'Mujeres-Signo,'" *Ancilla Cordis Jesu* 105 (1964): 30-44. Free translation done for me by Victor Reyes while he was a student at St. Meinrad School of Theology. A native of Venezuela, Reyes is now an ordained priest in the diocese of Atlanta.

15. Bianchi, *Il Postconcilio,* 75.

16. Interview, May 3, 1993.

17. Ibid.

18. Bianchi, *Il Postconcilio,* 260.

19. Ibid., 51.

20. WUCWO newsletter (January-April 1985, no. 91), special 75th anniversary edition.

21. Interview, May 3, 1993.

22. Brown, letter of April 11, 1989.

23. Ghanem, letter of April 30, 1993.

24. Aggeler, letter of May 12, 1989.

25. Guillemin, "Renewal," 16.

26. Interview, April 29, 1988.

27. Pamela Dowdell, letter and enclosure of February 20, 1993.

28. Interview, May 3, 1993.

29. Interview, April 29, 1988.

30. Daniel M. Madden, "Women at the Council," *Catholic Digest* (April 1965): 18.

31. Aggeler, letter of May 12, 1989.

32. Sr. Imelda Hennessy, letter of January 24, 1994. Imelda remained an active member of the Ballymahon community and played her favorite piano until three weeks before she died in August 1995, at age eighty-eight. She was a great Irish scholar, and in loving memory of her and of her nineteen years of teaching service in the U.S.A., I pray, *Go ndéanfaidh Dia trócaire ar a hanam* (May God have mercy on her soul).

33. Bianchi, *Il Postconcilio,* 143.

34. Interview, January 12, 1989.

35. Bianchi, *Il Postconcilio,* 171.

36. Ibid., 78.

37. Ibid., 79.

Chapter 6: Bridges Replace Walls

1. Mary Luke Tobin, *Hope Is an Open Door* (Nashville: Abingdon Press, 1981), 20.

2. Alberic Stacpole, *Vatican II Revisited by Those Who Were There* (Minneapolis: Winston Press, 1986), 13.

3. Goldie provided me with a list of the observers' wives who came to tea with the women auditors at the Foyer Unitas on October 14, 1964. They were Mrs. Robert E. Cushman (Durham, N.C.), Ms. Margaret E. Forsyth (New York), Mrs. Burns Chalmers (Washington, D.C.), Mrs. W. A. Quanluck (St. Paul, Minn.), Mrs. Walter Muelder (Boston, Mass.), Dorothy McConnell (Woman's Division, Methodist Church, New York), Mildred Horton (Randolph, N.H.).

4. Interview, January 27–28, 1989.

5. Ibid.

6. Ibid.

7. Tobin, *Hope*, 25.

8. Ibid., 28.

9. Ibid., 28–29.

10. Ibid., 26.

11. Interview, January 27–28, 1989.

12. Interview, January 12, 1989.

13. *Lay Apostolate Bulletin*, no. 3 (1965): 12.

14. Ibid., 13.

15. Ibid., 14.

16. Ibid., 16.

17. Cynthia Wedel, "Church Women and Christian Unity," *Catholic World* 202 (October 1965): 279–80.

18. Ibid., 280.

19. All information given here, unless otherwise indicated, is gleaned from unpublished photocopied pages obtained from Goldie's archives in the Library of the Pontifical Council for the Laity.

20. Wedel, "Church Women and Christian Unity," 280.

21. Ibid., 281.

22. Ibid., 280.

23. Ibid., 281–82.

24. Mary Daly, *The Church and the Second Sex* (New York: Harper Colophon Books, 1968), 6.

25. Minutes of meeting in Rome, October 29, 1965.

26. "Women's Ecumenical Meeting," *Lay Apostolate Bulletin* no. 3 (1965): 19; 18 and 19 record the event.

27. Wedel, "Church Women and Christian Unity," 282.

28. Rosemary Goldie, "A Woman at the Council: Memories of an Auditor."

29. Douglas Horton, *Vatican Diary* (Philadelphia/Boston: United Church Press, 1964–1967), III:165. This seems to conflict with Barot and Bührig's experience of being present for the rest of the session after Vicarello.

30. Ibid., III:165.
31. "Church Women and Christian Unity," 282.
32. Cited from a 1976 poster by Bonnie Acken, Red Sun Press.

Chapter 7: Bring the Council to the World

1. Léon-Josef Suenens, "A Plan for the Whole Council," in Alberic Stacpole, ed., *Vatican II Revisited by Those Who Were There* (Minneapolis: Winston Press, 1986), 94.
2. Ibid., 93.
3. Ibid., 102.
4. Ibid., 104. The quotation is taken from Montini's letter to Amleto Cardinal Cigognagi, which Suenens includes as an appendix to documentation on his conciliar plan.
5. Mary Luke Tobin, *Hope Is an Open Door* (Nashville: Abingdon Press, 1981), 30–31.
6. Emphases added are mine. Text from Walter Abbott, S.J., ed., *The Documents of Vatican II* (New York: Herder and Herder and Association Press, 1966), 732–33.
7. Eileen Egan, letter of April 12, 1988.
8. Eileen Egan, "To Recognize the Disguise of Jesus in the Enemy," *National Catholic Reporter* 25, no. 20 (March 11, 1988): 15.
9. Andrea di Montezemolo, letter of October 14, 1989.
10. Interview, January 27–28, 1989.
11. Ibid.
12. Ibid.
13. See *Gaudium et Spes* 90.1 and *Apostolicam Actuositatem* 19.3, 14, and 21.
14. Interview, January 27–28, 1989.
15. Ibid.
16. The whole issue of *Pro Mundi Vita* 108 (1987/1) is entitled *Women Appeal to the Pastors of the Church*. It includes important documentation on WUCWO and its consultation or lack of it in regard to Canon Law, *Inter Insigniores,* the 1971 synod, and, especially pertinent for my present work, "The Pontifical Study Commission on Women in the Church and in Society, 1973–1976," including "The Minority Note," December 29, 1975. It was signed by Pilar Bellosillo, Claire Delva, Marina Lessa, Maria Vittoria Pinheiro, Deborah A. Seymour, and Maria (Rie) Vendrik. Vendrik died before it was made public. There is also a letter from Karl Rahner to a commission consultant, information on WELG, and a women's meeting in Latin America in 1985.
17. Interview, January 1989.
18. Ibid.
19. Interview, January 1990.
20. Goldie, letter of September 18, 1995.
21. Interview, January 12, 1989.

22. Dr. Augustinus Frotz, letter of July 24, 1989.

23. Interview, September 21, 1989.

24. Ibid.

25. Ibid.

26. Marie-Louise Monnet, *Avec amour et passion* (Chambray: C.L.D., 1989), 222.

27. Ibid., 248.

28. Ibid., 247.

29. Ibid., 249.

30. Ibid., 255.

31. This contradicts a statement in Giuliana Bragantini, *Le donne nel Concilio Vaticano II* (Rome: Pontificia Università Lateranense, 1984), 150, where mention is made of twenty-one laypeople and women religious being appointed to the post-conciliar commissions in 1966. Luz-Marie Alvarez-Icaza is named, together with Bellosillo, Goldie, Monnet, Moyano Llerena, Vendrik, Guillemin, and Tobin. Luz-Marie herself has to be the final authority on this.

32. Interview, April 28, 1993.

33. Ibid.

34. Interview, May 2, 1993.

35. Moyano, letter of January 29, 1995.

36. Moyano, "A veinte años de Medellín," *Criterio* (September 22, 1988): 3.

37. Ibid., 4.

38. Parentelli, letter of January 18, 1991.

39. Interview, May 3, 1993.

40. Dorothy Vidulich, " 'Radical' IHMs Pioneered Religious Community," *National Catholic Reporter* 31, no. 33 (June 30, 1995): 19.

41. Chimy, letter in *Star of Mary* 32, no. 1 (January–March 1967) and a circular in preparation for the 1968 community chapter.

42. Ghanem, letter of July 5, 1993.

43. Archival text.

44. Ibid.

45. Suzanne Guillemin, "Renewal of Spirit and Structures," 12, a presentation given at a special colloquium organized by Pro Mundi Vita and held in Louvain, September 10, 1966.

46. Ibid., 13.

47. Ibid., 14.

48. Archival text.

49. Guillemin, "Renewal of Spirit and Structures," 15.

50. Ibid., 16.

51. Ibid.

52. Tobin, *Hope*, 43.

53. Ibid., 125.

54. Ibid., 119.

55. Ibid., 79.

56. Ibid., 100–101.

57. Ibid., 97.
58. Ibid., 131.
59. Joseph Dunn, *No Lions in the Hierarchy* (Dublin: Columban Press, 1994), 322.
60. *Pro Mundi Vita* 108:2.
61. Ibid.
62. Ibid., 4.
63. Ibid., 6.
64. Ibid., 7.
65. Ibid., 8–9.
66. Ibid., 10.
67. Ibid., 17.
68. Ibid.
69. Ibid., 18–21.
70. Ibid., 21.

Chapter 8: The Door Is Opened Too Wide to Be Closed

1. Seán Mac Réamoinn told me this story, February 7, 1989.
2. Casey resigned his bishopric in 1993 in the wake of much publicity and his admission that he had fathered a child eighteen years previously, when he was bishop of Kerry.
3. Just as women theologians have begun to make an impact in Third World countries, there is a backlash against them from Rome. Sr. Ivone Gebara from Brazil has been ordered to France to study "traditional theology," as recounted by David Molineaux, "Brazil's Gebara Bows to Vatican for Now," *National Catholic Reporter* 31, no. 33 (June 30, 1995) 15.
4. Robert McClory, *Turning Point* (New York: Crossroad, 1995), 86.
5. Ibid., 166.
6. Walter Abbott, S.J., ed., *The Documents of Vatican II* (New York: Herder and Herder and Association Press, 1966), 733.
7. Ibid.
8. Elizabeth Johnson, *She Who Is: The Mystery of God in Feminist Theological Discourse* (New York: Crossroad, 1992). Johnson is a highly acclaimed author and respected scholar, elected president of the Catholic Theological Society of America for 1995–96.
9. *Dublin Sunday Tribune,* July 16, 1995.
10. Someone at the Catholic University of America said this to Elizabeth Johnson because of her courageous stand for justice on behalf of Charles Curran.
11. Mary Luke Tobin, *Hope Is an Open Door* (Nashville: Abingdon Press, 1981), 41.
12. *Pro Mundi Vita,* 10.
13. Gladys Parentelli, "Teología feminista en América Latina," photocopy of text delivered at the Fifth International and Interdisciplinary Conference of Women at the University of Costa Rica, San José, February 22–26, 1993.

Postscript

1. The text appears in *Origins* 20, no. 8 (July 5, 1990).

2. All references here are taken from the ITC text as it appears in Francis Sullivan, *Magisterium* (Ramsey, N.J.: Paulist Press, 1983), 174–218.

3. The entire text of the CTSA's statement is published as an appendix in the *CTSA Proceedings of the Fiftieth Annual Convention,* ed. Paul Crowley (Santa Clara, Calif.: Santa Clara University Press, 1995), 326–29.

LIST OF AUDITORS

** Luz-Marie Alvarez-Icaza (Mexico; attended 4th session, 1965)

** Constantina Baldinucci, S.C. (Italy; 3d and 4th sessions, 1964–65)

** Pilar Bellosillo (Spain; 3d and 4th sessions, 1964–65)

** Jerome Maria Chimy, S.S.M.I. (Ukrainian rite, Canada; 4th session, 1965)

† Gertrud Ehrle (Germany; 4th session, 1965)

† Cristina Estrada, A.C.J. (Spain; 3d and 4th sessions, 1964–65)

† Claudia Feddish, O.S.B.M. (Ukrainian rite, U.S.A.; 3d and 4th sessions, 1964–65)

* Henriette Ghanem, S.S.C.C. (Coptic rite, Lebanon; 3d and 4th sessions, 1964–65)

** Rosemary Goldie (Australia; 3d and 4th sessions, 1964–65)

** Ida Grillo (Italy; 3d and 4th sessions, 1964–65)

† Suzanne Guillemin, D.C. (France; 3d and 4th sessions, 1964–65)

* Marie de la Croix Khouzam, R.E.S.C. (Coptic rite, Egypt; 3d and 4th sessions, 1964–65)

** Catherine McCarthy (U.S.A.; 3d and 4th sessions, 1964–65)

** Alda Miceli (Secular Institute, Italy; 3d and 4th sessions, 1964–65)

† Marie-Louise Monnet (France; 3d and 4th sessions, 1964–65)

† Marchesa Amalia di Montezemolo (Italy; 3d and 4th sessions, 1964–65)

* Margarita Moyano Llerena (Argentina; 4th session, 1965)

* Gladys Parentelli (Uruguay, currently in Venezuela; 4th session, 1965)

* Anne-Marie Roeloffzen (Belgium; 3d and 4th sessions, 1964–65)

? Hedwig Skoda (Czechoslovakia; 4th session, 1965)

† Juliana Thomas, A.D.J. (Germany; 3d and 4th sessions, 1964–65)

** Mary Luke Tobin, S.L. (U.S.A.; 3d and 4th sessions, 1964–65)

Sabine de Valon, R.S.C.J. (France; 3d and 4th sessions, 1964–65)

** Auditors with whom I met.
* Auditors with whom I corresponded but whom I did not meet.
† Auditors deceased (Ida Grillo died after I interviewed her).
? Whereabouts unknown.

Translation of Auditor Ida Grillo's Invitation to the Council

Gracious Lady,

The HOLY FATHER graciously has deigned to admit qualified representatives of the Catholic Laity as "Women Auditors" to the sessions of the Vatican II Ecumenical Council.

I have the pleasure of communicating that you, gracious Lady, have been included as one of the "Women Auditors."

As I inform you of this, I am happy to take the occasion to convey to you my profound esteem and best regards.

Most devotedly,
+ Pericle Felici

Copy of Auditor's Invitation to the Council

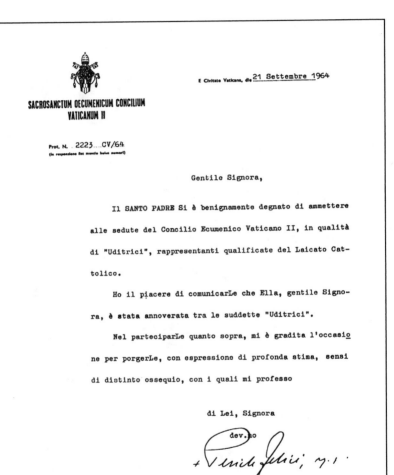

E Civitate Vaticana, die 21 Settembre 1964

SACROSANCTUM OECUMENICUM CONCILIUM
VATICANUM II

Prot. N. 2223 CV/64
(in responsione fiat mentio huius numeri)

Gentile Signora,

Il SANTO PADRE Si è benignamente degnato di ammettere alle sedute del Concilio Ecumenico Vaticano II, in qualità di "Uditrici", rappresentanti qualificate del Laicato Cattolico.

Ho il piacere di comunicarLe che Ella, gentile Signora, è stata annoverata tra le suddette "Uditrici".

Nel parteciparLe quanto sopra, mi è gradita l'occasione per porgerLe, con espressione di profonda stima, sensi di distinto ossequio, con i quali mi professo

di Lei, Signora

dev.mo

+ Emilio Julius, n.i.

Gentile Signora
Sig.a IDUCCIA MARENCO GRILLO

INDEX